# Through the Joy of Learning

## Diary of 1,000 Adult Learners

Edited by Pam Coare and Alistair Thomson

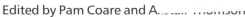

First published 1996 by the National Institute of Adult Continuing Education
(England and Wales)
21 De Montfort Street, Leicester LE1 7GE

Company Registration no. 2603322
Charity registration no. 1002775

Cataloguing in Publication Data
A CIP record for this title is available from the British Library
ISBN 1 86201 001 3

Designed and printed in England by Wilton, Wright & Son, Surrey

# Contents

Foreword                                              *v*
Introduction                                          *vii*
Acknowledgements                                      *ix*

## Part One: Dear Diary
*Twenty-eight complete Diaries*

Bernard Prunty                                        3
Liliana Fiorentino                                    6
Ann Mitchell                                          8
Nigel Padley                                          11
Christine Luke                                        20
Karen Holtom                                          24
'Something for Me' Group                              27
Hubert Jefferson                                      31
Barbara Hodgson                                       36
Bob Smith                                             41
Lesley Goulden                                        47
English for Work Course                               50
May Banham                                            57
Margaret Dobson                                       59
Peter Rolls                                           62
Silvia Schiavone                                      68
Celia Scott                                           72
Hayley Morris                                         75
Anonymous from Macclesfield                           79
Nan Lawson                                            81
Kathleen Chapman                                      85
Julie Smithson                                        88
Charles Nicholson                                     99
Mary Gilmartin                                        107
Joy Ball                                              112
Beginners' Drawing Course                             121
Sue Dyson                                             125
Janet Knight                                          128

A selection of facsimile pages and illustrations
from the Diaries                                      131–138

## Part Two: Adults Learning
*Extracts from the collection of Diaries organised into four thematic sections*

Introduction                                          140
Motivations                                           141
Challenges                                            155
Learning Experiences                                  169
Achievements                                          189

Afterward: Working with the Diaries                   201
Further Reading                                       206
Abbreviations                                         208
Index                                                 210

*Through the Joy of Learning*

# Foreword

I left school a week before my fifteenth birthday. I couldn't wait to get out of the place. My ambition throughout my childhood had been to become an adult. A **sophisticated** adult. I wanted to wear a cocktail dress and go to nightclubs and smoke cigarettes from a tortoiseshell holder. I also wanted a Vespa scooter, a french poodle and a flat of my own.

Unfortunately all of the above things had to be bought with money, and my qualifications (nil) meant that I was condemned to working for low wages in unskilled jobs. The only symbol of sophistication I could afford was the tortoiseshell holder. Within a year I'd enrolled myself at night-school for various 'O' level courses (but left before taking the exams, I fell in love and couldn't concentrate). I've been educating myself in various ways ever since: by private reading, by studying part-time for a Certificate in Youth and Community Work, by attending courses on poetry and script writing.

I recently attended a weekend course on interactive media where I was the oldest person in the room, apart from the lecturer who wore a cowboy hat and was drunk in the morning and even drunker in the afternoon.

I sometimes think that learning is wasted on the young. They are contained in these places called schools at exactly the wrong time. Their bodies and their minds are too fidgety to concentrate on things like the demography of Bolivia. It's we adults who benefit most from education. We bring our life experiences to the classroom, good and bad, and what's more we don't cheek the teacher, fight in the playground, or pass love notes round the class. We actually **enjoy** learning. We are motivated.

I know many people whose lives have changed completely since they became an adult learner. From those who have learnt basic literacy skills, to others who have taken degree courses. It's an extremely harsh world out there. Jobs are going, more computers are coming. But those people who are studying Cantonese at night-school are, I would say, in with a chance.

Sue Townsend

# Introduction

Many of us keep diaries. We confide our actions, thoughts and feelings to the page as a way of making sense of busy lives that do not contain the time for reflection. One woman writing for this project commented that keeping her diary was 'a useful thing to do. Time goes so fast and there is so much going on in my life that there is often not enough time to assimilate things'.

There is also something of the voyeur in us when we read someone else's diary. Other peoples' lives are interesting, exciting, awful, just different from our own and diaries, perhaps more than any other form, allow us an irresistible glimpse into the private thoughts of the writer.

NIACE, the National Organisation for Adult Learning, advertised their 'Diary of 1000 Adult Learners' project as part of the celebration that would accompany the 1996 European Year of Lifelong Learning and their own 75th Anniversary. NIACE was endeavouring to 'show how adults are learning in the 1990's, by taking a snapshot view of activities in any week' of the Autumn term 1995. Individuals and groups were asked to keep a diary for a week, 'showing your choice of learning and what it's been like for you.'

Many adult learners responded, writing of their learning experiences in a wide range of situations: the Open University, further education colleges, the Workers' Educational Association and the Women's Institute were just a few of those represented. Other diarists interpreted 'learning' in its broadest sense, exploring the variety and serendipitous nature of learning as volunteers, as club members, in social and leisure pursuits and at work. Few of the diaries received are a record of one complete week: many cover longer periods of learning, or draw on the experience of both childhood and adult lives to make sense of the present learning experiences.

Every diary is unique, and tells of an individual experience, and yet often that individual experience resonates with wider issues in adult education. What is common to all the diaries is a sense of purpose and achievement in the learning, and it is this combination of diversity yet commonality that has shaped the structure of this book.

The first section of the book is a small selection of whole diaries that illustrate the diversity of both style and content. Each was chosen for a variety of reasons, not all easily quantifiable. They were chosen primarily because they engaged us as readers and editors, by exploring the way formal and informal learning enriches and complicates everyday experience. They spoke to our understanding of what adult education should and can be. They also evoke a range of experiences and types of learning which, when seen together, illustrates the enormous variety of opportunities available to the adult learner.

The second section of the book is arranged according to significant themes that emerged time and again in the experiences of the diarists, about the motivations, challenges, experiences and achievements of adult learners. Shorter extracts from a larger number of diaries illuminate and explore these themes. In an Afterward about working with the diaries we write in more detail about the creation and use of the diaries. We consider how the diaries might be used by researchers, policy makers and participants in adult education, and we discuss some of the limitations of the diaries: what they are not able to tell us about adult learning and education.

We hope this book will encourage more people to recognise themselves in the lives described in the diaries printed here, and to discover the part that adult education might play in their lives.


Pam Coare and Alistair Thomson.

# Acknowledgements

We would like to thank Alan Tuckett and Helen Prew at NIACE for, respectively, initiating and coordinating the diary project, and the many NIACE staff members who supported our work on the book.

We would also like to thank the diarists who have shared their thoughts, feelings and ideas with us, and the tutors, Centre Heads, family and friends who have encouraged and supported their participation in this project. We have endeavoured to include all the contributors' names, but if we have failed to include you, please accept our apologies.

Jacalyn Aggett, M. Akhtar, Shamima Aktar, Nuzhat Ali, C. Allinson, Iain Anderson, Nancy Andrews, Irene Aptel, Mary Arscott, Gloria Ash, Zobina Aslam, Carolyn Atherton, Angela Mary Atkin, Joan Atkins, Jaag Baig, Diane Baker, Garan Bala, Genevieve Ball Joy Ball, Maxine Bancalari, May Banham, David Barber, Lesley Barber, Dave Barker, Michael Barker, Pam Barnes, Ruth Barnes, Hazel Batchelor, Fiona Bateman, Deborah Bellamy, Tajinder Bhurji, Linda Birch, Harriet Birungi, Sharon Blake, Pauline Blears Clare Borley, Jo Bousfield, T. Bowater, Freda Bowring, Eliane Boyet, Alan Brewster, Nina Brittain, Clare Britton, Mary Brokup, Debbie Brooke, Ian Brown, Doreen Bullock, Ray Burton, Atiq Butt, Fahmeeda Butt, John Cairns, Alasdair Cameron, Joan Chadwick, SheilaChadwick, Sue Chamberlain, David Chapman, Fiona Chapman, Kathleen Chapman, Johnny Chen, Chris Clifford, Ann Clowes, Deborah Coates, Caroline Cole, Tracey Collins, Brenda Connell, David Connor, Heather Corbett, Pauline Corcoran, Christy Cowell, Alistair Cumming, Joyce Cummings, Fiona Dale, Robert Darko, Rosalie Darlington, Neil Davies, Jean Day, Gloria Dayson, Jagjeet Dhanjal, Mary Diggle; Trudie Dixon, Margaret Dobson, Latife Dogan, M. H. Doughty, Jennifer Douglas, C. A. Durrant, Sue Dyson, Paul East, Barbara Evans, Maureen Fair, Jennie Farley, Anicette Fatusin, Kathleen Ferrelly, Leonard Field, Grace Fielder, Liliana Fiorentino, Alan Foreman, Marjorie Foy, Maureen Fradgley, Dawn Francis, Joan Francis, Stephen Francis, Lee Gibson, Frances Gilbert, Mary Gilmartin, Susan Goldsmith, Lesley Goulden, Liz Gough, George Graham, Gordon Graham, Dorothy Gravell, Brian Gray, Kevin Gregory, Grete Grove, Florentina Perez Guerrero, Sarah Guilbert, Billy Hammond, Margaret Hammond, Jeffery Handsford, Stewart Hardie, James Harkins, Peter Harland, Ken Harmer, Brenda Harper, Ken Harrison, Brenda Harvey, David Harvey, Sandra Hawkins, Lorraine Hayward, Marilyn Hayward, Gertrude Healy, Pat Heaps, J. Heath Cutler, Pauline Henderson, Jaqui Henry, Pat Hewitt, Daphne Hewlett, John Heywood, Jeanne Hillier, Rebecca Hilton, Charles Hincks, Carole Hoad, David Hoad, Carol Hodgkinson, Barbara Hodgson, Sheila Holder, Julie Holliday, Sally Holman, Karen Holtom, Stephen Hopley, Wyn Howley, N. Hubbard, Diana Hughes, Gwen Hunter, Paul Hunter, Joan Ims, Dawn Inns, Betty Isaacs, Sally Izod, Sally Jackson, Andrew Jameson, Hanadi Jardali, Doreen Jarvis, Hubert Jefferson, Jenny Jerrome, Barbara Johnson, Michelle Jones, Rosette Katambaye, Nicola Kavanagh, Amritpal Kaur, Balwinder Kaur, Fauzia Kazi, Tony Kelshaw, Janet Kenny, Peter Kern, Bilques Khan, Nafiza Khan,

Anne Kissane, Janet Knight, Rae Kozary, Sally Kulinski, Jacqualine Lamb, Pamela Lamb, Kevin Lange, Heather Lankshear, Patricia Latteman, Nan Lawson, Dennis Layton, I. Legg, Ginny Lloyd, Martin Locke, Margaret Lovell, Christine Luke, Suman Luthra, Jackie Luxton, Wilson McAnespie, Jim McCabe, L. McCreedy, Ian McCulloch, Georgina McGill, Rose McGuire, Sheila McKinnon, Mary McLean, Susan McLeod, W.G. McLeod, John McMillan, Tarquin Macadem, Ala Mahmood, D. Majoh, Hani Al Malah, Carl Malins, J. Marchant, Gulfraz Maroof, Carla Marsh, Lesley Marsh, Iris Marshall, Wendy Mason, Balbinder Mattu, Cynthia Mbah, Jane Meah, Jonathon Meecham, Geoff Meek, Sylvia Mendham, Ann Mitchell, Veronica Molloy, Margaret Montague, Vera Moon, Sandra Moore, Hayley Morris, Phil Morris, David Moser, Kate Mottershead, Albert Mower, Munira, Gaye Murdoch, Rose Muyingo, Jeno John Nagy, Charles Nicholson, Moira Nicholson, Ann O'Connor, Lisa O'Malley, Jane Oakshott, Annetta Owen, Dennis Owen, Nigel Padley, Barara Paige, Momin Patel, Steven Pattison, Dora Paynter, John Pearson, Rebecca Pearson, Tom Peel, Pat Penny, Margot Penrose, Sue Perrin, Pauline Peters, Suzanne Pezcod, Geoff Phazey, Emma Pickles, Karen Piesley, Angela Pinnell, Julie Pitre, Janine Poirns, Tania Post, Anastasia Prescott, Douglas Preston, Margaret Prett, Ester Prince, J. Prior, Bernard Prunty, Janet Ramsey, Eric Ratherwood, Catherine Rees Jones, Aida Rehmatullah, Isobella Renwick, Richard Reynolds, Lynn Rhodes, Keith Richards, Pennie Richards, Keith Riley, Kirsteen Roberts, David Robertson, Dorothy Robinson, Christina Robinson, Sarah Rogers, Veronica Rogers, Peter Rolls, Joslyn Ross, Beverley Rowe, William Rowland, Penny Rudkin, P. E. Ruffell, Sally Russell , Baseer Saad, Nazi Sereshki, Silvia Schiavone, Celia Scott, Jane Seaman, Brenda Sharman, Ken Sharman, Elizabeth Sharpe, Catherine Shaw, Gordon Shay, Eric Shier, N. R. Skidmore, Anne Smart, Anne-Marie Smith, Bob Smith, Colin Smith, Doreen Smith, Felicity Smith, Lyn Smith, Julie Smithson, Patricia Spence, Pauline Stack, Ann Stamp, Doreen Stowe, Judith Summers, David Swales, Glen Swan, Yuko Takayanagi, Christopher Tanner, David Tavener, William Taylor, Alla Tchyj, Narendran Thirunavukkarasu, Daniel Thomas, Keith Thomas, I. Thomson, Patricia Thornhill, Ian Tiffin, Lyn Tilbury, Joy Tomkins, May Walinet, G. A Walker, Bernadette Wallin, M. Wang, Barrie Wardell, Peggy Wardell, Betty Warner, R. Warner, Jeremy Wenckler, Dorothy Weston-Edwards, Elizabeth White, Doreen Whitehouse, Margaret Whiting, D. J. Wilkinson, Doris Williams, Lilian Williams, Nicola Williams, R. J. Williams, Theresa Williams, Edna Wilson, Sylvia Wilson-Prunty, Frances Withall, Winifred Wood, John Woodward, Sharon Woolven, Angela Wright, Beryl Wylie, Audrey Wythe, Rosemary Yonathan, and learners of the Adult College Lancaster, Carlisle College, Cottingham Adult Education Centre, Croydon Education and Training Services, East Durham College, Gateway Club Middlesbrough, Gillingham Centre Kent , Larchfield Community Middlesbrough, Macclesfield College, Menro House, Middlesbrough, 'Moving Out' arts project Stroud, Newcastle under Lyme College, Park Lane College Leeds, Penketh Adult Education Centre, St Mary's Mitcham, Sherringham and Holt Adult Education, Sittingbourne Centre Kent, Stroud College, Thomas Bennett Community College Crawley, Tower Hamlets College, Tresham Institute Northants.

# Part One:
# Dear Diary

## *Bernard Prunty; Rotherham, South Yorkshire*

*I was born in 1935, at Mullaghfard in Northern Ireland.*

*I now live at Goldthorpe with my partner who actively supports my return to learning, especially maths which have always been my nightmare.*

I was born in Mullaghfard, Co Fermanagh, Ireland on 23/6/1935. I was one of a very large family and my Daddy was a mountain farmer all his life. My mother also came from a small farming family. There was a large family of us and I didn't go to school until I was ten years old. Although I could read and write before I went to school, I left at fourteen, with a very basic education and a complete lack of confidence, feeling I was inadequately educated and it has been a handicap all my life. All my life I have worked as a labourer apart from seven years in the army. At seventeen I joined up saying I was seventeen and a half and they never checked up on me. I served as a private or fusilier in the royal Eniskillen fusiliers, where again I found my lack of education a terrible handicap. I married at 29 and my wife and I travelled up and down England working on farms and a spell back in Ireland working as a Council Warden i.e. Road Sweeper. My wife then became ill and I cared for her for five years before she died in 1992. I then sold up and moved to Wakefield. My life was in turmoil and to occupy my time I went to Wakefield Centre for the Unemployed and enrolled in a knitting class, I began to rebuild my life and meet and make new friends. I later joined a stained glass making class. I also met my partner and we later moved to Goldthorpe where we have been for the last year.

Here I received the encouragement to return to learning. I attend a Basic Maths and Basic English class, Knitting, First Aid, Typing and an Art class. I've also done some very basic learning about computers and attended a TUC/JSA weekend at Northern College. I'm also going back to Northern College to do a return to learning skills course.

## My week's diary is here.
## Monday 3/7/95

I went Typing today. Six weeks ago I'd never touched one and here I am typing. Using more than two fingers, it's great. I'm improving my spellings, I work at my own speed, the teacher is lovely and very helpful; so are the other pupils. My fingers don't feel so clumsy now and I really enjoy learning here. I just wish we weren't having the summer break …

## Tuesday 4/7/95

In English this week we wrote sentences, putting commas and full stops in the right places, using capital letters etc. My teacher then gave me a book to read for ten minutes and then she asked me questions about what I had read, asking me to describe things, to see what I had learnt from it (Comprehension). I also had to read something aloud. Others in my group were learning how to put on a plug or baking cakes in the microwave. My lack of education has always been a real handicap to me. It destroyed my chances in the Army because I lacked confidence. Here everyone is pleased to see each other learning! I really enjoy this class.

Knitting is as much a social occasion as a class. I am knitting a sweater and can now knit one row plain and one row purl, (stocking stitch). I like this group as everyone is friendly and someone will always help me out and explain if I get in a muddle or am stuck. We are a self help group and I am the only male in it so they like to encourage me. I also enjoy seeing their embroidery skills and I've also begun to realise I am using my maths and English skills counting rows and reading patterns ...

## Wednesday 5/7/95

I did maths today. It is opening up a whole new world for me as I always believed I was stupid. Especially with regard to timetables and railway journeys. Today my tutor taught me how to read a twenty four hour clock and work out times of buses, also how long a journey takes. Simple things that ignorance had made me hide my head in shame. I lacked confidence when in the Army and used to hide my head in shame because I could not grasp maths. Knowing I couldn't do it was always an embarrassment and often meant total humiliation too. I am also beginning to use a calculator and lose my fear of it. Each time I go I come away feeling I want the class to carry on all day. Maybe one day I'll know enough to sit my GCSE in maths.

## Thursday 6/7/95

I normally do First Aid but today I had a stomach bug so I stayed at home and did revision. I feel everyone should know basic first aid. Again I am the only male in a class of women but it's very friendly and I've missed seeing them and I won't see them next week as I'm off to Northern College for a Return to Learning Skills week.

## Friday 7/7/95

Painting or Art is at the Highgate base and I worked on a painting. I paint in oils and am learning different techniques. Melvin my tutor and I ate our sandwiches together at dinner time, then started a joint picture trying out different methods of painting trees and mountains. Beside the social side of meeting fellow artists/painters, I find great pleasure in it because seven months ago the only paint brush I'd ever used was to paint doors and fences. I'd never have dared to try art and here I am painting in oils. What's more, people who see them actually offer to buy them or scrounge them off me. Because they actually like them and want them!

Besides being relaxing and enjoyable, my partner and I also realise we're more observant of and appreciate more the things around us. We both look at things differently now. We enjoy and gain far more out of paintings, literature and architecture. Even TV programmes have an extra dimension.

So I thank God for the chance to return to learning. I feel like a sponge that's been squeezed dry and is now opening out through the joy of learning.

## Liliana Fiorentino; Crawley, West Sussex

*My name is Liliana. I was born 25 years ago in the Dominican Republic. My mother tongue is Spanish but I also speak fluently French and Italian. I have a university degree in Law. I came to this country two years ago after my marriage. My husband is Italian. He has studied and now works here in England. When I first came I did not speak English at all. I am still learning every day. I work part-time as a sales assistant and in my spare time enjoy reading, writing, painting and cooking. My aim is to return to the University.*

## Tuesday 12ᵗʰ of September 1995

Finally I have done it! I have joined an English class!

Today, exactly a year from my arrival in England, I have gone to the nearest Community College and I have paid, not for one, but for two English classes.

It has been the biggest decision I have taken since I have been in this country and I am very happy.

I am tired of living afraid and lonely, mourning in the corners of this house in an eternal depression. I have to realise that I am living in England now and that I have to adapt myself to this new environment and culture, building a happy new life. How can I do that if I do not speak English properly? How can I improve my English if I never talk to anybody? How can I talk to somebody if I am always afraid of making mistakes and being refused?

I hope these classes will give me back some of my lost confidence and will help me build the base for my new life in England.

## Tuesday 19ᵗʰ of September 1995

This morning I went for the first time to my "Spelling and Vocabulary" class. I was a little worried at the beginning when I saw that the other people in the class were all English. I was hoping to find other foreign people in my same situation which could share my feelings. But, after all, everybody was nice and kind to me, I did not make as many mistakes as I was expecting and when I took the bus back home I was very satisfied.

I enjoyed a rich, warm feeling sharing the experiences of learning. They did not care about my accent and accepted me immediately. It has been the first time since I have been in England that I have had a real personal contact with English people.

A little door has been opened in my heart today. Maybe I will be able to love this new country and people some day.

## Wednesday 20th of September 1995

My first "General English" class has been a real challenge.

I was a little nervous this morning thinking that maybe I would find my "General English" class too difficult. I have taken this class only to try if I will be able to cope with it. The other members of the group were all English people and I find it so difficult even to speak English properly! But when the tutor explained to us the object of the class I was very excited and happy. That was really what I wanted and what I was expecting: to be able to write correctly and with style, knowing new words, grammar, punctuation, to express myself in public with confidence, things I enjoy doing in my own language but which seem so difficult to me now in English.

I liked very much the other members of the group. They were open and welcoming people with an admirable wish of improvement. I am sure I am going to learn wonderful things with them, not only about the English language, but also about England, English people and general life. You cannot learn a language if you do not love it and it is impossible to love a language if you do not know, understand and love the people who speak it and the land where the language was born.

I enjoyed particularly doing the exercises, looking for synonyms and writing sentences. It was very hard for me because I could not think so quickly in English as the other members of the group did, but I was proud of myself in my little success.

I have always been too exigent with myself, wanting to do everything perfectly. Now, I have realised it is better to be patient, to give me the opportunity to make mistakes and to learn from them.

## Friday 29th of September 1995

This has been only my second week studying English and I have already received so many benefits! I am beginning to feel much more confident. It is not only what I am learning, but the fact that I am going out, meeting people, being forced to talk and understand what people say to me.

I have been in England for a whole year and in all this time I have not made any friends or spoken to many people. I have been living a very isolated life, with a deep feeling of being too different, with the sensation of not belonging to this place and with the sad certitude that I will have to live here for a long time, maybe all my life.

Now, for the first time since I am in England, I feel I belong to something. I am part of a group of students, people in some way like me, eager to learn and improve every day. They are real people, with families, dreams and worries, not the distant human shapes I used to see through my window.

The true help these classes are giving me is not just the confidence to write a piece about a passage. They are building a bridge between me and this new world where I am living, so different from the one where I come from, and between me and the people of this world, their feelings, aims and particular vision of life.

I am filling my brain and my heart with wonderful, new knowledge every week and the more I learn, the easier is the next lesson.

## *Ann Mitchell; Stockport, Cheshire*

*I am just entering the second half of my life having just turned '50' so I definitely qualify as an adult learner. I have sampled quite a few evening classes over the last ten years and find them most satisfying.*

*When I have completed my part-time work for our business I have some time to myself; my daughter is married and my husband encourages me to do my own thing as he likes flying. So learning to create and perform relaxing activities is a pleasure that I will continue for many years to come.*

## Introduction

"What shall we take up this term at night school?" Bev asks Julie and I.

"Well let's see" answers Jooles as she looks in the College Prospectus, "There's mmm … 'Singing for Pleasure'." "Not for me Julie I can't sing. I thought I could but I have been told otherwise," says I. "Stained glass, no can't do that night, how about you Bev?" says Julie, "Is there anything you fancy?" passing the booklet to Bev, who scans the pages. "How about Tai Chi?" "What exactly does one do in Tai Chi?" I enquire. "Well its slow, relaxing movements together with breathing exercises" they both say, they are cleverer than me. "That sounds good to me, let's go for it."

## WEDNESDAY

I always feel so good after Tuesday evening – "chilled out" is the expression that comes to mind. I stretch like a cat and lift myself from the comfort of a warm bed. My husband has gone to the office so I have the luxury of the house to myself. While last night is still fresh in my mind I slip into loose, comfortable clothes. A large glass of water accompanies me as I venture into the "Torture Chamber". This is my daughter's ex-bedroom, she was married recently. In the room is a multi-gym, exercise bike, treadmill and rowing machine. Hidden in the corner are some barbells and dumbbells. But there is still room for me in the middle to carry out my "Tai Chi", "Wonderful."

With the window open, I begin the gentle warm-up session. Feet, legs, thighs and up to the waist are secured by imaginary roots spreading from the feet and the rest of the body is suspended from the ceiling by a thin, silk rope, also imaginary. My breath is gentle and deep, my body relaxed and my whole being at peace. It is a wonder I don't keel over and fall asleep. But I stay firmly upright – it must be the roots. At this point in the class, Christine says, "Remind yourselves where you are in the room and slowly open your eyes." I have great difficulty in opening my eyes, when I'm not in class, the relaxation part for me is quite hypnotic, but I must press on.

We learnt another movement of "The Form" last night. This is the part of Tai Chi that is performed in parks by the Chinese, but is becoming popular around the world.

## THURSDAY

I repeat the movements of Tai Chi much the same as yesterday. This is the secret, perform as often and as long as possible. Because I have now the opportunity to stay at home 3 days a week to write instead of "going out" to work, I am about to carry out my wishes, which are to look after my body, mind and spirit. After 30 minutes of Tai Chi, I force myself into a less gentle pastime in the "Torture Chamber", but it all adds to one's fitness.

## FRIDAY

This is one of my days spent working, but because I travel about I'm able to mooch around book shops. I find a book on Tai Chi which covers the form that we are learning at night school; this is great because there are such a variety on offer. I can't wait to read it.

## SATURDAY

Saturday is the shopping and cleaning day, so to enable time to perform Tai Chi, I have to force myself out of bed earlier than usual, which isn't that early. As I didn't get a chance to practise yesterday, I have to concentrate on the movements, but they eventually flow. Later I find time to read "Tai Chi" by Robert Parry, a really well set out, easy to follow book. The introduction in the book reads as follows, "Tai Chi is many things to different people. The beautiful controlled movements have for centuries inspired men and women from all walks of life, people of all ages and all levels of fitness. Vitality, relaxation, tranquillity, enhanced personal creativity and a sense of purpose – these are just some of Tai Chi's enduring gifts." Works for me.

## SUNDAY

Pop around to my sister's. She thinks I'm very laid back and asks my secret (I have had rather a stressful three years). "No secret" I say "Just Tai Chi". After I tell her more about it, she wants to try for herself. Because it is on my mind I go home and practise some more. That's what the book says, "PRACTISE, PRACTISE, PRACTISE."

## MONDAY

Today is another "out of house day." Because of the nature of my work, I travel to Oldham, Buxton and Hanley. On my travels I look for videos demonstrating Tai Chi, but so far I'm unlucky. There aren't any television programmes relating to anything similar either, not even on Sky television. No practise today as we eat out early evening and I have to give some of my time to my husband.

## TUESDAY

This is my serious, get down to writing day. If I get a good start on Tuesdays it usually stays with me Wednesday and Thursday. So I ignore the Tai Chi today in the knowledge that I can resume it in the evening.

Seven fifteen to nine fifteen at Poynton school in the Drama workshop is where we, (we being, my friends Julie and Bev, Christine our Tai Chi teacher and a gathering of new friends) congregate for our lesson. After the initial chit chat and the calling of the register, we begin. Two hours of gentle but effective movements under the supervision of Christine who has been performing Tai Chi for eleven years and says, she is still learning. It is like being on a journey – a journey which is interesting because it is into the self. The study of Tai Chi takes forever.

*"Perseverance is one of the fundamental requirements in practising Tai-chi Ch'uan. No results can be obtained without it."* Yearning K Chen

## Nigel Padley; Scunthorpe, Lancs.

*I am a forty two year old steel worker married with nine year old twins and a mortgage. I am finding life a lot more fulfilling since learning how to read and write. Among other things I now do surveys and other conservation work for butterfly conservation, as well as being a volunteer. Adult Education has taken me from being illiterate to may be having a piece of work published.*

*The photo is of Ruth Pownall my first teacher and myself. I think Ruth deserves a mention because she got me through my initial unsure stage at the beginning.*

## Foreword

Learning to read and write at forty was the hardest thing I have ever done. First I had to admit to my self that I needed help, then I had to ask strangers for that help.

It was hard work and up hill all the way for the first two years, but I think it was the best thing I have ever done.

In this diary I have talked mostly about my fears and how I reacted to those fears. I think I should say that I had count less good happy times that far out weighed my fears, but it's the fears that most people miss out when recalling memories. Thats why I have written about them.

After reading through my diary, I think it ends better than it starts and I repeat my self a little bit. But I think it changes as I changed.

It's been another hard thing to do because I'm not sure who's going to end up reading it.

## Monday 25th September 1995

I have been day off today.

I have been working in the living room all morning, I will be glad when we have finished the decorating.

When I took the oil painting off the wall to put it in a safe place, it triggered memories of where and when we had bought it. It was from a week end we had spent at Hartsholme country park near Lincoln in the little caravan we had at the time. Jenna and Christopher our twins were about eighteen months old and my most vivid memories are of them and how we could not work out why when people walked past our caravan at night they would start giggling and saying things like. "Ah look."

Then we realised that as soon as we closed the curtains that separated Jenna and Christopher's bed from the rest of the caravan so we could not see them, they would pull themselves up and spend most of the night looking out of the window. It looked funny because all you could see of them from the outside of the caravan was their little hands gripping the bottom of the window and two pairs of eyes peering out.

I had fish and chips for my dinner. After which I walked up to The Old School House on Rowland Road for my creative writing class. It was the start of a new term. It's only a short walk from our house of which I am glad because I am sure if it was any further I would not have started the course last year, of which I missed the first class because I was afraid that as soon as the class started writing every one in it would notice that I still had a big problem with my literacy skills.

I think I will always remember how I spent the next week tossing the fors and againsts about in my head and how I was still unsure when I set off to enrol at the second lesson. I think it was the thought of being in a class on my own with a lot of strangers and not knowing how they would react if they found out that I had been almost totally illiterate just over two years ago. I think that at the time I would have given my left arm to have Ruth or Wendy (my two Adult Education teachers) with me that after noon.

The first thing I did when I got the creative writing teacher on his own, at the end of the class was to tell him about my educational back ground. It was one of the hardest things I have ever done. He did not seem interested at all.

Even today I was still a bit nervous on my walk up there. David the teacher thrust an enrolment form at us all at the start of the class. The way he gave them to us put me back about three years and I was racking my brain trying to think of an excuse why I could not fill it in. It must have taken me about ten minutes to get my act together and start filling it in. Apart from that the class was very enjoyable.

When I got home I started on the decorating again. Liz went straight from work to have a look at one or two carpet shops. She picked a carpet which when I saw it I thought was very nice. A man came from the carpet shop to measure the living room after tea. Liz had just got back from taking Christopher to Cubs when he came.

## Tuesday 26th September 1995

I have been day off again today.

This morning Christopher came through into our bed and got talking about his school work. That's one thing we never thought he would do because he did not like school at all until Liz and I went to see the head master and got him put into another class.

I have been using what I have learnt at first as a student and now as a volunteer at adult education to help him, because I do not want him to be forty like I was before he realises what he's missing out on. One of my main aims was to get him up and running. Which I think we have done, because he will sit down and do some home work with Liz or I every night.

After breakfast, I had a walk up to Ancholme House. Where on a Tuesday when I'm not at work I'm a volunteer in Ruth's E.S.O.L. class.

When I walk into Ancholme House for what ever reason, my thoughts always seem to drift back to the first time I walked down the corridor looking for room 6 to see some one called Viv Thorpe. I had spoken to her on the phone the week before and she had sounded alright, but I was still very much on edge. She took me from room 6 into the creche, because there was a class going on in room 6.

After a chat with her which I think was partly to put me at ease and to find out a bit about me, I think in a way she was trying to find out how bright I was with out being too obvious. She then said, "I think I will try you in Ruth's class."

Then she took me back to room 6 and introduced Ruth to me and gave me a card with her name and phone number on (which I have still got) and on the back she wrote the days and times of the classes she thought would be the most suitable for me. Ruth, Viv and I agreed that I should start the next Monday (which I did).

I nearly ran out of the place after the meeting. I felt quite proud and pleased with myself as I walked home because I was pretty sure that was the hard bit over with.

When I got home Liz my wife, who I had only told about my reading and writing problem about two weeks before asked how I had gotten on.

"It went alright I think, but the teacher at first glance looks just like our Lynda." (my sister).

It was at the start of today's class that Ruth gave me the letter about writing a diary. After reading the letter I put it on a pile of Ruth's paper work and said, "I was not really interested in it."

Ruth just said something like, "OK it's up to you."

As the class went on, I started thinking about it again and the only reason I could come up with for not having a go was that I did not think I would do any good. But then I thought that's what's held you back in the past, just look at where you are now compared with two years ago. So at the end of the class I told Ruth that I would have a go and that I would try to write my diary in a chatty flash back style. We ended up having a long chat about this and that, we got talking about wild life after I told her that I had had my photo taken for the steel news because I had found a colony of rare Butterflies on the steel works.

I think that sometimes after classes I keep her chatting too long but she's too polite to say anything. I think that's one of the things that makes her a good teacher, because she is easy to talk to.

It was not till I was in a shop getting some chinese chicken and mushrooms to cook for my dinner that I thought, I bet Ruth knew all along if she left me to make my own mind up about writing a diary I would do it, but if she had tried to talk me into it, it would have put me off.

I also bought myself a cartridge pen from the stationary box, to write my diary with. I tend to buy a new pen when I start a new project I'm not sure why. I think I bought a cartridge pen this time because I think that the people who read these diaries will think it's the sign of a good writer. That just shows you how daft I can be sometimes.

After cooking and eating my dinner I started writing my diary.

After tea I set out in the car to go to a Butterfly conservation working evening near Wragby about forty miles away. I was only about five miles from home thinking about how I could write a piece in my diary about how I would never have dared join something like this at one time, because it was always at the back of my mind that I would get caught out and every one would know that I could only just write my name and read about the same. I had it worded quite well when the car started to smoke and pull to the left. I drove it about another half mile to a lay by and stopped.

The left front brake had seized up and the wheel was red hot. I took the wheel off and poured the container of water that we keep in the boot over the brakes.

Then after it had cooled down I freed the brake off and put the wheel back on and drove home and try as I might I could just not get back to the same train of thought.

## Wednesday 27th September 1995

I have been at work on six till two this morning. It went pretty much as normal.

Through the post today we received Jenna and Christopher's Young Ornithologist club new membership cards.

I enrolled them in the R.S.P.B.'s children's section two years ago for two reasons, firstly I think that all children should be involved in conservation because it's their future and secondly because I was a member of the R.S.P.B. and I could not understand a lot of the articles in the magazine. Ruth knowing that I was interested in wild life brought me some of her children's old Y.O.C. magazines, which I thought were very good. So I enrolled Jenna and Christopher so that I could get the children's magazines to read.

After work Liz took the car to have the brakes checked. We need a new calliper which they are going to fit tomorrow.

Christopher was real proud of him self to night when he got home from school because he had got a sticker for reading, I think that means we've got him through the learning pain barrier. I always thought he would end up like me and I used to say to Ruth and Wendy that they would be teaching him in about twenty years time, but with their help Liz and I seem to have got him on his way.

I called it the learning pain barrier because I think when you get to a certain point in the learning process it seems harder and harder to make any progress and it would be so easy to quit, which I thought Christopher had done at seven years old.

I started writing a book called through the pain barrier after I had finished as a student at adult education because looking back I took a lot of my frustration and anger out on Ruth but mostly I think out of Wendy as if it was their fault I was not making the progress I thought I should have been.

I think they had seen it all before, but I thought if I could write down what I felt and thought at the time it would some how make amends.

## Thursday 28th September 1995

I should have been at work on six till two again this morning, but I have taken a lieu day because the carpet fitter is coming at about one o'clock to fit the living room carpet. It also meant that I could go and help out at the special needs class run by Hilary and Wendy. Of the two classes where I am a volunteer this one is by far my favourite.

It was at the induction course run for new volunteers that I put my hand up to help out at this special needs class. I think the only reason I volunteered for this class was that no one else put their hand up for it. At the time I could not see any thing good about it. It was run by Hilary and Wendy.

Hilary had always stuck up for Wendy when I was giving her a hard time. I think it's fair to say that at one time I tried to bully my way through Word Power. If I thought that Ruth or Wendy were going to knock back a piece of my work I would snap at them as soon as they started to talk to me about it. This did not put them off though and they always had their say. I think that at that point, I thought they were asking too much of me. But I am sure now they knew just what they were doing.

I don't know why I thought they would hold it against me because they had always been alright with me and Wendy and I had got on great at the induction course.

The thought of helping people with special needs was a bit off putting as well. I was not sure what to expect at that first class. Wendy introduced me to the class and straight away three students gave me their work to look at, I was touched at how friendly they were and I do not think I had ever felt at ease so quick before with so many strangers. By the end of the first class I felt like we were all old friends. I now plan other things around that class so I can attend as many as possible. (I some times wonder if Wendy and Hilary were expecting the old me to turn up at that first class or the new grown up me.)

Today at the class another volunteer and I took four of the students around town to take some photos for a project they are doing.

At tea break Wendy was asking me about the creative writing course I am doing at the moment at W.E.A. She also wanted some information about it for another student of hers, I am going to take her my file in next week.

The carpet fitter got here on time, he has made a good job of fitting it.

I took the car to have the brakes done after Liz had got home from work and she picked it up later.

Then we put the furniture back in the living room.

## Friday 29th September 1995

I am nights tonight.

Last night while we were laid in bed drinking our Ovaltine (God that makes us sound old) I got Liz to read through what I had already written, for her opinion and to check my spelling. Liz has helped me from the start and I am sure that I would not have got this far with out her help. She thought that my diary was going to be too long for a week. So I spent about the next half hour explaining to her that it was not just one week's diary, but one, that I tried to put years into a week of flash backs. From my first lesson at Ancholme House with Ruth that I nearly bottled out of because as I was walking in the main door of Ancholme House a man I worked with was on his way out. This encounter sent all kinds of thoughts racing through my head, what if there's some one I know in the class? What will happen if work finds out? Then I thought if there was some one in the class I knew I could just pretend I was in the wrong room and walk out.

I think the fear of being found out was the main reason I was aggressive to my teachers because they were trying to get me to use my new found skills out side the class room, but I thought if I'm going to get caught out this would be the time, but after a while I realised that this was the only way forward.

At one time I thought I would be able to stop or turn back at any time, and that thought in a way kept me going.

The worst moment I ever had was one Sunday morning, just after I had started at Adult Education. I had just started to do some home work at the kitchen table, when Jenna our daughter started to cry in the back garden. I rushed out side leaving my home work on the table, she had fallen off the slide. While I was seeing if she was alright one of our neighbours walked in the house straight into the kitchen for a coffee as she often did. When I walked back into the kitchen there she was standing near the sink. Liz was up stairs in the bath and I felt sick. I did not know if she had seen my home work or not. I was not sure if I should try to move it or not because if I did it might bring it to her attention. Then I thought if she has seen it and she tells her husband he will tell every one where we work.

I do not think she saw my home work because no one has said any thing about it.

I was two till ten that day and when I set off for work I got Liz to go down to M.F.I. and get me a desk and chair for our bed room and that's where I have done my home work ever since.

After I had explained to Liz what I was trying to do with my diary I think she quite liked the idea.

I have spent most of the morning working on my diary.

I had a toasted egg sandwich for dinner before going back to bed to get some sleep ready for work to night.

I did not sleep too well this afternoon, I had just got back in bed and the window cleaner came.

Then I got thinking about writing a foreword for my diary. Which was going round in my head. I was also clock watching because I had to be up to let Jenna and Christopher in from school, because Liz had gone straight from work shopping with her Mother.

Jenna and Christopher brought some conkers home with them, which they said I had to put in vinegar for them.

After Liz had got home from shopping she took Jenna and Christopher for their Kick Boxing lesson. We are trying to get them involved in as many things as we can hoping that it might keep them off the streets when they get older.

## Saturday 30ᵗʰ September 1995

I am nights again to night.

Last night at work during my meal break I had a walk round looking for some aluminium drink cans for Jenna and Christopher to take to school. Their school is collecting them to try and raise money to buy a new computer. I was surprised how much Christopher is doing to help, he looks in every road side bin on his way home from school at night and he is asking every one for them and when we think that only four months ago he would not have urinated on the school to stop it burning down. Liz and I think that the change in his attitude is to do with the fact that we went up to school and got the head to put him in another class with another teacher. I think that half the battle is getting the right students and teachers together. I think that most schools could learn a lot about that and other things from Viv and her team at Adult Education in Scunthorpe.

Last night at work I picked up a copy of this months steel news and the article about me finding a colony of Grayling butterflies on the works was in. I have been looking at wild life on the works for years, and I did a project on it for my Word Power, but if I had found this colony back then, I would not have said any thing to the bosses about it just in case there might have been a form to fill in to get the works photographer to cover it for the steel news.

I have not slept too well again. Next door's phone keeps ringing and their dog keeps barking at it.

I got up about 10.30 am and had two rounds of toast and a cup of tea. After which I had a quick walk in the garden and there was the most gorgeous Red Admiral butterfly I have ever seen, on the lawn. I rushed in and got my camera which I had to put a film in, batteries and a different lens. To my surprise it was still there when I got back outside. I used the film up on it.

I'm not sure what the pictures will turn out like, but it was good practise for me because one of my aims is to enter a photo of a butterfly into a photographic competition run by The British Butterfly Conservation Society – Lincolnshire Branch. That's another thing I would not have dared do because of the forms involved.

While I was writing about the photo competition I got thinking about the first time Ruth got me to try and write something in class, and after she had read it she said something like that's alright.

But I could see from the look on her face that she could not read a word of it, which made me realise just how bad I was. At that point I was not sure whether to go on or not. I thought if I've got to forty without knowing how to read or write why learn now.

I think what made me continue was that in the short time I had spent at Adult Education they had given me a glimpse of what I might one day be able to do.

I went back to bed at 1.30 pm. I was a long time getting back to sleep.

By the time I got up again Liz and the children were home from spending the day at Brigg with my family.

## Sunday 1ˢᵗ October 1995

I am nights again to night.

I have not slept too well at all. Jenna and Christopher have been real pains this morning. I was a long time getting to sleep because of them and I was up by 10.30 am.

The first thing I did when I got up, was to put a peanut feeder on our bird table. I think I should explain, I have set a bird feeder up outside our garage next to a hole I have made in the garage door to put a camera through. I am hoping to get some good photos of birds feeding. Then I can show them at next years A.G.M. of the Scunthorpe's Museum Society, (which is another thing I have joined since starting at Adult Education) where members can show their own slides. After a cup of tea, Jenna and I took some stuff to the tip for recycling. Christopher was at church with the Cubs.

I got into recycling after doing a work sheet on it at adult education, and now I am trying to get Jenna and Christopher into it. There were 12 people at the recycling bank and apart from Jenna they were all men. I wonder if they had all done the same work sheet as me.

I went back to bed after my dinner for about two hours.

While I was laid in bed, I got thinking back to when Jenna and Christopher were born and how I got Liz to go and open them a Building Society account each so if ever I needed to spell their names I would know where to look.

Then I got thinking about how at one time all I wanted was the Word Power certificates to prove I was no longer illiterate, how I got them did not seem important.

I always used to write on any thing I sent to Liz (i.e. cards on her birthday) "To Liz, all my love, from Nigel." She once asked me if that was all I could spell. It was years before she found out it was.

## Monday 2ⁿᵈ October 1995

I should have been quick turn round today, nights back two till ten, but I booked a 39 hour day so I could attend my creative writing class. But I am full of cold, so I am staying at home today and I might miss Ruth's class tomorrow, because I do not think it would be fair to give my cold to the whole class.

I am thinking about dropping my creative writing class any way. Because I think it's about time I moved on, in the field I would like to end up in which is conservation. I would like to be the Manager of a Nature Reserve one day and that's why apart from the creative writing class every thing I have joined since starting at adult education has been to do with wild life.

Thinking back I could write a lot more about my time at adult education but my diary has got to finish some where and I think me planning my next move is as good a place as any.

I think I should say that I got a lot of help from volunteers and other students, but I thought I better not name them in my diary.

This is the longest piece of work I have ever done and I think it shows what adult education can do if you give them the chance.

The End.

## Christine Luke; Frome, Somerset

*Until recently, I worked in administration for large and small enterprises including the last nine years with Social Services. The knowledge and experience acquired over the years enabled me to use those skills when I returned to education. In September 1996, I start a new career as Deputy Director of Vocational Education at a comprehensive school in Bristol.*

*My interests include listening to music, reading, travelling abroad, cycling, information technology and being involved in my children's activities. After working for several years, I hope to enrol on a course to develop my skills still further.*

I took up adult learning, believe it or not, as a hobby. I was working in an admin job which suited my circumstances and one which I enjoyed although there would never be any opportunities for promotion. I decided to enrol on a part-time BTEC Business and Finance Course, Ordinary National Certificate at Trowbridge College in Wiltshire in 1990 just to prove to myself that after completing formal education in 1969, I could still learn at 37 years, hold down a job and raise two children or, in other words, I wasn't 'brain-dead' and I needed to upgrade my qualifications (which comprised a mix of GCE's and CSE's ranging from 4 'O' Levels to varying grades and various shorthand/typing and wordprocessing certificates)!

Nearing the end of the ONC, my tutor commented that several previous students had gained entry to universities and the seed was sown! It had been a personal ambition from a child, to study for a degree but I had been a late developer and didn't show the 'potential'. However, again through circumstances, such as needing a salary, I decided to enrol on the BTEC Higher National Certificate in Business and Finance, for a further two years. During the last year of this Course I also studied GCSE mathematics. This was because I had applied for, and been accepted on, the two year BA Business Education Course with Qualified Teacher Status at the University of the West of England in Bristol. I next arranged 'unpaid leave' with my employer, which means that after the course, I can return to my old job if I so wish.

Life since September 1994, when I re-entered full-time education, has obviously changed significantly for me. I am now a 'mature student' in a mixed group of around 25 – the youngest being about 22 years and the oldest when the course completes will be 48 years old. I drive to Bristol daily to attend lectures etc. This is a round trip of about 48 miles from Frome, Somerset, takes approximately 90 minutes each way and I pick up another student along the way. Some students travel daily even further than this – Bridgend, Ross-on-Wye and Yeovil for instance.

As mainly 'mature students' with other commitments, I feel one of the major experiences we miss out on is not living in 'digs' with peers and being closer to the campus so we can take advantage of the different clubs and hobbies (such as scuba diving and gliding), time simply doesn't allow. However, I feel very lucky and privileged to have been offered the chance to experience a lifestyle which I thought had long passed me by and perhaps the shortage of time will ease up later so I can pursue some of those things eventually.

We are a very diverse group, educationally and socially, coming from a wide variety of backgrounds and several different nationalities; some with lots of work experience and life skills and others with different experiences. Initially this caused some problems with the group 'gelling' but we have always found that in times of crisis we are 'there' for each other and this has been my most compelling experience – camaraderie – working with and for other people in a similar situation all sharing the same problems and pressures and dealing with them together even though we have come from varying backgrounds.

The two year course structure has taken different formats. Indeed, each term has been different. During the first year, university attendance was either three or four days with the remainder being allocated as 'study' days. The first term of the second year has been two formal days attendance and the other days used for group and individual assignment work. This is partly due to the changing way that teachers are now being trained which has decreased professional studies teaching time in the university and is, instead, the responsibility of our school placements. Most of our subject lectures are divided in such a way that opportunities are found to show how students can apply different methods of teaching in schools other than didactically. Therefore, we experience a wide range of different learning styles which have included, as well as those already mentioned, role-play, presentations, seminars, discussions, debates and being put under exam conditions to remember what it is like for the student under pressure.

Overall, there has been much independent and self-supported study and I think this is because of the type of profession and subjects we have chosen to teach. My qualification will enable me to teach Economics, Information Technology and Business Education at GCSE, 'A' Level and GNVQ standard. All these subjects change practically on a daily basis so it is important to be self-motivated, committed and be able to work independently to keep ahead of the changes, and future pupils!

## A 'typical' day at the University may comprise:

9.30 am:    Two hours subject lecture. First hour mainly didactic delivery with some whole group participation, questions/answers. Second hour may include group work set by lecturer such as using the computers in economics or finance to set up work such as a profit and loss account and ratios which could then be saved on floppy disk to be adapted as teaching resources in our future schools/colleges. Alternatively, a student may deliver the second hour especially if they have a good working knowledge of the subject. For instance, one student has worked extensively in marketing and another is an ex-accountant so they would prepare and take the respective lecture. This, again, is good preparation for teaching – we all agree it is far worse teaching peers than pupils any day! Subject notes are

|              | photocopied and distributed because this helps to build our resources when teaching. Always, our key focus is to build resources ready for when we 'go out' on Block School Experience (BSE). |
|--------------|---|
| 11.30 am:    | Short coffee break. |
| 11.45 am:    | Individual or group tutor time. This time is used to discuss assignment/project work, difficulties, problems, etc. Each student is assigned a personal tutor who will eventually write allocated students' references when applying for jobs. |
| 12.30 pm:    | Lunch. |
| 1.30 pm:     | Professional studies – looking at aspects of teaching, such as monitoring and assessment, differentiation in the classroom, different teaching styles, dealing with behavioural problems, etc. Role play may be used or perhaps organising a teaching aid game such as in a production line/organisational skills, to see how the game works and assess whether it is worth using in the classroom – setting up simulations so schoolchildren can actually participate aids learning because the experiences help memory retention so it is a much more effective method of teaching. |
| 3 pm:        | Tea Break. |
| 3.15 pm onwards. | Time used for tutor appointments, library research, reading, etc. and homeward bound when everything is accomplished. |

During the first term at UWE, I spent six weeks leading up to Christmas (1994), at a large inner city mixed comprehensive school teaching 'A' level Economics, Business Studies, Intermediate GNVQ, keyboarding and I was also allocated to a tutor group. Some of the time was also used to observe other classes such as careers, mini-enterprise schemes, etc. Student teachers are expected to take a full and active part in school-life and to build good relationships with both colleagues and students – I even attended the sixth form Student Ball – a very high profile occasion and also the staff disco! The Block School Experience (BSE) gives the opportunity of participating in school-life to see if the right choice has been made. It also allows the university lecturers and school-teachers to observe student teachers taking classes to see if they will make good teachers. When student teachers return to university, BSE help us to focus much more clearly on aims and objectives to be achieved over the entire two years.

What has University life given me? Well, it has given me the chance to fulfil a life-long ambition. I love every day I am on the campus, the excitement, the atmosphere, meeting new faces and the overall learning experience. It has given me the opportunity to break out of the mundane routine; university life opens doors to meet people who otherwise would not be encountered (for instance I have just completed a major assignment which involved a complete company appraisal so I had to contact the organisation and build relationships with key personnel so I could gain their confidence to interview and question them in detail to gain a true perspective of the company to write the assignment); forge new and lasting friendships; work with like-minded people; try new experiences and rise to sometimes difficult challenges set by the assignments such as running our own 'mini-enterprise' over a term so we can empathise with pupils when they encounter problems in business enterprise schemes. The feeling of meeting and fulfilling those challenges is euphoric!

The Course, as with the ONC and HNC, has had a big effect on my personal development. It will enable me to qualify as a teacher, gain 'professional' status and hopefully, progress onto a new career which will allow me to demonstrate my love of learning and knowledge which will hopefully have an impact on, and bear fruit in time, for my own students. The beauty of my main subject, Business Studies, is that it encompasses many aspects of business life. At the same time as teaching the subject, the teacher is also developing, encouraging and preparing students for their future work-life roles.

I have been lucky to have both my partner's and children's support to be able to fulfil my ambition. Obviously education is a high priority in our household and I hope that my own study is an example to my children. So far, they have been luckier than me in that they are being given the chance to fulfil their potential because they have the backing at home by being given the facilities and resources. And, most important of all they are shown interest and given encouragement and support – things which I did not really have when I was younger. Currently my son, who is now sixteen, won a scholarship to a local music school to pursue a musical career as a cathedral organist and is studying for three 'A' levels. My daughter, now fourteen, has just moved to the local community college where she starts working towards GCSE's next year. She shows more confidence daily, and is also demonstrating musical ability in clarinet and piano. At the time of writing, I will be in my final two terms at the University of the West of England in Bristol and preparing for my final Block School Experience. I will now only spend odd weeks on the campus as I commence my final teaching practice in January until June 1996 and return only to UWE during half-term and at the end of the practice. Two more assignments to go and Qualified Teacher Status (the final school placement tutor passes or fails us) so there is a considerable amount of hard work to do yet! Then our group splits to pursue careers and lifestyles across the globe once again but now all the richer for our common experience.

A conversation I had recently with my tutor when I summed up that "I felt as though I would always be a student learning because we never know enough especially when teaching" and he replied "that is indeed how it is!" Once a student, always a student, whether to gain qualifications or satisfy self-interest, the thirst to learn is never quenched.

Now, nearly six years later, my hobby is nearing completion for a while but one day, who knows, maybe the Masters ...

## Karen Holtom; Moseley, Birmingham

*My name is Karen I am age 39. I live in a flat in Moseley in Birmingham with my friend Mary.*

*My hobbies are reading and writing and going out with my friends. I also like animals. I am a member of a Support Group because I love helping people get what they can out of life. I like going to night school and some of my work I am doing is reading other people's diaries and I enjoy reading them. I am also an Advocate to my friend Gwenie. We have been friends for three years. I enjoy everything I have done.*

## My Life

I left school at 16. At 17 I went to Bellbarn Centre for 4 years. I didn't like it sometimes because we didn't have a choice in activities and we had to do what they said. The Centre was in Edgbaston, Birmingham.

When I was 21 I left Bellbarn Centre. Then mam went back to work and I had to look after my brother Daniel who was 5. Sometimes I liked and sometimes I didn't. I did it because I had no choice.

After two years a Social Worker called Betty got involved with my family and she said I should be with people of my own age.

Now I have changed Social Worker because I was very upset at home. Her name is Jean Bishop and she is very nice. I went to live at Allens Croft Centre in Kings Heath, Birmingham and I was very happy there.

## My home at Allens Croft

In 1990 I started to go to Allens Croft for weekends then a week then for 10 days. After that I had a week at home from Monday to Friday and I went to Allens Croft on Friday to Monday night. This lasted for six weeks.

I was waiting for a permanent room. When I was there I did jobs on the rota like setting tables and washing up etc. Then I finally got a room and I had two key workers. They was John and Arley, were nice.

When I finally was living at Allens Croft I started to learn to cook Sunday lunch, one week with Eileen and one week with Bridget. They were the cooks. Then also I did tea on a week day.

Then I had some training to catch the bus to Kings Heath and the Centre. One day I had to meet John at Selly Oak Hospital and I did it. I felt good.

One day I went shopping for my food in the supermarket also. I did my own washing and ironing. In time I was good enough to go into the training kitchen and I was able to do all my own shopping, cooking, washing and ironing and I felt good and proud.

## My New Home

In December 1991 I had a chance to live in a flat with Mary.

One day Lea phoned Mary and arranged a meeting and Lea showed me the flat. One day I came with Arley to meet Mary and we had a cup of tea. I liked the flat and Mary. Two weeks later I moved in for a three month trial and I was very happy and it was successful.

Now I have been there for five years and now I am able to go away on holiday on my own and I don't need any more training in housework, shopping, cooking, washing, ironing and I can handle my own money as well.

I see PCO Lea Birford and she gives me support once per month offering emotional support and training in crisis management using Diary.

## On Holiday in Blackpool

I went to Blackpool in 1990 with PCO's Eileen and Ineth. We went on the coach from Digbeth Coach Station in Birmingham.

When we got there we got off the coach at the Lonzedale Coach Station in Blackpool. Then we went to the house where we stayed. The house is called Lauren House. It is owned by Mrs Janet Barott.

I have been two times with the Centre, then I went with Mary.

When I knew we was going I phoned Janet to ask if she had any room. Then I went to the travel agent and booked my coach.

Last Christmas I went again and had a good time.

In August I went on my own. I phoned for a taxi to go to Digbeth Coach Station. And I am going for Christmas 1995.

## When I Started Night School

In 1990 I started night school at Wheelers Lane School in Kings Heath. I went on the 35 bus from Allens Croft to Kings Heath, then I walked.

In 1992 I moved up into Wyn's class. In 1993 we moved to Swanshurst School in Billesley, Birmingham.

In September 1992 to July 1993 I did my City and Guilds Wordpower Foundation Course and it was successful. I enjoyed it. I came almost every week and I obtained a Certificate.

From September 1993 to December 1994 I did my City and Guilds Wordpower Stage 1 again I was successful and I also obtained a Certificate.

In December 1994 I also obtained an adult learner award and we had a Presentation evening in February 1995 and I obtained a Certificate.

I have also done Keyboard Skills at Trittford Centre in Billesley. I enjoyed it and I obtained a Certificate.

## Gwenie

Gwenie is a friend of mine who I go and see one day a week. She lives in a Hospital called Monyhall Hospital in Birmingham she has lived there since she was 18.

She is a nice lady and she has trouble talking and walking.

When we go out she likes going and having a cup of tea. Sometimes when I am not looking she will have my tea. When she sees me she is happy, also it makes me happy to see her.

I work for Citizen Advocacy South Birmingham as a Volunteer.

I have been an Advocate from 1993 to Gwenie and I have enjoyed working with her. I am glad to see how well she has done.

Everyone who sees her are very pleased with her and me and they say I have worked very hard.

> ### 'Something For Me'
> ### Adult and Continuing Education Group;
> ### Cottingham, Yorks.
>
> *We planned this group to meet the needs of women "returning to life", as one of them said to me, after being very involved with home and family for years. Hence the title, based on their frequently expressed desire … "And now I want something for me".*
>
> *Although we were only together for a summer term, it was a very supportive and pleasant group, in which I observed personal growth and development of confidence. All the students subsequently moved onto mainstream Adult Education and some made significant employment progress.*
>
> *The diary was written by the group at my suggestion in order to encourage other learners.*
>
> *Patricia Crowther, Course Tutor.*

**Situation:** An Adult and Continuing Education Group of 6 women students looking to return to paid work. A confidence building course offering job search and interview skills with additional options in word processing. A negotiated agenda.

## Diary

Before we started

We felt very apprehensive about what we would be doing and what the other people/tutor would be like and whether we would be able to cope with the work.

## Week 1

All our worries disappeared when we saw everyone was very friendly and the working atmosphere would be relaxed. First the tutor talked about herself, then we all took our turn. It was embarrassing at first but, once we got into it, we were fine. We discussed why we had come on the course and what we were hoping to gain from it and by the end of the first week we had drawn up our agenda about what ideally we would like to gain from the course:

Confidence – Job Search – Interview Skills – Curriculum Vitae – Career plan – discussing issues – sharing difficulties – increasing assertiveness – presentation skills.

We realised that this was a lot to cover and that we might not make it all.

## Week 2

Pat was absent and Denise took over. We listened to part of a tape but wished that we could have listened to it all because it was interesting. We then discussed what skills and strengths we had gained through our different experiences in life and started to realise that we had a lot more than we had first thought.

## Week 3

Pat was with us again and we began to look at job search. We discussed where to look for jobs, what employers are looking for and what we have to offer. We talked about Equal Opportunities.

## Week 4

We looked at job adverts, application forms and began to think about compiling a C.V.

## Week 5

We looked at how we would write a letter to apply for a job, how it would be set out and how we would word it.

## Week 6

We prepared our C.V.'s with Pat's help then made up a mock advert for two jobs by splitting up into two groups. Group one planned one for a children's clothes shop and Group two for a receptionist in an opticians. We discussed how we would apply for the job and also how we would conduct our interviews.

## Week 7

We wrote our letter to apply for our imaginary job and then, splitting into two groups we planned the questions we would ask. We were using Equal Opportunities documentation modelled on the Adult Education Service's procedures so we also had a Job Description and a Personal Specification. Everything to do with our job was typed up and looked quite professional. We rounded off the session by looking at the photocopier since we needed copies of everything, and also the fax. We managed to fax Carol's husband's office!

## Week 8

We were all very nervous this week as we split into our two groups again to conduct interviews. First one group interviewed and then the next. Afterwards we discussed that it wasn't as hard as we thought that it might be. We had been very worried that we might giggle and spoil it all but we didn't. People really came through well in interview both as interviewers and interviewees and we felt quite professional. We had immediate feedback on our performance and Pat promised also a written diagnosis of how it went, to be typed for our portfolios.

## Week 10

We looked at our portfolios and agreed that there is a need for them to be organised. We realised how impressive they can then be as a record of what we have achieved. We talked again of the need to prepare for interview, of open and closed questions and of rehearsing our responses with a friend. We discussed the role of non-verbal communication in terms of how we present ourselves. We looked again at our agenda to see what we had covered and realised that we had been rather ambitious for a ten week course. We could see how much we had managed to cover, which was a surprising amount. We decided to spend a little time on assertiveness although as Pat said we had been quietly developing this on our course anyway since it relates to self-confidence and valuing ourselves.

We prepared a summary of our course as part of the end of the course evaluation as follows and gave feedback to Pat to help to shape other courses.

## Summary

We enjoyed learning and getting new ideas about job search and courses because it gave us something to think about and another interest outside the home and children. It was definitely 'something for me'. We had all enjoyed the many discussions we had had and felt that we had learned things from listening to each other. Pat was extremely helpful and made us feel at ease and gave us confidence. She persuaded us that we have many more capabilities than we think that we have and made us feel important.

We ourselves made outside links with other agencies such as the Job Centre and the Careers Office and became aware of other qualifications such as the new NVQ and GNVQ. We learned a little about Equal Opportunities and the law of employment which will help us when we get back into work.

Those of us who have done the word processing and computer course have really enjoyed it and have been well taught by our tutors and the rest will take the plunge next term. We are all signing up for at least one class in September and some of us for two or three. Two of us have been offered better jobs because our employers noticed that we were taking our careers seriously.

We felt sometimes that we were a bit rushed and would have liked more time to give us, say, an hour to talk about our personal lives and things we have done in the week and to plan the next week, then a coffee break and a second session to get down to the hard work and decide on the next week's session. Perhaps two hours is too short, maybe we need two and a quarter or two and a half, and we would all like a second term as a group because we feel that we work well together.

Most of all we have gained confidence and a little assertiveness. We know that when we move on, there will be some support for us back here either formally through workshops or informally. And we fancy the idea of a weekend away at a residential weekend if it could be arranged with next term's group.

And then we wrote this Diary because we felt that it might help other students to see what they can do through the Adult Education Service.

## Tutor's Comments

They have been a lovely group to take, with the only problem being the amount of absences due to holidays, sickness, children's mishaps which have slowed our progress. I am rounding off the course with a one hour's tutorial for each of them to tidy their portfolios and to check how much each had covered individually of the small competence based booklet which I have designed and use for this type of group. I expect to see them around the Centre in the future doing other things and I am pleased that they feel that they have had such a positive experience on this access back to learning/ work course.

## Hubert Jefferson; York

*Born 1924. Trained as a pharmacist. After service as a photographer in Fleet Air Arm, married in 1950 and took over family business of village stores.*

*Two sons – Roger, 24 years service in Police.*

*Roderick, BSc, ARICS, Chartered Quantity Surveyor.*

*After 3 coronaries, I retired and sought fresh interests, through WEA classes. Local history, family history, oil painting, medieval wills, the way we lived 16th – 18th Centuries. Published history of my home village 1993 and followed with a C20th social history. Other hobbies: photography, York city archives, parchment craft.*

*Intend to follow new classes as long as possible!*

## SUNDAY

Had a full day in checking, and correcting where necessary, the computer print-outs of TWELVE WILLS from Probate Register 14, held at the Borthwick Institute of Historical Research, York.

Held in conjunction with the WEA, with Mrs Ann RYCRAFT as our tutor, a changing group has, during the past five years, been reading, discussing and summarising the wills of York craftsmen and York women from the fourteenth to mid-seventeenth centuries. The aim of our group is to complete entry of our summaries, which have of necessity had to be updated regularly as we met different challenges, and put them on computer, and to make our work available in printed and disc form. This allows us to improve our reading of documents, and to research individual historical interests. As a founder member of the group, I have been totally fascinated throughout, and found it a most challenging task which has been of great encouragement through a period of ill health. The number of parish churches within the city, together with their numerous different names over the years, has been a challenge in itself. Following our research in one parish alone, it was found that no less than thirty eight bodies were buried in the church porch – a rise in the base level must have occurred …

## FROM PROBATE REGISTER NUMBER 14, Borthwick Institute.

| fol 50. | Robert JACKSON. | Tanner. | Made | 26.3.1554. | Proven | 11.10.1554. |
|---|---|---|---|---|---|---|
| 53. | Thomas WRIGHT. | Haberdasher. | " | 14.3.1554. | " | 9.4.1554. |
| 74. | John WOOD. | Innholder. | " | 28.3.1554 | " | 28.4.1554. |
| 61. | Robert PYNDER. | Glover. | " | 4.4.1554 | " | 20.4.1554. |
| 81. | Nicholas TESTES. | Glover. | " | 13.6.1555 | " | 10.7.1555. |
| 129. | Richard WILLIAMSON. | Cord/ner. | " | 30.8.1552 | " | 3.4.1554. |
| 163. | James JORDON. | Merchant. | " | 20.1.1551 | " | 28.3.1554. |
| 148. | Peter ESSHE. | Fisher. | " | 30.6.1554 | " | 20.8.1554. |
| 156. | Richard HUTON. | Tapiter. | " | 4.10.1553 | " | 7.4.1554. |
| 182. | John BACHELER. | Cordwainer. | " | 13.11.1555 | " | 22.11.1555. |
| 213. | William BASSLER. | Butcher. | " | 5.9.1553 | " | 22.3.1554. |
| 269. | Robert FORGAILE. | Butcher. | " | 22.5.1554 | " | 22.8.1554. |
| 240. | Robert RAWCET. | Weaver. | " | 6.8.1554 | " | 27.8.1554. |

Total checking time amounted to some seven hours. Delivered by hand to Mrs. Rycraft.

## MONDAY

Typed up these notes referring to work done yesterday, then spent around two hours searching through my own collection of photographs of my home village of Elvington. About two years ago I published 'STORY OF THE HISTORY OF ELVINGTON', which, more or less, I ended at the end of the nineteenth century, primarily to avoid any embarrassment to relatives still living, of one or two particular events. Used the bench mark of the Census returns for my excuse …

Since that time, there has been an immense feedback of requests to complete a social history of the twentieth century, avoiding in that way the delicate ground. Earlier this year of 1995, I gathered a lot of material from personal resources, and from lifelong friends in the village, and put them together into a book form. My previous book did not contain any photographs even though very many were available dating from around 1860 – an almost incredible statement, but in the census of 1861, the former headmaster of the village school has recorded himself as a 'photographic artist', and many of his prints had been retained by members of the family resident at the Rectory, and whose family still retain the gift of the living.

After all that explanation, I trust the reason for it is now obvious! An exhibition of photographs of the village dating from the period, is now on display in the parish hall, and also in the village school. The pictures which I intend to photocopy are not in such a display, and will be new to readers. There is one drawback to all this … I shall not publish it in printed form, but hope to donate copies to the parish council, Hull University, who have records for the East Riding, where Elvington always was!! The Borthwick Institute, and York Central Library, whilst retaining one copy for my family, in order to show them what poor old 'grandad' did in his dotage! Today has gone past without much to show for the time spent, but I have enjoyed very many happy memories of my youth, and remembering absent friends …

## TUESDAY

With the weather too hot to do any physical effort, I have decided to type up all the handwritten notes, so am sat in a darkened room with artificial light! It gives one the feeling of doing something useful, yet not overly strenuous. Being a very amateur typist, I find that I have already spent over three hours and only reached the fourth page, BUT, I have had to decipher my handwriting also!

However, I also find that I have written a number of notes from an old school friend, and never entered them into my system of preservation – I dare not call it a filing system, since that would imply that they would always be ready to hand as required which never is the case … Betty was vice-captain of the Ladies cricket team during the 1930's, and has a fund of stories from those days, and when I complete the diary for today, I shall be writing them up into something resembling a story, before committing them to memory on the word processor for future use in the book.

## WEDNESDAY

Another extremely hot day, the whole morning of which has been taken up with a hospital appointment, including tests on the heart scanner, to check whether I shall stand up to severe surgery in the near future. From remarks made to junior doctors who were present, it appears negative. A relief in one respect but it may prevent me attending any courses during the winter months – shall just have to wait and see.

Last evening I got engrossed with the notes from Betty, and wrote several pages, principally in recording names of members of the team, their exploits in various cup and league matches which were played all around the East Riding of Yorkshire, and the celebrations held upon the occasion of trophy success. As she was also a Girl Guide Leader, and a member of the Girl's Friendly Society ( a Church of England society for teenage girls at that period) she had also kept a very well written diary, full of information which is invaluable to me in the social history of my native village. Altogether a very long day, and quite tiring. I shall need a rest after these few lines. Think the heat makes one feel worse!

## THURSDAY

Received the WEA list of courses by post this morning, and must admit that I fancy one or two of them, especially Art. It must be almost thirty years since I first studied oil painting in class, but have continued to practice whenever the time is available. During the past year or more, John Rayson, a member of the Guild of Aviation Artists, has come to live in the village. We have been very good friends for several years, and he has given me much good advice – especially, that I should devote one day a week AT LEAST, to art. John died in May from Motor Neurone Disease, and I miss his wit and help greatly. Whenever I am able, I try to spend a few hours at the Elvington Air Museum helping in the Gallery, John being a Founder Member of the Museum, and an Honorary Vice President, whilst I knew the airfield as farm land before the war, and spent many a Saturday afternoon there shooting rabbits. The days of carefree youth! I beg to be excused from expressing such memories, but they tend to come to mind very readily as the years pass …

I MUST complete the story of TWENTIETH CENTURY ELVINGTON, get it edited and photocopied, and then I can move on to 'pastures new', and who knows, maybe have a period of concentrating on painting.

## WEDNESDAY … of the following week …

The heat in the latter part of last week was so overpowering for a couple in their seventies, that we got in the car, complete with suitcase, and drove over to Bridlington to escape!! Now refreshed, and it being a little cooler, I feel more like returning to some work, but before starting anything else, felt that I should update the diary.

I have spent most of the few days in the cooler atmosphere, reading and resting, so the first job this morning was a visit to the local Library, where I discovered a new list of adult education courses, and have brought it home to study to see if anything desperately appeals or shall I continue with my painting. Took some nice photographs of sunsets last week together with a range of subjects which may prove suitable. It is the lazy man's version of sketching I'm afraid, but does take up much less time when a wife is hoping to do something which she especially likes! Having been a Fleet Air Arm photographer fifty years ago, it still attracts me as an amateur.

Have had a good look through the LEA list of evening classes, and found some most attractive. Being considerably less active I put aside pottery as a complete change, and have selected a Monday evening course at Burnholme Community College, entitled 'Parchment Craft' – an entirely new challenge which I know nothing about! "Learn how to make Victorian style embossed greeting cards and pictures" … I'll try!

Have made arrangements with printers to have 'Twentieth Century Elvington' photocopied and bound at a special price, and take them today, to collect tomorrow. I have agreed for ten copies to be done, only three of which will be sold to close friends who are keenly interested, and the others will be donated to University Libraries, York Reference Library and Elvington Parish Council, and probably the village school. At a cost of £6.00 each for 130 pages of A4 script, plus photographs, it seems quite reasonable.

## SUNDAY

Collected booklets and feel very pleased with end product. Must make arrangements to get them out in the next few days. Took the three copies to friends who are delighted with the reproduction of the old photographs by photocopier they are quite surprising for prints dating back before World War One.

## FRIDAY

Had to have a swab taken and a course of antibiotics this week, so not done what was intended. Bed rest does not encourage serious reading in this very hot weather. Am knocking about again now but must do very little other that sit around. Expect the TV will get well warmed watching the Test Match …

## WEDNESDAY

Much better health again, and finally have sent off the remaining books to Hull, York and the Reference Library. Had two most appreciative letters by return of post from the two University departments, and the Chairman of the Parish Council intends reading it himself before handing over to the Clerk …

This really completes my 'work' before the new term starts in September, and hence, the end of the diary. Get a canvas out!

## Barbara Hodgson; Leeds

*I was born in Leeds. After leaving school at 15 without any qualifications I started work in a mill. I married at 18, had 2 children and moved to Newcastle.*

*The next 30 years were spent raising a family and working in shops.*

*I enviously watched my daughter go through college and university.*

*We moved back to Leeds in 1995 and because I had always wanted to return to learning, my neighbour, who was already a mature student, introduced me to the local college. The friendliness and standard of teaching are excellent.*

*At 50 this is just the beginning!*

## THE DIARY OF A NOBODY (Who Will One Day be a Somebody!)

First and foremost the reasons why I decided to undertake the monumental task of going back to learning.

We have to go back to 1961, the year I left school. I had been to grammar school but, for family reasons, I had to leave at 15 years old, before I had taken any 'O' levels. I married young and had a family, which I don't regret, but as the years went by I wished I had some sort of qualifications. I always read a lot and did plenty of crossword puzzles and quizzes. This probably kept my brain from stagnating. I sort of promised myself that I would, one day, go to night school or something similar. I didn't know anyone who did this but every year I collected all the prospectuses from the local schools and colleges. The years went by and despite all my good intentions I never did do anything about it.

My daughter left school at 16 years old with only a few CSE's though I thought she was capable of much more. When at the age of 26 she wanted to go into nursing, she decided to go to college and work for 6 GCSE's. I enjoyed seeing her work every night and really took an interest in what she was doing. I found myself seriously thinking about joining her, but again just let it slide. Michelle did really well and when she gained 6 really good passes she decided she wasn't as interested in nursing as she once was. She had done a psychology class and realised that this was the direction she wanted to go in. She went on to do an Access course with a view to going to university to study for a psychology degree. I was quite envious at this point and wished I had the bottle to do something myself. It was as this point that my husband and I moved from Newcastle to Leeds so my ambitions went on the back burner again.

We bought a house, and as luck would have it my next door neighbour was seriously into adult education. She had done lots of courses over the years, and she persuaded me to go for it. She took me up to the local adult education centre which happened to be Park Lane College at Town Street.

I decided to take an English course that was working towards GCSE. This was a year long course that I felt would ease me back into learning, because after 34 years out of school I didn't have enough confidence to plunge straight into a GCSE course. I needed to re-learn all the basics again before I could possibly begin to think about exams. I also needed to prove to myself that I could do something along these lines. I have always loved words and writing and at 49 I thought, now is the time to go for it before I get too old. At the end of the year I would hopefully sit an RSA exam and achieve something at last.

On the prospectus was a course called 'Getting a Certificate in Maths' which seemed complimentary to the English course and as both classes were free I had no hesitation in enrolling for this one as well. I don't find maths particularly easy and had forgotten just about everything I had been taught at school. I needed to start right back at the beginning and I thought this course sounded ideal. This would be an accredited Open College course and preparation for GCSE next year. My appetite was now well and truly whetted.

My friend had already done both these courses so she enrolled on an 'Options' course which consisted of a mixture of books and authors, videos and discussions. It was another Open College accredited course. It sounded really interesting and was again a free course so I added this to my list.

We also spotted a Local History course and this took our fancy as we are both really interested in knowing how things develop and grow. Another friend decided to join us on the 'Options' and History courses.

I called a halt at this point and couldn't wait until term started.

The first day arrived and I was so nervous as I made my way to the Centre. My first class on this Monday was English and I didn't know what to expect. I needn't have worried, it was great. The tutor, Chris Busby, was excellent, she really explained things and tailored the class to individual need as well as general topics. I thoroughly enjoyed the whole experience and even welcomed the homework!

My next class was on the Wednesday. This was Local History and though it wasn't quite as 'local' as we first thought, it was nonetheless very interesting. I think we were under the impression the area to be covered would be our immediate surrounding area of Leeds, but it was actually about Yorkshire in general and Leeds in particular. We found it very interesting.

On the Thursday I went for the Maths class, and again I found it very enjoyable. Marnie Draper was the smashing teacher, so patient. She explained each step very carefully. We were all at different levels, so it must have been very difficult for her doing individual teaching, but she didn't get flustered at all!

When the Friday arrived I was feeling a bit mentally battered after the homework of the night before, but I was looking forward to 'Options', whatever that was. Once again I was really pleased and surprised. We had a video of a modern fairytale and a paper and discussion to follow. The teacher, Chris Osborne, was very nice and made us feel really at ease. The class probably fell into the category of English Literature with a twist. We were told Shakespeare was also on the agenda.

All the teachers were so approachable and down to earth. I had thought they would all be very clever, aloof and distant which was how I remembered teachers from school. I certainly couldn't have been more wrong! Clever they most certainly are, but very down to earth and enthusiastic about their particular subject. They all treat us as equals and don't talk down to us. They just treat us as friends, which is great, it's so comforting and it makes the learning so much easier.

Following is a typical week in my learning calendar:

## MONDAY 13th Nov '95

Today in English we began by doing some vocabulary work from the worksheets Chris gave us. I enjoy this type of work very much. We had to match words to definitions on the first paper. Then we had to use a dictionary to match hard and easy words together, on paper number two. I now know quite a few different words and their meanings. Next we discussed and practised how to write a standard letter. I always thought I knew how to do this but how wrong I was! In business these days all letters are churned out by computers and word processors so the format has changed. I had noticed, but didn't think it applied to a letter a customer would write to a firm. As Chris, my teacher, pointed out, more notice would probably be taken of a well set out letter than a personal note. It looks as if you know what you are talking about and would be dealt with accordingly. This makes sense, so I'm really pleased to have learnt this. We had to write an example letter asking about holiday accommodation. I was quite pleased with mine and got 'well done' when it was marked. We were also taught how to make sure we set the letter out in paragraphs first as we would an essay. This does look much better, so well structured. Chris gave us a sheet on how to start and finish a letter as well, which will be really useful. There are some questions on this paper and we have to do these for homework. I thoroughly enjoyed today's lesson, we seemed to have covered lots of things and clarified a lot more.

We are all at different levels in the class but Chris handles it with ease, doing overall class work when appropriate, and then one to one as we do the tasks set. Its nice to talk to my classmates as well. We are all from different places and we have many reasons for wanting to learn. I really admire some of them because the subject doesn't come easy but they are determined to master it.

I handed in my homework from the previous week, which was a passage and questions about a young lad's first day down the pit years ago. We also had to write an essay on a first day in our lives. I got good remarks on my paper and I was really pleased, it makes all the hard work worth it.

## WEDNESDAY 15th Nov '95

Local History is the subject today. This is a very large group of mainly retired people. Today's topic turned out to be about the Brontes. Kath the lecturer is a Leeds City Guide and really knows her subject well. She escorts parties of foreigners all over Yorkshire and really has an enthusiasm for her job. She is very knowledgeable about all things Yorkshire, and so are most of the people in the group. A lot of them had been there last year and enjoyed it so much they were back again. They all seemed very well travelled in the county, maybe this is Kath's influence.

I joined this group with two friends and we are complete novices in this game.

It was very interesting, I knew a few things about the Brontes but was pleased to learn a lot more. We tend to go off on a tangent in this class, someone will ask a question and everyone starts reminiscing and adding their own little anecdotes. It's super hearing all the stories but Kath has to call a halt and get back to the subject in hand. This is not so much a formal class as an informal gathering of people interested in their ancestry, with a very informative speaker.

## THURSDAY 16th Nov '95

Maths loomed, perhaps my least favourite subject. Marnie the teacher is great and so enthusiastic about her work, but it hasn't rubbed off on me yet!

For the last few weeks we had been covering the whole subject of percentages. I had done some homework and was pleased that I got them all right.

Today we started with percentage change and all that it entailed. I don't find percentages particularly easy for some reason, but I think I've finally grasped what Marnie was trying to get at.

She must get exasperated sometimes trying to get through to us but she certainly doesn't show it. She keeps smiling and bubbling away all the time. We are all at widely differing stages and it's a one to one situation all the time. She moves around the room all lesson, from chair to chair. We have a good laugh because while she's with us we think we have it, and when she moves away the light goes out and we go blank again. If I ever take an exam in this subject, I'm going to gag Marnie and strap her to a chair next to me. I'm sure I'll sail through with no bother, then. It must be her presence that gives us inspiration.

I took lots of homework home from today's lesson, just to make sure I really have understood how to do them.

## FRIDAY 17th Nov '95

My last lesson of the week is 'Options'. So far this has consisted of an adult fairy tale, Shakespeare's 'Romeo and Juliet' which were both followed by a discussion about what we had seen and a written paper asking questions. Then we read a poem based on 'Fanny Hill', I loved reading this. We then asked if we could do more Shakespeare and Chris chose 'Macbeth', which was brilliant. We again watched it on video first and then discussed all the implications of it. We did a test paper to make sure we had understood what we had seen and read. Never in a million years would I have thought I would understand and make sense of Shakespeare, never mind actually enjoy it. All the class, including my two friends really enjoy the banter and discussions.

Chris (not my English teacher) really enjoys a good discussion and she draws answers out without us realising it. We all see things differently, in the class, which is good because we get so many points of view.

After a lot of work on 'Macbeth', Chris decided because we have just had Armistice Day, and its very topical, that it might be an idea to start looking at the poets and poems of World War One. She gave us copies of poems by Rupert Brooke and Wilfred Owen. We read them together and commented on the content, the war and Remembrance Day in particular.

For homework, we were given a worksheet with plenty of questions about the poems we had read.

I've never even looked at, or thought about poetry before. I always tended to dismiss it as boring, but I even went to the library and found some books on First World War poems. I thoroughly enjoyed reading them. I have totally amazed myself! I am really looking forward to next week.

You can see what a busy week I now have. This time last year I would never have thought I would have the courage to do something like this. I'm so glad my friend, Pat, gave me a nudge in the right direction. I feel as if there is no stopping me now, I've got the learning bug and I think I would like to go on and maybe do some GCSE's. After that who knows?

I think I am capable of much more than I gave myself credit for. I've become so much more confident, not just in college but in my every day life as well. I can handle so many different situations now without being overwhelmed. The only thing I haven't quite mastered yet is how to run a home efficiently while doing classes and homework. I'm sure I'll be organised before long, much to the relief of my dear husband, George. He's being really good about it, but he's not sure why I'm doing this. I haven't been able to make him understand how important this is to me.

I'm not sure what my ultimate aim is but this is certainly the first step towards it. I'm just sad I didn't do it years ago. Why did I wait so long?

## Bob Smith; Trowbridge, Wilts.

*Hi. My name's Bob Smith. I'm 47 years old, married and have two teenage daughters. Just over a year ago I became unemployed for the first time in my life. This caused me some consternation and hardship. I was conspicuously unsuccessful in finding another job that paid enough to keep up the mortgage.*

*I decided to change the direction I was headed in, i.e. downhill fast. The way I felt able to change direction was by turning my hobby into a living. My hobby is computing, I'm actually quite good at design and problem solving on computers, but I have nothing on paper to prove it. So the answer I came up with was go back to school and get something, (anything) on paper.*

The following is a personal account of what happened when I got to Trowbridge College. I hope you enjoy it, I enjoyed the course and writing about it.

People are named in here, so if anyone is upset by my comments, feel free to sue me. But bear in mind that I am still unemployed, so you won't get much.

### It beats sitting on your butt at home

Well! What would you do? You arrive at the decidedly middle age of 46 and find yourself unemployed for the first time in your life. Do you rant and rave? Do you worry yourself slim? (by about ½ a stone in my case). Do you pretend it will all be all right as soon as you find another job? (at this time, in this country?) Do you get so angry it eats away at your self control? Do you rewrite your CV a dozen times? Do you stop and take stock of life, death and the universe? Do you find out who your real friends are?

I did all those, and then some. Then I did something else all together, I decided on a complete change of career direction. I decided to try and turn my hobby into a living, the only problem was that although I am very experienced on, quite skilful at, and really enjoy my hobby, I have nothing on paper to prove it, apart from copies of design work I have done for friends. So what to do.

In my case, I decided to go back to school, or more precisely, to Trowbridge College. One of the advantages of being unemployed is that the fees for vocational courses are paid for by someone else. (By the way, for the first time in years I could afford to have my teeth done properly, that's paid for as well if you're unemployed). Back to the main thread of this account. The courses I chose in the end, after looking through the, (to me) vast choice available to me, was the BTEC IT for Business, 6 month mountain. This particular course takes the kids, (16 to 18 year olds) a whole year to complete.

### Well, why not?

I had spoken to a not very tall, not very thin bloke who was very excited about this new course the college was running, his commitment and enthusiasm were catching, I caught it, and signed up, after all his name was the same as mine. Now something the reader should be aware of was that I signed for this course in June, the course didn't start until the following September. The reason I mention this is because when I signed up, I believed I would have a job before the course started, so I wasn't really expecting to have to find out if I could still learn anything in a classroom again. Silly, wasn't I? Surprise, surprise, September rolled around and I didn't have a job, so I got myself a rucksack like my kids have. Put in my pens, ruler, rubber, a few Esseltes and anything else I could think of, and set off for a completely new experience. I had been a caretaker for 9 years at a large comprehensive but to be one of the students, well, that's something else again.

## Here we go

We were to start our odyssey in the interestingly named room, E105. We were greeted by Mary Wood and Bob Willcox, there was also a mini whirlwind in the background that we found out later, is called Mari Pearson. I can remember looking around and making a number of snap judgements about the people in the room. You know the sort of thing. She's not bad looking. He looks thick. I'd like to get to know her. Why on earth has he bothered turning up? You can probably tell from this that I was taking the educational content really seriously at the time.

Our first lesson; wasn't. By that I mean we were informed about the colleges policies about this, that and the other. We were marched round to various places of interest like reception, the library, the orbit centre, the local pub ... Just a joke, I already know where that is and don't use it very often, I mean £1.65 for a glass of wine, I can buy a bottle of the same stuff for £1.99.

## The agony and the ecstasy

The second lesson turned out to be a mixture of agony and ecstasy. This was because "keyboarding", the lesson title, involves pounding the keyboard until your arms, fingers and shoulders are screaming for mercy. Against this, the lady taking the lesson is the sort of teacher I wish my daughters had been exposed to more during their school years. My youngest in particular might even have enjoyed some of her education. I, and I think all in our group certainly enjoyed Mari's classes. George Bright please take note.

That ended our first day. I went home to my wife and said quite truthfully that I didn't know what I was going to learn on this course. As it turned out, quite a lot more than I thought, not all of it academic.

So the next day I duly turned up again and this time I took a bit more time to evaluate my class mates. The mix was very broad, and this actually proved to be a very good mix of "varicose" people. There were three blokes around my age, a couple of women about the same age, two girls, two lads, and one guy of indeterminate age. Added to these there were a couple who never turned up and another bloke who came to one session several weeks into the course, we never saw him again. All but two of us were unemployed and hoped to improve our chances of finding a job, the other two were students waiting for a university place to be offered.

## Make do and mend

The second day was to begin with Business Technology in the excitingly named B202. It was in here we found out that Information Technology included stuff which cannot be considered, "state of the art". In this room we found antiquities like 286 computers with mono screens and only running DOS programs, antiques like … YUK … type writers and worst of all, WordPerfect 5.1. Added to this we had to use pen and paper as well, God … whatever next. Whatever next, turned out to be finding out that even clapped out equipment like this doesn't always work when you turn it on. That was the first time we experienced Mari's ability to be frustrated by the equipment, cross about the equipment, have her lesson plan totally wrecked by the equipment, and yet still deliver an interesting and sometimes gripping lesson. As we progressed through the course we discovered that all our teachers had plenty of practice at this skill, some with considerably less success than others. That is apart from Ruth Berken who never had this problem, mainly because she has not yet learned how to use the on/off switch on most of the equipment, (she says she has – but won't). Sometimes her hand written assignments were almost readable even after they had been hand turned through a lytho copier. She had to use this because her photocopying card is permanently empty of credit.

The next class was IT Fundamentals, this proved to be more or less what I had expected it to be. Some pretty basic information on what the various bits of a computer are called, what they look like, what they do, (or as is the case with the college network, sometimes don't do). Plus some, for me, fairly heavy stuff on how organisations are set up and how they communicate.

The third and last class on the second day was more agony and ecstasy keyboarding. You, the reader, can have no conception how much I hated the ACU-TYPE program we used in these lessons, its smart-arse comments, ("You must have two left hands", "Are you wearing gloves" etc.) when I inevitably got it wrong. Its unwavering patience waiting for me to catch up. (No, this dammed program never caused the system to crash). Plus the fact that I didn't want to be able to type quicker that I can think. By the way, if Mari is reading this, I'm typing this account using my normal hunt and peck system of typing, and really enjoying figuratively "flicking the V's" at ACU-TYPE.

## The WORD is

During the first section of the course, (there are three sections of 8 weeks each) we only had two classes on Wednesdays, they were in the morning so we got the afternoons off. The upshot of this was we spent the whole morning with Mari, well there's worse ways to spend a morning. We were introduced to room E115 where we were in turn introduced to Word 6 for Windows, and the computers in here ran Windows, sort of. It is to Mari's credit that it was several weeks into the course before I realised she was winging it on Word, she had only just started using it herself. For me this made the lessons more interesting because when we wanted to find out how something worked, or in some cases, didn't, it became a race to see if the class could find out before Mari did. I believe we all learnt more that way than if it had just been shown to us.

The Thursday of the first week was when we met Ruth for the first time. Her lesson was sandwiched between two more sessions with Mari, one of the dreaded ACU-TYPE and one on Business Technology. Ruth's forte is communications, this covers a much wider range that I had realised before, but she quickly made me aware of memos, reports, business letters, memo reports, telephone manner, how to sit in interviews, (we learnt how not to sit from watching a video of Steve's interview), plus all manner of bits and pieces that had never really crossed my mind before. The fun thing about Ruth's classes was the way the discussions would suddenly fly off in totally different directions than Ruth had intended.

So ended the first week. I finished the week even more convinced that I wasn't going to get much out of this course other than a certificate. I decided it was better than sitting on my butt at home and came back the next week, and the week after etc., etc.

During the first 8 weeks we gradually found out vital facts like which computers run fastest in the orbit centre, like how comfortable the seats are in the library and how they have free papers for students, (hey! student; that's me). Like how you can get a filling, tasty meal in Pegasus, like how there is no point whatsoever of trying to run PowerPoint in room E115. How it is almost impossible to find a parking space, and if you do you're likely to get wet feet because you've parked in a puddle.

One thing which impressed me was the visibility of the principal, he often eats in Pegasus and always acknowledges people. In my experience in an establishment like the college this is very unusual, and very welcome. By the way, Ruth tells me that if a member of staff smokes, it is easy to talk to George because you can often find him having a drag behind the bike sheds, (are there any bike sheds in the college?). Also during the first 8 weeks it became apparent that not all of us were giving our all to the course, (this is an in joke, the Royal Air Force has a lot to answer for). I was impressed by Karen's ability to catch up after missing several days at a time. I have never met anyone who asked more questions than Steve. Then there was the one day that Mark didn't try to out talk Steve he, (Steve) managed to beat himself in a discussion, in fact he talked himself round to the opposite point of view without any input from anyone else, at the time it was quite fascinating to listen to. Glyn never seemed to pay any attention to what was going on but always handed in perfectly acceptable assignments. Ian's sheer dogged persistence in all the work also started to become apparent, of all of us Ian had to work the hardest to achieve an acceptable result. Alice just kept doing the work and getting the marks, she kept saying she couldn't, then went and did it. Leza, well I still haven't figured Leza out. And there was the quiet menace of Tim. Tim felt the course was not what he wanted so he just sat there and stewed. Sue also decided this wasn't what she wanted and left. There was one guy called Derek I think who appeared for one class and never returned.

## Part two

By the end of the first 8 weeks we were becoming a self supporting group, we were working well as a group and at one time or another we had or would all receive help, or a kick up the backside from someone else in the group.

Then the second 8 weeks began and we met John Godfrey, he of the purple shoes and fruit salad ties, who is so laid back he nearly falls on you. Now when I was at school we has a subject called sums and when it got complicated like fractions or algebra, it became arithmetic. I have also been introduced to the same subject called maths as my daughters progressed through the education system. So you can imagine my confusion when the same subject reappeared on this course as "Enabling Principles".

This section got us started on programming with Cath Shaples, Cath mothered us and never seemed to get cross when we had trouble telling a DO WHILE loop from a VARIABLE, or a STRING from an IF THEN statement. I think she got just as frustrated that she couldn't make me understand sequential files as I did that I couldn't, not that I ever showed it ... Much. And then, (yes Ruth, I do know you're not supposed to start a sentence with "AND") there was Bob WiLLcox, with 2 L's. We started an excursion into all sorts of software with Bob, spreadsheets, databases, presentations, CAD and all sorts of sexy stuff like that. Of course Ruth was still there, out in the cold and damp garden sheds with no equipment to go wrong. Apart that is from the plug sockets which Mark discovered were as safe as a condom in a drawing pin factory. Kick it once to turn it on, twice to turn it off, and three times to set fire to the building.

As our marked assignments were gradually returned to us, (in the case of John Godfrey and Mary Wood, very gradually) we discovered we weren't as thick as some of us thought we might be. This in itself was a great confidence booster, and this time was for me certainly, and I think probably for the others as well, the high spot of the course. We were doing the work reasonably well, (between us we finished up with more distinctions than merits and passes put together). We had got to know each other and our teachers. We had found our way round the place. We felt comfortable in the establishment and part of it.

Also around this time Cath came up with a work placement for me which meant I had to show one of the college secretaries various bits and pieces of Word 6. Now I may be old fashioned, but I felt that if the college was going to stick a complex piece of software on its staff, it, (the college) should train them to use it. Not rely on its students to teach its staff, cost effective as this may be. Having said that , I have heard that there is going to be a proper training course for the staff. I'm available, affable and I work cheap. Having done that small job Steve and I were given some quite interesting extra curricular assignments. I grabbed the really good one, work up a presentation about the college on PowerPoint 4, and left the hard graft to Steve. Evaluate and report on a number of management/database programs. Steve always surprises me with how thorough he is on any given task, he wrote to, rang up and generally cajoled umpteen companies to give him details of and in some cases, working demos of their software. Me, I sat at a computer and played with PowerPoint, and if I do say so myself, I was quite pleased with the result.

## Happy New Year

Christmas came and went, and so finally did Raf. Those of us who got past Christmas and into the new year were the ones there for the long haul. And believe me, that last section was a long haul, for one thing we started a module I dreaded almost as much as

ACU-TYPE; electronics. We continued seeing Ruth once a week and had lively and sometimes heated discussions about all sorts of things like child molesters, why newspapers aimed at the "workers" didn't survive, Steve's body language at interview, sometimes it even related to stuff about the course. We and Cath staggered to the final program. Bob manfully tried to turn Ian into a design expert. His biggest problem proved to be getting any of us to understand electronics. Mark had a basic grasp at the start, the rest of us had barely grasped, "BASIC", never mind making burglar alarms and the like.

Karen, Steve and myself were having so much fun learning we all enrolled in a Saturday course on DTP with Pagemaker 5 on the Apple Mac. We all started three weeks into the course, and poor old … well, young actually, Maggie Dolman got a real culture shock when we turned up and transformed her peaceful well behaved class into BTEC part two. In fact the third week she buggered off to France to get away from us … well not so much from Karen, more Steve and I.

Karen then had to drop out of the BTEC course because she got a job, well that's what we joined for. She had managed to do enough to get a certificate anyway.

The course and us arrived at the end together on March 23rd, (the date's not house style is it Mari?) Our teachers arranged a last supper at nunch time, and true to the rest of the course, we finished up in the wrong room. Even so it was a fitting conclusion and we all shook hands and said keep in touch, maybe we even will. Steve and I may be going to keep pestering the college staff because Bob, with 2L's, wants us to try and make a training video, should be fun.

## Anymore?

Just a few observations about the last six months about bits and pieces I've missed. I wonder how many forests have been cut down to enable us to finish this course. The staff at Trowbridge College have in almost all cases been helpful, supportive and smiled a lot. The whole experience has shown me that in middle age I enjoy the learning process so much more than when I was at school. It also reminded me how much I missed being around the little animals we grown ups refer to as kids.

There were occasions when Cath and John's idea of "fun", was, to say the least, a little perverse. There were other times when for one reason or another we behaved like … kids, and on these very rare days, our teachers screamed for help, and the room would finish up with more teachers than pupils. On that subject I felt a bit sorry for Mari when she sometimes sat in on our lessons to brush up her own knowledge, and we immediately treated her as a second teacher and kept asking her questions about house styles, punctuation or spelling. Looking back over the last six months, I have gained much, knowledge, friends, a wider outlook on many subjects, a reason to get up in the morning and at last, a qualification. If, as seems likely, I'm still looking for work next September, I'll be back for more.

## Lesley Goulden; Bramhall, Cheshire

*Little education due to ill-health as a child. A secretarial course led to employment with 20th Century Fox, EMI, Halle Orchestra and Sheltered Housing.*

*Discovering it is never too late, fulfilled ambition to extend education; starting with "O" and "A" levels with NEC, followed by OU studies, gaining BA, (1st Class Honours) aged 45. I also fostered children.*

*I enjoy gardening, drama and travel, and am a long-standing member of a Writers' Circle. After retirement, for health and fun, joined a "50+ Keep Fit" class. Now intend to pursue physical and academic education indefinitely.*

## DAY 1 – Class Session

I chose my class because, being over 60, I did not want anything over-ambitious. At the first session I learnt that joints are like door hinges – if you use them they stay lubricated and if you don't they seize up. You need to be taught to do appropriate exercises properly and safely by a qualified person.

In that first hourly session I was taught exercises to do at home and that strain is not the name of the game. If it hurts then you must stop or modify the exercises. Some exercises, such as leaning forward "skiing" arm-thrust, can be done either sitting or standing (so you can still practice this even if you are never likely to get out on the piste).

Useful also was the realisation that to exercise need not be costly and you don't need to be either youthful or have a body in the Princess Di mould. There were no Peeping Toms watching our session. Not surprising – no fancy leotards here. We were an all woman group who came in whatever we had – track suits, shorts, leggings, pirate pants and a colourful selection of holiday T-shirts.

We had expected sessions to be something of a chore but it was fun. Rousing music and dance rhythms and plenty of laughter in a very friendly group. We finished that session and all subsequent lessons with relaxation. (Something I have found useful in the pre-Christmas build-up). The instructor turned out the lights and we lay on the floor on our backs and sighed our tension away, relaxing every part of our bodies. After relaxation you first roll over on your side and then get up slowly to avoid dizziness.

## DAY 2

Started to put techniques into practice. Had learnt that you don't need fancy equipment. Plenty of items in the kitchen can be used. I often have a tin of baked beans in one hand and a tomato soup in the other, using them as dumb-bells for arms exercises.

And, as I do not have an exercise mat, I use a piece of silver radiator foil for floor exercises when there is no-one to see me lying on my back looking like an oven-ready turkey.

Reading a magazine article about keeping healthy, I decided to extend my range and planned regular walks with my husband who is also retired and a member of the Ramblers. In the summer I will arrange to go swimming with some of my friends. Will investigate opportunities at local Leisure Centres. Walking and swimming are both extremely good exercise.

When I walked to the shops I hurried for a few steps to increase my heart rate a little and then slowed down again. I planned to try to take a walk every day – even if only to just post a letter.

## DAY 3

Up with Mr Motivator on GMTV. Exercise session only lasts for ten minutes but it gets your circulation going on winter mornings. Husband lies in bed laughing. Must try to get him to join in. Have asked him to get me a skipping rope for Christmas. Thinks I am entering second childhood. Not told him yet about broken vase – casualty of my efforts to juggle with bean bags.

Anyway last laugh on me. He doesn't know it but I have been collecting recipes to cut cholesterol, reduce salt in diet and slim down a little. We both need to be healthy.

## DAY 4

As well as trying to get rid of tum and bum bulges, I am also doing exercises to get rid of "Dracula-wings" (loose skin that takes to hanging around upper arms once you are no longer in your first flush of youth). Must investigate if there are any videos which can help you with this kind of shaping-up.

At the session we did many exercises in a group or with a partner. Some of these were dances. This morning I am standing in front of my bedroom mirror trying to remember the Hawaiian dance we were taught. It was very good for exercising hands and posterior. The hand gestures mime such peaceful activities as smelling flowers and listening to the ocean and every time the song mentioned "old Hawaii" (which was just about every other line) you did a figure of eight with your hips. Consoled myself that I might have looked more fetching on a palm-fringed beach in a grass skirt. (You have to use your imagination sometimes).

## DAY 5

TRIUMPH! Ran for a bus without getting breathless.

Went walking with husband. Makes us feel fresh and alert. Will investigate group activities which involve walking. Libraries and Advice Centres useful for finding out "what" "where" and "when".

## DAY 6

Exercises indoors. Stairs and chairs useful. Rose twenty times from sitting on dining room chair to standing. Bought magazine with exercises illustrated. Did finger, neck and wrist/ankle movements.

## DAY 7

Saw Mr Motivator in the flesh! Very firm muscular flesh, wore snazzy Lycra one-piece. (That's him, not me!) We went with a party from Poynton class to Macclesfield's Leisure Centre where he was taking an "Ageing Well" session. Hall had an air of crowd-excitement. Hundreds of people moving in unison to stirring music and Mr Motivator shouting: "Take it hup, hup, hup – come on lets do it!" Amazingly we all DID it.

I don't just mean those on the main floor, there were also people in wheelchairs (some in sparking bowler hats) who enthusiastically did arm exercises and clapping. It made me realise that exercise is important to everyone! There was a sense of exhilaration and achievement for us all. It was literally a lesson for life.

Afterwards Mr Motivator was mobbed by us golden oldies, struggling for autographs like hysterical teenagers at the height of Beatles mania. *Now who says exercise doesn't make you feel young!*

*'English for Work' Course; Croydon*

## Victor
### 30 October
It's very interesting to be at school at this stage in my life. It is a rich experience to understand people of many nationalities, with their customs, religions and different life-styles. It's easy to learn, because the time passes in an informal way. I never thought I would live in a foreign country, and now here I am!

I have great difficulty in a different language, but with a small effort I think I'll win the challenge. It's easy to learn, because the method of learning is clear and interesting. We learn computers, too. To learn to work with computers is attractive and a challenge. Naturally this school is very, very different compared to my old school. This morning we had computer practice, and in the afternoon we had a visit by Angelina Purcell, organiser of the course "Business Start-Up." She spoke about the advantages of this course. I think it sounded interesting and exciting.

### 31 October
To continue my dairy, today I am going to speak about myself. I am Portuguese, 56 years old and in my country I was a warehouse manager. I'm married with four children (one boy and three girls) and five grandchildren. I have lived in the UK since September 1994. Two months after I arrived I started to work in a factory as a packer in a video cassette factory. The pay was very low and I had great difficulty in managing, despite working 50/60 hours per week. So I decided to study in order to speak better English and to have a better job.

At the Training Centre today, we had a visit from Gisela Wrest. She spoke to us about the NVQ Administration Course, but I think this course is not of great interest to me. Then Elizabeth told us the origin of Halloween and it was very interesting to know its roots.

### 2 November
To continue my "Dear Diary", today we had a strange exercise. Joanna brought a cassette with a song called "Don't Cry for me, Argentina," and a worksheet. The worksheet had blank spaces which we had to complete after listening. I completed about 30% unfortunately badly. The song was about Evita Peron, first wife of the dictator Juan Peron, President of Argentina between 1946 and 1955, and who was dismissed in a military coup. After spending 18 years in exile, this man returned to power in 1973 and died in 1974. The story of this woman was very, very interesting. With her beauty and charm she used various men in order to get power, money and lots of

luxuries. Using cheap popularity, because she was a daughter of the people, she deceived the people, organising charity parties, giving away part of the money (the smaller part of course) and with the other part buying jewels, dresses etc.… for herself. If anyone criticised the situation they were silenced, arrested or killed, typical dictatorship solutions. But despite this, when she died in 1952, the people cried about her death.

After lunch, we had a visit by Christine Sampson. She spoke to us about "Information Technology", which is a course beginning after Easter. It looks interesting but I don't know what my situation will be in the future, and I'm going to think about which decision to take. I'm going to speak, too, about a custom in my country on 1 November, which is All Saints' Day. On this day, it's usual (I think in all Catholic countries) for everyone to visit the cemeteries, put flowers on the graves, and remember their dear ones who have died. It's an unhappy day, because you cry a lot and have red eyes etc …

But naturally, it is a good day for the people who sell flowers, it's a day for great business, and today that's everything …

## Parshotam

Since I lost my job last year I have been looking for another one. I could not find another job so I joined the English for Work course. I have been doing this course since last September 1995. At the CET Centre I learn computers.

I am looking for the job which I want. Last week I went to the Job Centre to find a job. The job was not suitable.

## Bindu

I am Bindu. I come here from India. I came here on 14 May 1995, because I got married. When I came here it was very difficult to understand people's accents, and I knew it was very difficult to get a job without correct language, and I wanted to continue my studies here. These three factors persuaded me to go to classes here. I could not join a course when I came here because it was the wrong time. That is why I went straight to language classes at the Oshwal Centre. Three months later I went for a two weeks' summer course. After finishing that course I went to Ambassador House for Guided Study.

Now I am doing English for Work, a six month course. I haven't any experience and I haven't done any work yet. The course is very interesting. The teachers are very co-operative and teach a lot of vocabulary and grammar. And I am able to improve my pronunciation.

On this course we study computers and typewriting. I think this will help us to find a job. We learn some office skills, too. That is why I have really enjoyed this course very much. I have learned a lot about computing in a short period. The students' adviser, Elaine Shaw, has told us about courses for further study. This is useful too. Our good teachers are also helpful in improving our speaking.

Oh! I nearly forgot to write my teachers' names: they are ELIZABETH GOLDMAN and JOANNA LANE.

Another thing I would like to say is sometimes the Student Advisers from other colleges and some teachers come here to give advice and speak about other courses.

## Najah

My name is Najah Alchamali. I come from Syria. I have four children. I have been living in England for two years. I live alone with my children so sometimes I feel bored and depressed because I left all my family behind in Syria, so I decided to do something to get a job to improve my life and my children's lives.

So I am doing the English for Work course. I am doing this course not only to get a job but also to meet people from different countries. I like learning English with a group because I find it more useful. Also I like class conversation, especially when we are talking about something important for our lives, which will help us to organise our lives and make us try to do everything right.

I would like to say I have learned a lot of things on this course. For example, I feel more confident when I talk to people, and my English has now improved. This helps me in dealing with people and with problems that arise. Also I am learning how to use a computer and how to type a letter or something else.

The thing I enjoy most is that our teacher is always cheerful. My present experiences are very different from how I learned in the past. In the past I couldn't speak to my teacher and I felt shy when I wanted to ask a question because she was always angry. I had to stand up if she asked a question, but here the teachers give the students more confidence to talk fluently.

I like my course because I meet lots of people from different countries and different religions. This has broadened my knowledge. Today our lesson was the story of Eva Peron. This story was really interesting for me and I think for all of us, because that lady was nothing from her birth until she was fifteen years old. Then in a few years she became president. That was really strange. Today I had to leave early because I had a lot of things to do, but this story fascinated me so much that I stayed until two o'clock. I like this kind of lesson, because it involves all of us and it is useful for everyone to give his or her opinion. It gives them more confidence. Finally our teacher Joanna is very clever. She knows what subjects are most important for us.

## Catherine

My name is Catherine. I am 24 and I come from France. I have come to England to improve my English, because I used to work in several international transport companies and, in this area, you must speak English. It is really useful. Then, when my English skills have improved, I would like to get a job, maybe as a freight controller, shipping clerk or a secretary. But one thing is sure, the better my English is, the more chance I will have of finding a job …

So, at the moment, I'm on a training course called "English for Work". On it, I have learnt how to use a computer and I am very glad about that. Moreover, I am very satisfied with the way they have been teaching me. I have really enjoyed being with students who come from different countries. Everyone can talk about his or her culture. Besides I have been learning a lot of vocabulary and it enables me to read and understand almost everything now.

The last thing is that this gives you the opportunity of getting on another training course like NVQ, Enterprise, computer-courses and many other things … I have had real support from my teaches and it is very encouraging.

In conclusion, EFW course is interesting basic training and essential if you want to go on training courses afterwards.

## Rekha

I'm Rekha. I came to England in 1981 because I got married. I worked for International Stores Ltd for two years. I have one son who is eight. I thought that now I could do something for myself. What I have I need to brush up and to learn new systems (Information Technology). I started EFW on 4 September and this is the 9th week. I'm really enjoying this course very much. When I'm in the computer room, I like it very much. We do some English work in pairs, sometimes in groups and sometimes on our own. It's interesting because my teacher always says 'Two heads are better than one'.

On Mondays we do Computers in the morning, and in the afternoons some grammar. On Tuesday morning we do Jobsearch Skills and in the afternoon this week we're going to write a diary for 15 minutes and do Listening and Speaking. The teaching method is completely different from when I was at school. In class, there were nearly fifty of us children and if we didn't understand, we still didn't ask the teacher. I've found that in the training centre there is a very friendly atmosphere. I'm sure I'll gain more skills and experience.

On our Training Course, there are fifteen students and they all come from different countries, so we learn about each other's religion, culture and little bits of language. Today is Thursday. In the morning we did dictation. I like doing dictations very much but I missed it because I went to watch my son's assembly at his school. We read a passage about Eva Peron and the teacher explained hard words and talked about it. We listened to the song about Eva's story (which was really interesting) filled in the gaps and answered the questions. At 1pm Christine Sampson gave a talk about the Computer course. She explained all about Computing and we asked some questions on what we wanted to find out. I found it interesting. Now it is time to write my diary.

Today is Friday. We are in the Computer Room. Everyone is so keen to learn computers. If you come and look in the Computer Room, you can hear a pin drop and students are busy with their work. Soon we are going to have a cup of coffee. In about 5 minutes the teacher will say, 'Chai break!' but still nobody bothers to go. So you can imagine how interesting it is! The teacher and students are friendly. If I don't understand something first time, I can ask a few times more and the teacher will explain to me until I get it. She tries to give me a full answer.

## Monika

I'm Monika, an Italian girl who loves England very much. I came to this country without any reason, as an adventure, but I've found something not very easy – the language. I started work a week after arriving and it was a nightmare for me, so I wanted very much to get into a school, but it was impossible because of my shift, which was different every week. After a long visit to Italy I came back to England; this time no luck, no 'yes' from employers. I was lost for a while until the Job Centre suggested what I should do. Finally my life was saved and I had an interview at Ambassador House to get into the English for Work course, which I thought would be the most helpful in my case.

I've found the course very interesting, especially the computer, which before was another world to me. Another reason why I like the course very much is the teamwork, when we have to help each other. With this system I think, the time is not very hard and is very enjoyable. I especially enjoy it when we talk about our life-stories, religion, country, crime, so different from each other's. So we can discover different cultures, which is much more exciting to find out from real people than to read in the newspaper, where most of the time we don't read the whole truth.

On Thursday we have to write on a set subject and next Thursday we read it aloud as an exercise.

## Nagalingam

I am Nagalingam Sivbalan from Sri Lanka. I am studying the EFW course at Ambassador House Thornton Heath. Last week I missed attending the classes because I had more work to do at home than usual. Usually my wife does all the work, but unfortunately she was sick and I did all her work, such as dropping the children at school and picking them up, cleaning, cooking, shopping and looking after the children.

The week before last I learnt a lot. I got a lot of information about an INFORMATION TECHNOLOGY course from a South Northwood Tutor. She explained clearly so that everybody on the course could understand. I think this course is very useful at the moment, because we are in a computer world. Everything is computers nowadays.

## Sylvain

I am Sylvain. I come from France. At the moment I'm learning English for Work. It's very interesting for me and I'm interested in everything. It isn't like a typical school. Today we all did a CV on the computer using a word-processing package (Word for Windows 6.1). I started 9 weeks ago, and now I know how to print, close Windows, make a calendar etc.

My English is better than before and I am more confident in speaking. Now I am not afraid when I see a computer. We all learn in a group of 2, 3 or four people. It's very easy to learn that way.

## Shushila

My name is Shushila and I come from Kenya. At the moment I'm learning English for Work and it is very interesting. I learn English in groups and sometimes by myself and we help each other. I started Computing eight weeks ago and it is very interesting. On

Monday morning I do computing and in the afternoon I do Grammar. Today we discussed with Gisela Wrest about her NVQ Administration course and we asked some questions. Today is Thursday. I did a dictation and now we are reading the story of Eva Peron. It is very interesting and we listened to the song about Eva and I like it very much. In the afternoon we had a talk from Christine about her Computer course and we asked some questions. On Friday morning I did Computing and in the after noon I talked about Guy Fawkes. On Saturday morning I did my shopping. On Sunday evening we had fireworks in the garden.

## Moira

I come from central Italy and I've already been living in England for a year. When I first arrived here, my English was very bad and sometimes when I wanted to talk to people I didn't know how to express myself to them. More often than not, I used to gesticulate instead of speaking English which I really didn't know very well and that period of my life was very hard for me.

Afterwards, I said to myself: 'If I want to continue living here in England, speaking to people, making friends and finding a job, it's better for me to start quickly' and so I did that.

Unfortunately, in colleges it's only possible to find part-time courses of about three hours a week and it really wasn't enough for me. I mean my English wasn't good enough for a job, or rather for the employers who I wanted to ask for a job. I tried to find something more helpful and I went to find information from the same college where I used to study. They told me about a course called "English for Work" and so I applied for it straight away because I thought it sounded very interesting. Now, in fact I am doing this course and I can say that I have done the right thing. It's a very interesting and helpful course. In particular, the teachers are very good and they give us their full attention all the time and that, I think, is wonderful. They know us and our weaknesses and how to remedy them. The way they teach is very different from what the teachers used to do when I was at school in my own country. In this class, our rapport with the teachers is very friendly and not formal as it used to be when I was at school in Italy.

There are times when the teachers organise pairwork for us and sometimes in groups and that's not only helpful for everybody, but in particular we have the opportunity to get to know more about each other and so the atmosphere in class is very friendly, something very important, too.

About the course programme, I can say it's very general and complete; to be precise, we study a lot of things such as; Computing, Business Vocabulary, Grammar, Jobsearch Skills, Listening, Speaking, Reading and Guided Writing. In addition to this course, they arrange guidance which provides us with the type of advice and assistance that's right for us and we work together with the guidance worker to work out what we can do next.

Actually, this week we had three teachers from different courses in our class: Ms Gisela Wrest from the NVQ Administration course, Ms Angelina Purcell from the Enterprise course and Ms Christine Sampson from the Information Technology course. We had the opportunity to ask them everything about the course, for example: what are the skills we need to get on that course? What kind of qualifications will we get at the end? And so on. I found this very interesting and useful and I think all the information that I received from the teachers will help to prepare me to enter the world of work.

## *May Banham; Bournemouth*

*Educated in Blackheath. Served an apprenticeship with Fortnum and Mason to study buying. Later, took a modelling course and was engaged to appear on television in their first fashion show in 1937.*

*Married in 1939. Worked in the Ministry of Supply, London, during the war. On my husband's demobilisation from the army, our home in Farnborough, Kent, was where we brought up our two children.*

*Started my own business in the sixties, employing forty women. This brought world wide travel in the fashion world.*

*Retired to Dorset in the late seventies, where sadly my husband died in 1986.*

## A Potter's Diary

Some six years ago, I became a student of pottery. As I was in my seventieth year, it may be useful, at this point, to give some explanation for my late start.

As a member of **Shoreline**, I had for some years contributed to sales of work by making craft items for the RNLI. On the death of my husband, I immersed myself more in this work, holding an annual sale in our village hall. My sale at Christmas time was well attended and the handicrafts sold. However, I needed to come up with new ideas each year in order to stimulate sales, and my regular visits to libraries provided me with the necessary inspiration. On one of these visits a poster on the notice board caught my attention – it also changed my life. This poster announced pottery lessons at the Punshon College of Further Education in Bournemouth.

I had never studied this craft before, and it was with some trepidation that I joined in the Autumn Term of 1989. However, once ensconced in the class, apron donned and faced with a lump of clay, I began to work. Hey! Why hadn't I done this before, I asked myself? It was to be the first of many invaluable and enjoyable lessons.

My contributions to the RNLI continue, but the sales of work came to an end. Ceramics were to fill every spare moment. It was my great good fortune to have the guidance of an excellent tutor. Her students are motivated and encouraged to ever higher standards of work. My day at college is the highlight of my week – superseded only by visits from my family and grandchildren.

In order to gain greater knowledge of the creative techniques, I began to work at home. Clay was delivered from a local merchant, whilst a large slab of heavy chipboard made its home on the surface of a kitchen unit. I would work right through the day practising joins, coiling and eventually slabbing. Where did the hours go? Did I stop for lunch? This latter thought would strike me as my energy levels started to flag at around 4pm!

Now, after six years of study, a great deal of my work is derived from the slabbing method. Buildings have always fascinated me and fit this process well. I love making pots too and anything else that arrests my attention. Visits to the museums and art galleries are rewarding and informative, giving me endless ideas. Books are also a joy, and I go back to those I possess time after time.

As in all crafts, disaster lurks unseen. I'm reminded of some of these, such as, at the point of pouring white glaze into a large pot, the base parted company with the body – leaving me looking like a Dickensian wraith, not sure whether to laugh or cry! I remember also, the great feeling of achievement during my first year, on the completion of a swan – the feeling was shortlived, when five minutes later the neck fell off! Then there was the uncontrolled laughter of my son when I demonstrated throwing on my new wheel. Such was the momentum, that my clay was unseated and whizzed past my ear to smack against a far wall. I have to say that I collapsed with laughter too.

On the plus side, an early commission came my way in January 1991. A puppet of mine had been seen in a college exhibition, and I was approached to make a Nativity scene for a church for the following Christmas. The request was for heads and hands – the bodies and garments were to be made by my new patron. I ended up making eleven heads, twenty-two hands, Joseph Mary, Christ-child, kings and shepherds! I was invited to attend the Christmas Carol Service at the church and it was there that I saw the completed Nativity scene, which was beautifully arranged and truly lovely. The warmth of that gathering will always stay with me.

I'm sure that this material, that I find so captivating, inspired my old hands to produce a standard of work that was reasonably acceptable. I would that I had found this course many years ago. Adult education is a gift not to be missed, whatever one's age.

In 1995, I was nominated for an award by my tutor, Angela Wiseman. I felt very honoured to have been selected for this prize, and indeed quite overwhelmed, when informed I had won the NIACE certificate for outstanding work.

One never knows what tomorrow will bring.

## Margaret Dobson; Stockport

*I was born and brought up in Bradford, Yorkshire. An early inclination towards languages was suppressed by a scientific education. At Leeds University Medical School, took B.Sc. 1st Class Hons. Anatomy (1948) and M.B; Ch. B.2nd Class Hons. (1951).*

*After marriage and hospital jobs, settled into General Practice while bringing up a family. In 1963 started my own practice in Marple, Cheshire, which became a Group Practice.*

*After retirement, 1986, my linguistic interests reawakened. My husband had four French correspondents (non-English speaking) whom we visited regularly.*

*An excellent French teacher enthused my love of French literature, poetry and art.*

## Mon. Nov. 6

The week begins early on a Monday, with BBC 2's "The Learning Experience." At 4 a.m. they put on "The French Experience" which I record for later viewing. While my washing-machine functions, I sit and watch my video in comfort. This week, there are fifteen minutes of "Les Benevols du Coeur", a voluntary organisation in large French towns, running soup kitchens for the unemployed and homeless. Often in a marquee, they dole out wholesome adequate food to down-and-outs. The helpers obviously enjoy the camaraderie and the feeling of doing good. Three bijou snips of French life follow, excellent for listening to French conversation and observing different ways of life to our own.

## Tues. Nov. 7

I'd better get on with my French homework today, ready for Wednesday's class. The task is to write a brief essay on the Dictionary, the use thereof for the meaning of words, etymology, pronunciation and how the use of words alters over the years e.g. the innocent word "gay" which has acquired quite a new connotation. New editions of the dictionary are needed as new words are introduced into current use from other languages, or new technical processes necessitate new words to describe them. Older words become obsolete. This exercise involves composing a literary piece, stretching both my powers of composition, spelling, punctuation (and French).

The evening warrants a little mental relaxation, so I attend a Scottish Country Dancing class. After all, physical exercise is essential to our well-being and it is excellent memory training to remember the movement sequences of so many intricate dance formations. In my youth, we had a Scottish teacher who schooled us in the basics e.g. "Paddy

Basque" step. For years, I thought this referred to an Irishman on the border between France and Spain, but now with my French learning, my accent has improved to "pas-de-bas"!

## Wed. Nov. 8

The French class. One and a half hours of intensive French conversation; audiotapes of native French speakers with their fearsome speed of enunciation and devastating local accents; perhaps a dictation of a sixteenth century poem; or excerpts from Cyrano de Bergerac.

This is indeed Lifelong Learning, since I commenced at age ten, at school, and am still learning at 69! How the language has altered over that period. With having become more proficient in speech, my husband and I have made many friends in France. They cannot converse in English, so the relationships have matured purely by our ability to understand and keep us talking on quite intellectual subjects with people of very differing backgrounds. One friend, a Norman, worked on the Isle of Reunion for years, marrying a Creole wife. Now he has retired home to Normandy with her and their offspring, but returns regularly to their tropical roots. Another, a Lyonnais, joined up with De Gaulle's Free French forces in N. Africa in 1940, was decorated by Haile Selassie with the Star of Ethiopia, fought in all the campaigns up through Italy e.g. Monte Cassino, landed at Toulon and fought through Provence. After the war, he continued in the Gendarmerie in Reunion, the Comoro Islands, Djibouti and Martinique. What a fund of evenings conversations lie there!

## Thurs. Nov. 9

Another day of relaxation at my Bobbin Lace making class. Once more working out patterns as in dancing, but translating them into lacework on my pillow. The quarterly bulletin of the Lace Guild had arrived which includes a letter I had written to the Editor – (something I never dared do previously). In a previous copy, a member has sent a photograph of an old piece of lace she had found in France, depicting a quaint figure, "Riquet a la houppe." She had asked "Who was Riquet?" So I researched the Larousse Encyclopaedia, found the seventeenth century, author, Charles Perrault, and a copy of his Mother Goose Tales on our bookshelves with the complete story of the ugly, intelligent prince who loved a beautiful but stupid princess. Under his influence she grew to be quite sensible, while in her eyes, he became handsome. I wrote off a précis of this moral to the journal.

## Sat. Nov. 11

Sadness comes with the post today, telling us of the death of an old French priest we had come to know. He had been writing his memoirs of the wartime years, had just prepared them for going to press, but not survived to see the finished book. His parishioners had dealt with the manuscripts and now were sending us a copy of the book. This is learning life indeed – he had been in church, marrying two couples at the moment the Gestapo had walked in to arrest him. One couple was married but they would not wait for him to complete the second service. He was bundled into a train of cattle trucks going east, but managed to scribble a note on a scrap of paper and address it to his mother. When they stopped alongside wagons travelling westward, he pushed his note through the slates into one of the trucks. The "letter" reached his mother. He arrived in a forced labour camp at Melk in Austria, to work in a subterranean factory making ball-bearings. One day, all the priests and pastors were separated out to be sent to Auschwitz but his name was left off the list. Thus he survived. Towards the end of the war, American planes flew over, one day, and all the prisoners ran out to wave. Tragically, the Americans saw rows of army huts and people in khaki uniforms, assumed it was a military camp and bombed it. When the American land forces were near, the Germans were planning to drive all the detainees into the underground passages and blow up the entrances to the mines. Once more, he was lucky. Life surely has some meaning.

## Sun. Nov. 12

The week has come round to "The Learning Experience" again on T.V. Calamity! The French Experience has been replaced by "Deutsch Direkt". A hint to learn German!

### Peter Rolls; Camberley, Surrey

*I retired as Head of Printing and Photography at RAE Farnborough in 1990. As a 'life-long learner' (photography, media, communication, social research), my first instinct was to find a class to join. Fiction-writing seemed OK, despite lack of 'literary' background.*

*Surrey Heath Adult Education Institute was starting its 'Power of Words' programme and I joined Leslie Buckwell's group at Chobham. Since then, I have written poems, play-scripts, diatribes, monologues and short stories. Now a diary.*

Mrs Cribbin's experience bears no relation, need it be said, to Adult Learning in Surrey Heath. I cannot vouch for elsewhere.

## Mrs Cribbin's Chronicle

This is a really daft idea. Keeping a Learner's Diary. It's hard enough to crank up your Urge every week. But now they want us to sit down and write about it. Record our impressions – what it's like to be a Learner etc.

Well, I can tell them: Creative Writing is hard going. Especially with Miss Wigmold and her vowels. I can't get the drift half the time.

But I suppose a Diary will be practice at the writing. It's for some outfit called Nice, so I said I'd do a bit each week. Nothing creative, mind. I'm calling it Mrs Cribbin's Chronicle – although I might change my mind about the apostrophe. I think we're doing them in Week 4.

## Enrolment Day

We had to go down to the Church Hall and sign on. It's not as though I wanted to do this class at all. I fancied the Country Cooking – but it was full. It's always full. The same women every year, baking great puddings and cakes. No wonder they look cheerful and rosy-cheeked; it's indecent. Education is for improving your mind, not stuffing your face.

The Enrolment people were keen to push the Yoga. No chance. All those hard floors and draughts. And that Zelda, nagging about keeping the thoughts Pure and the Mind free. Mrs Bleasdale did a week of it last year. Stiff as a board she was, and got a great splinter in her leg. And her Mind's never been the same since.

So the only thing going was this new class on Creative Writing. Which sounded a cushy little number. And it will be one up on her next door; she's been uppity since she got that Book Club circular.

I paid for the 8 lessons. Then they mentioned this Diary thing. I asked about getting a discount out of it, but no dice. Anyhow, here we go. See how it works out.

## Week 1

The first thing I did was arrive early and sharpen my pencils. Not to suck up to Miss Wigmold, but to get a seat near the fire. This Hall's bitter first thing. Thank God I'm not stretched out next door with Zelda and her zombies.

I looked in at the Cookery people with Mrs McSweeney. All those ovens warming away, full of bun. No wonder they look pleased with themselves. Sickening, it is.

Our class started off with a real squeeze – twenty people, which is a record for anything around here. All women, of course. It's that TV thing that's given them ideas of pen to paper. Fair enough. Mind you, after Miss Wigmold had done her words of welcome, six of them left, which made things a bit easier.

A bloke called Spivey came out from the main Centre and we filled in forms for a while. He said how glad they were to be expanding classes in the villages. Just the one morning a week, but it was a 'key element in their outreach policy. Improving their demographic profile and financial viability …' In other words, his job is on the line.

Then he gave us a pep-talk on Learning as a Way of Life. Plus a few house rules, such as no alcohol, no mocking at the Yoga and making sure we cleared up afterwards. He looked a bit pointed at my pencil-sharpenings and you could tell he is more of a petty-fogger than on the creative side. Thin, spindly bloke, he is. I did a doodle and called it 'Spider Spivey'. Funny, isn't it, how the Urge takes you in different ways sometimes.

Anyhow, when he'd gone, we got down to it with Miss Wigmold. People introduced themselves and said why they'd joined a writing class. You never heard such a lot of twaddle in your life. 'Expressing oneself,' they said. 'Emotional release'; 'stretching the mind'; 'reaching for the stars'. Always keen to write, they said; ever since they were young. I couldn't believe I was hearing it. When I knew them at school, they thought that into-lectual was two words. And their idea of 'free expression' was chalking on the toilet wall.

But I told her straight. I come to get out of the house for a morning. And for a bit of a chin-wag. She didn't go much on that: 'We're not here to chatter', she says.

'Hang on,' I says, 'surely we get to talk about our work – have a bit of a laugh.' And then she went on about laughing – not constructive, she says. *Miz, miz, miz* seems to be her motto.

I said no more. Let her prattle on, I thought. I'll do a bit of Nice's diary. I was still doing it when the others started packing up. I think I missed something, but I wasn't going to give her the satisfaction of asking.

## Week 2

It's all puddings and steam next door and like a morgue in Yoga; rows of stiff bodies. In here, it's chaos. Only 10 have turned up and she's wittering about the Numbers. 'Budgetary short-fall …', she moans. 'Productivity quotient …'

'What are you worrying about,' I says. 'You've got your money. Never mind your quotas and quotients. Let's get on with the biz.'

She didn't like the prodding. 'Right,' she says, 'let's be hearing your Topic from last week. Perhaps Mrs Cribbins would like to go first.' And she looks at me meaningful- like.

Well, it was news to me. 'Topic?' I says. 'What Topic?' And then, of course, it turns out that I missed it last week , while I was doing this.

'Oh, never mind, if you can't manage it,' she says, all ippety snippety. 'It's quite voluntary…' But you could see she was feeling a bit Wackford.

Her Topic had been 'Winter – a seasonal poem', so we heard nine epics about robins and holly. I reckon half of them were pinched from Christmas cards, so you can tell what it was like. Paralytic.

I did a doodle of a woman with a giant hair-do. Wiggy Wigmold.

## Week 3

Only 6 of us today, so she's not quite so full of herself. Probably terrified of old Spivey finding out. But after about 10 minutes, the Major joined us; which was a bit of a downer. He says he wants to brush up on his writing before starting the memoirs. Then he comes out with the old patter – 'Such a bevy of lovely ladies,' he says, with a twirl and a wink. 'Bound to find some inspiration here.' Of course, most of us have given him the elbow, or worse, in the past. But old Wiggy took a bit of shine to him and we spent a long time hearing about life on Luneberg Heath and Catterick camp, or whatever.

Eventually, my clock-glances and paper-rustling sunk home. She got the message that some of us hasn't paid good money to hear how the Major tore aside the Iron Curtain. He's already emptied the *Red Lion* of a Friday night. And with her number being only 6 students, she's a bit vulnerable.

'Yes, Mrs Cribbins?' she says, a bit coolish.

'Far be it from me,' I says. 'But I've got my Topic on Winter and I was hoping…'

But I never got any further. Next thing, the ambulance came hooting up outside and there was men rushing in and asking the way to the Yoga. They'd come for Zelda. Done her back in, apparently. And her lot had just laid there for twenty minutes, purifying their minds and thinking she was doing a demo. for something more advanced.

We all went for a good oggle, of course. And I had to go home, what with the laughing being forbidden. So I missed another Topic.

## Week 4

No Zelda, so they've put the Yoga lot in with us. There's 7 of them lying in the corners and we're down to 4 around the fire. So that's 11 all together, plus Wiggy dodging about, relaxing and stimulating in turns. She doesn't look too good. Her Number may be up in more ways than one.

She gave us 10 minutes of the writing. Doing a story about an animal, using all the senses. Well, I knew most of the others would be on the mimsy side – robins and kittens and that. So I chose something a bit more carnivorous – a eagle. How keen its eyesight was and how much it liked the taste of robin. But as I put pen to paper, I noticed her next to me, that Doris Fishwick. The <u>nerve</u> of her – she was looking at my pad. 'Here,' I says, 'mind your own. This is 'c', this is.' And I did one of those little circles ©. That showed her.

Anyhow, I was a bit cheesed about my 'Winter' thing; still stuck on line 1. I've tried it on my Wilf, but you might as well shout at the wind. So I sat Wiggy down and gave it to her straight:

*'Oh, wondrous land of snow and ice.'*

Well, you never heard such a nit-picking performance. All I needed was a bit of help with a rhyme for 'ice'. 'Nice' and 'mice' are on the feeble side, and 'lice' and 'vice' seemed a bit sordid. So I'd thought of 'twice' and had been working backwards along line 2, trying to get some sense into it. But no; we never got that far. Old Wiggy seized on *'Oh'* of all things.

'Shouldn't it be *'O'*,' she says. *'O wondrous land…'*

'Stone me,' I said. 'Does it matter? It's just a sound: 'Oh' or 'O'. It's all the same.'

But she wouldn't have it, rambling on about the rhetorical tone. And the others joined in, chipping away until I offered to have a vote on it, sarcastic-like. 'A, E, I, O, or U,' I said, 'it's all the same to me. But let's get that tone just right, whatever we do. And then we'll all do alternate words. Make a real Committee job of it.'

Well, they didn't go much on wit, so it got a bit fractious. And then the yogas sat up and said would we turn it down; they were losing touch with the Infinite. I told them straight. They could do their Infinite anywhere, anytime. All I'd got was two hours of a Monday morning and I wasn't getting very far. Four weeks and I'd only done one line – and now even that had got whittled down.

'I'm doing a Diary,' I said. 'National thingummy, I'm supposed to put down my Aims and Achievements. How's it going to look if I've taken 4 weeks to achieve the letter *'O'*?'

Well, they're a huffy lot: all 'A' levels and avocado. So they swept out, vowing to complain to the Top People. Good riddance, I thought. But Wiggy was in a state, weeping and wailing about her Numbers. At which point, the Major came into his own with the manly charm and comfort. She sobbed a bit and he ushered her out on his arm: we could see them heading for the *Red Lion*.

'Well,' I said, 'there go the apostrophes. Can we get on to line 2?'

But the others said the Urge had gone and they were going as well.

## Week 5

No Wiggy, no Zelda. In fact, no-one at all. Just me. But I don't see why I should give up. I've paid my money for eight warm, Wilf-free mornings and I'm sticking with it.

As you can tell, I'm keeping up the Diary. So if old Spider comes, he can see I'm not wasting my time.

The Cookery lot are doing bread. Which is very nice for them, I'm sure. But that waft doesn't half come down the passage. Warm and yeasty it is, makes your mouth water something cruel.

I'll have another go at line 2 … trying to end with *'paradise'*, or possibly *'edelweiss'* …

It's no good, I'll have to go and complain to Mother McSweeney about the waft. All the saliva is damping my Urge. I'll ask for a slice or two of freshly-baked, to get things going again.

No dice, she said. And her lot giggled. Little, piggy eyes, they've got; and spotty necks. It's all that cholesterol.

## Week 6

I had a letter from Spider on Thursday. The class is finished. Lack of demand, he said. But there's no refund, so I'm here anyway. The Hall's open and I've got the fire to myself. He won't be up here checking on a cancelled class, will he?

I had a squint at the Cookery. I'm due a bit of 'own back', after last week's brush-off. So I was glad to see they're doing Caribbean Chocolate Carnival. 'Oh, yes.' I thought, when I saw their stuff on the table. 'We'll soon sort you lot out.'

No messing about, I swept straight in. 'Ah,' I says, 'Caribbean is it? All the finest ingredients, I suppose?'

She gave me a look like scrumpled lemons. But she could hardly dodge the point. 'Of course,' she said. 'Nothing but the best.' And the others all smirked and licked cream and cocoa off their spoons.

'Ah,' I says, 'In which case, it'll be the proper rum, will it?'

She fell straight in the deep end. 'Yes,' she said, sniffily, 'none of your substitutes here.'

'In which case,' I says, fingering her bottle of the Captain Morgan, 'you're breaking the Church Hall rules. No alcohol on the premises. Very strict, they are. You and old Spivey will get done for it.'

Well, that knocked her sideways. And the rest of them, too. I left them to it, squittering away like a lot of pricked baboons.

As I got up the road, I decided to put the knife into Week 8 likewise. So I went back. 'And don't think,' I says, sticking my head round the door, 'that you'll get away with real brandy in your Christmas doings. Rules is rules; festive season or not.' At which all their ruddy faces went grey, like heaps of cold porridge slipping into the washing up. 'Have a merry.' I said, and left them to it.

## Week 7

Another letter from Spider. All the classes is cancelled for the duration: Cookery has been banned by the Vicar and the hall is locked. So I'm doing this last page at home.

Spider has asked me not to send this Diary directly to Nice. Will I please let him have it for vetting? No chance, matey. If he's stopped reaching out, he's not putting in. I'll send him a copy, of course. But he can't go quoting bits in his prospectus, unless he checks with me first. One thing I have learned about is copyright. The whole thing is ©.

Nice have sent a form to go with the Diary, so I'll fill it in and get everything off pronto.

Their first question is: *'How would you quantify your Achievements in relation to your Aims ?'* Well, in my situation, it's a plus to get a few mornings out of the house. But I never got started on my eagle. So, on the creative side, it's all come down to a discussion of *'Oh'* or *'O'* and finding a rhyme for 'ice'. Not very quantible, really.

The second question is : *'Have you any complaints ?'* Well, I'm not a natural moaner, but it has to be a 'yes' to that one. Old Wiggy's idea of a writer is your lonely quill in a garret: no chat; no questions; head down and churn out your Topic. Whereas I'm on the Bohemian side, looking for a few laughs and the odd, inspirational drink. Another time, I reckon the upstairs room at the *Red Lion* would be favourite.

Yours sincerely,

Myrtle Cribbins (Mrs)

<u>PS to Nice.</u> I'd be pleased to do more Diary, but there's no classes left . I blame old Spider. If I were you, I'd strike him off your list. He's got shifty eyes; d'you know what I mean? If you're handing out any cash, I'd make sure it goes direct to the students. Cheers.

## Silvia Schiavone; Worthing, W. Sussex

*I'm 59 years old. I came in this country from Italy in 1964. I couldn't speak a word in English. I have four children and four grandchildren.*

*I attend three courses at Northbrook College, Worthing: Brush up your English, Wordpower and English for Speakers of Other Languages. Later I would like to do an art course and to write children's stories.*

## Monday 18th September 1995

This morning I was very excited to go back to Northbrook College after such a long summer break. When I went into the classroom I was glad to see all my friends from the previous term. There was an introduction for new students and then we started our Brush Up Your English session.

We started with Skimming and Scanning. We had to read through a text rapidly to get a general idea of what it was about. Then we had to look for information and answer some questions about the passage. It was about cooking and we had to find out how to prepare fresh pineapples, pears and passion fruit. I answered all the questions correctly and I found it really interesting.

After lunch I started my Wordpower class. This is a new course for me and I felt a bit nervous and confused at first because there was a new tutor and new students. We introduced ourselves and I told my group where I am from and how long I've been here. I said I wanted to be able to speak better English and I also want to be able to read and write more.

We visited the library and then we went back to the classroom. I wrote about the day I came to England. It was quite difficult and challenging to think about all those years back but I managed to do it. My teacher said I did very well.

## Tuesday 19th September

Today I haven't got any lessons, so I set myself some study at home. I did some exercises out of Essential Grammar in Use – this is a self-study and reference practice book. I worked for about 4 hours. When I checked my work with the answers at the back of the book I found I got all my tenses right. I felt very happy and proud of myself.

## Wednesday 20th September

Today I went to college for my ESOL class. I got there an hour early so I could go to the library. I managed to read a book called The Ear. There were some difficult words in it so I wrote them in my exercise book and I looked for the meaning in my dictionary. I learned them and memorised them in my head. I find that using books in this way is a wonderful way to learn new words.

In the classroom I met some students from the previous term. I was happy to see them again. We did an introduction for new students. We worked in groups talking about the things a student should do to learn and the things a tutor should do. We did a tour of the college and we visited the computer department. A man explained how to use the computers and he said we could go there anytime. I enjoyed today, I'm feeling confident and I've learned quite a lot.

## Thursday 21st September

Today as I've got no lessons, I've decided to write about the book I read yesterday. I put the story into my own words. I wrote it in draft first, then I corrected my spelling mistakes. When it sounded good, I wrote it in my exercise book

I was pleased with what I wrote and I was pleased that I understood what the story was all about. I will take it into my Wednesday class next week for my teacher to look at. This homework lasted four hours. It's a long time but I feel I have learned things and difficult words which I never knew before.

## Friday 22nd September

Today I did some homework for my ESOL class. My teacher asked us to find a picture of a room, from a magazine, and describe what I can see in the room using – there is and there are. I also had to describe a cottage using a picture and some information that she gave us.

## Monday 25th September

In my Brush Up Your English class we worked in groups doing some dictionary practice. I had to find the meaning of four words from a newspaper article. We also had to look for words starting with 'un'. I found this very helpful and I was pleased I did it correctly.

## Tuesday 26th September

Today Jan came to see me at my house. She used to be a volunteer tutor in the ESOL class. She is now doing a TEFL course to become a qualified teacher. She needed a student learner to work with and she asked me. She taped a short interview with me and she asked me to write a short story for her to check. I felt pleased and confident about all the things we did.

## Wednesday 27th September

This morning I went to my ESOL class. We worked in pairs and practised a conversation which we could put on tape and listen to. It was to help us assess our speaking skills. We did some grammar practice describing pictures of rooms using there is and there are. This was an enjoyable lesson.

### Thursday 28th September

This morning I decided to write a short story for my granddaughter. The title of the story was The Wolf and The Fox. I started writing early in the morning. When I read it over, I was surprised that the story sounded really nice. I corrected it and wrote it out again. I'll give it to my tutor to correct next week. She takes it home and checks it in her own time. I will give it to one of my granddaughters for her birthday as a present to remember me by. In the future I would like to write more children's stories for my other grandchildren on their birthdays.

### Friday 29th September

Today Jan came to see me again. She brought back the short story I wrote for her last time she came. She said I answered the questions in the interview well and she said my pronunciation was good. She said my handwriting was fine and she said there were just some spelling and grammar mistakes. She thanked me for letting her work with me. She said she was pleased to work with me because she knew me before at the college.

### Monday 2nd October

I'm glad to go back to class after the weekend. I miss the good atmosphere in the class with my teacher and my friends. Today we worked in a group doing some spelling – long and short vowels. Then I wrote a letter to a friend, imagining I was on holiday and I addressed it properly. I also practised some punctuation. I feel more confident about writing letters.

In Wordpower I did an assessment activity. I brought in a newspaper cutting – it was an article which interested me about a mother who lost contact with her daughter. I had to read the story to my teacher and then she asked me some questions and I answered them correctly. We were pleased I understood it all.

### Tuesday 3rd October

I studied at home today. I wrote about the most exciting day of my life. I had to remember what happened 39 years ago. I practised using the past simple tense.

### Wednesday 4th October

My teacher gave me back the description of the room. She said I had used the grammar – there is and there are very well and she said my paragraphing, use of commas and full stops was very good. She also looked at the piece I wrote about My Most Exciting Day and she said it was a lovely piece of writing. She said I described the day very clearly and that I used good grammar and vocabulary. I feel happy because I know the more I practise the better it gets.

## Friday 6th October

Today I was waiting at the bus stop and I started a conversation with another lady. We continued talking on the bus. I felt very confident speaking to her. I think she understood me very well. Before I started these classes I was unable to start a conversation like this because people didn't understand me very well. Now I know I can speak with more confidence.

## Celia Scott; Norwich

*I'm 64, a widow with 4 children and 5 grandchildren.*

*Left school at 15, later trained as occupational therapist working in the psychiatric field.*

*Like gardening, singing and painting furniture.*

*Have always lived in Norfolk and been interested in the landscape and why different plants grew where they did. When my pension arrived I wanted to keep my brain engaged and the trailer for the Open University Ecology course saying 'Do you want to know why the landscape looks as it does?' caught my eye. Now I'm hooked by the amazing complexity and beauty of it all.*

## "Do you want to know why the landscape looks as it does?"

Diary of an O.U. Earth Sciences Student
February – October 1995

### February:

At last we're off again. I really don't like the O.U. academic year not starting until February just when I want to start getting out into the garden again. The boxes with the manuals have arrived, I'd been told it was a very full course and gosh the files at least are heavy, 2 ring backs about 3 inches thick, each crammed with information. It's called 'How the Earth Works' and should follow on well from last year's Geology with all its Geophysics and Geochemistry … So I've started in earnest now with a bang, the Big Bang in fact, it is interesting, but … there is so much information which as usual I forget as soon as I've read it. Plus ça change. At least the Maths isn't as daunting as I'd expected, perhaps I'm getting better.

### March:

First tutorial, new tutor, mostly new faces but luckily one familiar one from near here so we shall be able to work together again sometimes, our phone bills roaring up the while. I think I shall put J. down on my family and friends BT list.

### April:

First assignment due; really working hard for it not knowing quite what the tutor wants. Large part based n the first video, they really could have found a better presenter. But at least we've been sent all the videos in advance this year and shan't have to remember to record them each week. The seismic part has gone O.K., is very interesting I'm finding, more so than the Earth's early formation …

## May:

Both TMA and CMA returned with very good marks, what a relief, I feel I'm on the right track at last and am beginning to look forward to the next section, it really has been hard going so far. Second tutorial was really helpful. K.G. very good at explaining complicated concepts. This year I'm the only old granny again and still find I'm the only one saying 'Yes, but?' and thinking I'm the only idiot and then finding that no one else has understood either; how nice to be old and not care if you're thought a fool …

## June:

An OUGS field trip to Assynt to see the Precambrian basement and Moine thrust. Very nostalgic seeing all our old haunts, but so interesting with two marvellous leaders; have learnt more in this week than I thought possible and will never look at a road cutting with the same eyes again. Suilven, Canisp and Quinag, those names are magic and I'd always remembered them. Reading 'do you want to know why the landscape looks as it does?' in that O.U. pamphlet has got me here now in the oldest part of the British Isles and what's more, beginning to understand it … Back to books again with my notebooks and samples to remind why I'm battling with these wretched Variation diagrams. I've enjoyed the tectonics – I like big things which I can imagine happening like India trundling up the Indian Ocean from below the equator and crashing into Asia and scrunching up the Himalayas, or all those downgoing slabs hoovering up the ocean crust, but this geochemistry is so specialised I feel I'm losing sight of it all. There's so much to do in the garden never mind all the rest, I do feel I'm neglecting my friends – not the family, I don't let that happen – how these girls with families and jobs manage I can't imagine, they're absolutely fantastic.

## July:

Second lot of assignments back, again ridiculously good marks, if only I could remember it all as well as they seem to think that'd be something, still it's beginning to tie together better now and it's a surprise how keen I am to do it right, none of 'that'll do' like I used to have … Everywhere is hot, and learning about all that mantle convection and conduction doesn't make this heat wave any more bearable.

## August:

A break at the beach with all the little ones, already they're interested in the stones and the beach shapes and how the sea makes the sand ripples; walked with G. for miles looking for mermaids tears, totally non geological but never mind that, she's only 3, fossils next year.

## September:

This distance learning is sometimes jolly lonely, thank heavens for the phone, but I'm looking forward to the weekend at Lancaster, everyone says it's so helpful.

Well it was. Never mind calling it a revision weekend, that rather presupposed we knew it in the first place; but it was good using the equipment for real and lovely to see old friends and make new ones, some really fascinating people. I knew one of the tutors had a real gift for making even the most daunting work seem fun so chose to do the gamma ray spectroscopy with her group in the a.m. It was most interesting and Shap Fell was hot and sunny, is this a record? For the p.m. we lugged large bits of seismic recorders up the fell, (some bright spark found a barrow), and then back down again, a fuse had blown and there were no spares, blast. But next day tying together our data on K TS and U was absolutely first rate, our group really worked together as a team and made a jolly good presentation, we really felt chuffed, all thanks to G. How nice it is to think of we and not me …

Back home revision proper now, we've been told to really concentrate on Block 5 and Heat; watched all the videos over and over, at last I feel I've got the general picture, applying all this enormous amount of information is the difficult part but is getting easier. Have dared to look at past exam papers; have had a good session with J. on them, it is a great help to have someone else there to explain to you or be explained to.

## October:

I am truly bored to sobs with revising and wish it were all over. I feel fairly well prepared, at least as well as last year.

Exam day. Standing outside Cromer A.T.C. hut I think that of all the silly things I have done in my life this is probably the silliest. 3 hours later it's over. Some was alright, some downright impossible and some just O.K., not time to think, you just had to read and dash it down. I know I've made some absolutely stupid mistakes …

Packed up the books, cleared the dining room table; must return the Home Kit and wait for Christmas Eve and the results. Roll on next February and 339, but now they say it's oversubscribed, so disappointing, but perhaps this'll be the year to do Physical Resources plus The Rise of Scientific Europe, must keep on track to graduate by the Millennium.

### Hayley Morris; Crawley, W. Sussex

*I have been married for twenty-one years and I have two teen-age sons.*

*I did not reach my full potential at school. I was bullied every day, which shattered my confidence. I made certain my work was never good enough to win praise, because I couldn't bear to be the centre of attention.*

*Recently, however, thanks to Olive Huston, an excellent tutor, and the friendly support of my fellow-students I successfully completed an English course at my local community college.*

*I am proud of my achievements and I intend to go on to pursue all my ambitions.*

## Friday 3rd November, 1995.

For the last few weeks, I have been taking an English course at the local community college. I have always been interested in English and I've been yearning to do a course on the subject ever since I left school.

I am very happy with my progress so far and, if all goes well, I hope to go on to take a GCSE course in the future.

## Saturday 4th November, 1995

11:07 p.m.

I spent some time revising my English coursework today. I have had five lessons so far and I have enjoyed them, but I must participate more in group discussion. Most of my fellow-students cope quite well with this, but it is proving difficult for me – difficult, but not impossible. I am determined to master the problem, which is why I decided to practise on my family this morning.

Normally, when we are seated at the breakfast table, we are too sleepy to manage anything more than a brief chat about our plans for the day. This morning, however, with my English lessons in mind, I wanted to discuss something a little more thought-provoking.

I sat up straight, steepling my fingers, as some people do, when they are trying to look intelligent and self-assured. Then, in a voice that sounded clear and confident, I attempted to open a discussion on ways in which the local shopping parade could be improved.

Christopher and Stephen looked at me as if I were a 'verb short of a sentence'. What did they expect at seven o'clock in the morning – Abraham Lincoln's Gettysburg Address? In future, I'll practise my vocabulary on our rabbits. I'll probably get more response!

### Sunday 5<sup>th</sup> November, 1995.

10:30 p.m.

This evening, we attended a firework display on the green at the end of our close. It was exhilarating to watch the fireworks whirring through the air and exploding into a kaleidoscope of colour, lighting up the night sky. We enjoyed it very much.

I decided to write about the firework display because Olive said we would be doing some descriptive writing as part of our coursework. I need to practise this as much as I can.

### Monday 6<sup>th</sup> November, 1995.

9:23 p.m.

We had a discussion about diaries during our English class last week. Anne Frank's diary was mentioned and it sounded interesting, so I got it from the library. Late last night, I started reading it and the next thing I knew, it was five o'clock in the morning and I hadn't had a wink of sleep.

Anne and I went swimming today. I was so tired, I could have fallen asleep whilst we were queuing for our tickets.

We enjoy going swimming occasionally. We intend to take lessons next year. At present, we are learning as much as we can about it from books and we are very pleased with our progress.

I regret staying up all night. It has made me feel jittery and quite unwell.

### Tuesday 7<sup>th</sup> November, 1995.

4:30 p.m.

I am in Crawley Library. I like nothing better than sitting here, studying. I am revising and making sure my folder is all up to date for my English class tomorrow.

This evening, I read a little more of Anne Frank's diary. What an excellent writer she was, for a girl her age!

### Wednesday 8<sup>th</sup> November, 1995.

I had my sixth English lesson today. I was pleased with the marks I received for last week's homework on Alice Taylor's autobiography and an article on Humphrey, the Cabinet cat.

Olive is a brilliant tutor. She is patient and helpful and she explains everything in a way that is easy to understand. She praises us for work well done and when we experience difficulties, she praises the effort we've made and offers constructive suggestions as to how we can improve.

I was very nervous about doing this course, but I couldn't have asked for a better tutor than Olive. She has inspired me with confidence and enthusiasm.

## Thursday 9th November, 1995.

I spent some time in the library today, writing down my thoughts about town and country living. We will be discussing this topic in class next week. I find group discussions rather nerve-wracking, but I am determined to participate more. It will all come right in the end. I will not give up until I have got the hang of it.

## Friday 10th November, 1995.

*A noun names a person, a place or a thing*
*A verb tells us what is happening*
*A pronoun is used in place of a noun, as in 'she saw the film' or 'they went to town'*
*A sentence makes complete sense on its own, for example: 'Vanessa is travelling home'*
*Consider the word group: 'on her feet', its a phrase, for the meaning is incomplete*
*I've learned all these things and much, much more, yet a few weeks ago, my English was poor*
*Writing was a daunting task, until I joined Olive's English class*

## Saturday 11th November, 1995.

9:18 p.m.
I did my homework early this morning and then I practised playing my keyboard. I learned how to play a few years ago and I derive a great deal of pleasure from it.

Sometimes, when I get into difficulty with my English homework, I put down my pen and I play my keyboard for a while. It relaxes me and it clears my mind.

## Sunday 12th November, 1995.

11:32 p.m.
We went to church this morning. As I listened to the speaker, I made a mental note of any words he used that were unfamiliar to me.

I am very interested in new words and punctuation now that I am studying English. It is amazing what you can learn from reading and from listening to people when you pay more attention to grammar and vocabulary.

## Monday 13th November, 1995.

Christopher and the boys don't like going to the barber. They bought some hair clippers and elected me to do the job. I have no experience whatsoever in cutting hair.

After I had read a small leaflet and watched a five-minute video, they seriously expected me to create fashionable styles, with the speed and dexterity of Vidal Sasson!

Stephen was my first victim. He wanted a style like Sean Maguire's. He ended up looking like a plucked chicken.

If only I had had my pen and notebook to hand, when Stephen looked at his reflection in the mirror. The adjectives he used to describe my efforts taught me things about the power of the English language that I never knew before!

## Tuesday 14th November, 1995.

11:50 p.m.
The group discussion is very much on my mind at the moment. I've talked myself hoarse about town and country living this week, but now that the lesson is only hours away, I feel nervous and apprehensive.

## Wednesday 15th November, 1995.

12:30 p.m.
I did it! I participated in the group discussion about town and country living. I was really nervous, but I was determined to do it. I am very proud of myself.

*(See page 134)*

## *Anonymous; Macclesfield, Cheshire*

### Adult Education by a student who wishes to remain anonymous

The problem with Adult Education – if problem is the right word – is that it can become addictive. The convert is prone to the missionary zeal normally associated with religious converts or ex-smokers. I left school, at seventeen, with five rather mediocre "O" levels. I didn't dislike school, but money interested me far more. By the time I'd reached twenty-three it had gradually dawned on me that, whilst I hadn't exactly missed the boat, I would be travelling steerage on any further educational journeys. Six years later I disembarked with "A" levels and an honours degree.

Twenty years have since elapsed. This includes seven years living in the USA – a learning experience in itself and another story. I haven't attempted anything particularly ambitious since my degree, but I seem to be hooked on the intention of learning – including omitted child-hood pursuits such as ice skating and swimming. To the undisguised delight of my son, who was five at the time, my wife and I, complete with inflatable, "dayglow" orange arm-bands, splashed and spluttered through the kiddies pool.

Studying is much lower key now. I struggle with a distance learning course in English literature, and attend evening classes, in conversational French (another subject treated with contempt at school), at Poynton High School but everything still has to be learned by experience. I'm conditioned to read only books that will teach me something – not that this is necessarily restrictive. I usually have three or four books on the go simultaneously. At the moment "Readings in Classical History", "Lord Jim", "Vanity Fair" and Virginia Wolf's short stories. All rather pretentious I suppose, but most of the classics didn't attain their status by being boring. I don't have much time for reading so why waste it?

I don't buy a newspaper, If one is available I turn to the science, sports, arts and entertainment sections. Current affairs I receive from the radio which, I like to believe, is less likely to be politically filtered.

Television has a wonderful capacity to inform but there's so much trivia. I have virtually no control over the program selection and consequently watch very little. I made an exception on Sunday and insisted on watching "Galileo" – I even managed half an hour of the "Beatles Anthology", until my wife realised that "Coronation Street" was on. Radio is my preferred medium – science/history, music, sport, current affairs plays etc. Radio 4's OU programs on Sunday evening can also be quite illuminating. As "Background" learning, often as an accompaniment to washing pots, decorating and similar "mindless" activities, it's almost subliminal and therefore "free" time.

Active learning on the other hand is much more problematical. Keeping a specific time and evening available, as any part-time student knows, often requires considerable diplomatic and organisation skills. Then there's homework. I believe in homework. Knowing that shortcomings will be aired in front of the class is an incentive to complete assignments. Finding the time is another matter. There are so many distractions at home. Sitting quietly invites hints of more useful employment – washing up, decorating, gardening. "Yes dear, I know you have French homework but you did promise to finish the kitchen three years ago." My wife has already put up with "A" levels and my degree so its difficult to be too insistent.

Even the dog regards inactivity as a signal for playtime. Consequently most assignments tend to be completed over a cheese sandwich during lunch at work – with greasy fingers an optional extra!

On Mondays and Thursdays I parade my innate lack of rhythm across the dance floor. This may qualify rather loosely as adult learning and is more in the interests of marital harmony than realising missed opportunities, but easy it isn't.

Because I tend to espouse the advantages of achieving qualifications whilst at school my daughter thinks I'm a bore – she's probably right. To her "A" level history essays, are at best uninteresting. That I find the subject diverting is a mystery to her. She was unwell on Saturday and anxious about a particular assignment. My offer of help resulted in four sides of A4 on the early reign of Henry VII. My daughter didn't learn much from the exercise but I thoroughly enjoyed it. I was a little disappointed, however, that it only merited a B+.

Sometimes, as I rush between crises, panic to complete homework, or trample on my wife's toes, I contemplate an alternative existence as a couch potato. But I know it wouldn't work – I haven't learnt to play jazz piano yet, and French is only one language. And if I ever master the waltz, fox-trot , samba, etc. there's tap dancing and some of the Open University courses look rather tempting ...

## Nan Lawson; Glasgow

*Born 1930 in Fife on east coast of Scotland. Left school at 14 – first job school Clerkess in junior Secondary Schools. Following employment in Local Government Officers and National Coal Board.*

*Married 1955 – met husband George at Scottish Country Dance Class. Son born 1958, daughter 1971 – by now living in Paisley, 7 miles from Glasgow.*

*Have always attended Continuing Education Classes and now member of Senior Studies Institute, University of Strathclyde.*

*Main interests reading (especially historical novels) and Scottish Country Dancing which she has been teaching since 1957.*

## The Diary of a 3rd Age Volunteer Heritage Guide

### Sunday 4 June 1995.
### On duty from 1.00 – 4.00 p.m. with David at the Ramshorn.

Our visitors today included people from Canada, Ireland, (presently students at Strathclyde University) Bishopbriggs and Glasgow. All "chance" visitors who just happened to be passing and saw the notice outside. Generally showed more interest in the stained glass than in the historical background of the building, but most interest shown in the Graveyard. One visitor was a man professionally involved in museums and historical research with a strong interest in stained glass. In fact, he has produced a book on "Glasgow Stained Glass". It's amazing the information we tap into from our visitors – this particular man was able to point out that one of the windows was wrongly attributed. I'll put a note on my return to Clio who will be able to have it rectified. Got so carried away with all the information that I went home to tea and forgot that Jennifer and I had tickets for a Concert in Paisley Town Hall for 7.30 p.m.!

### Wednesday 14 June 1995.
### On duty at the Ramshorn, 1.00 – 4.00 p.m. with Betty Jack.

Our visitors included an elderly priest who was very deaf. He just wanted to look round on his own but chatted on his way out. He has been in Glasgow for over 30 years but I'm sure his Irish accent is as strong as the day he got on the boat to come over. The heatwave continues which makes the walk round the Graveyard much more pleasant than the days we've gone round in bitter cold and rain. They've made a grand job of cleaning it up – so much so that people from the surrounding workplaces pop in to sit on the new benches and eat their picnic lunches. Wonder what David Dale would make of that?

### Wednesday 28 June 1995.
### On duty at the Barony with Maureen.

Our visitors today included an American, an Argentinian, two from Australia, one from New Zealand, several from England but mostly local. We find that Strathclyde students and staff members (both Academic and Administrative) are showing interest. Although some had attended commemorations there, and sat exams! – they were taking the opportunity to have a proper look round. Today's visitors showed particular interest in the mural of Christ in Majesty which is a very unusual if not unique decoration to have in a Scottish Presbyterian Church Building. The little window on the Burning Bush in the John White Chapel attracts a lot of interest.

### Wednesday 16 June 1995.
### Ramshorn 1.00 – 4.00 p.m. with Bob Kutner.

Wrote down the details as 4 Glasgow, 8 other Scottish, 1 Turkish, 3 English, 2 Dutch, 6 Canadian, 1 American. One of the Scots was a Scottish Tourist guide who would have stayed longer but her parking ticket was running out. Says she'll come back again, probably on Doors Open Day in September. The Canadians were an adult with a group of teenagers who had been on the Open Deck Bus Tour and returned to see the church with the plaque to Sir John MacDonald who emigrated from Glasgow and became first Prime Minister of Canada. When we did the walk round the Graveyard they were thrilled to see dates on the stones which pre-dated the founding of Canada. They gave me a lapel badge of the maple leaf.

### Wednesday 23 August 1995.
### Ramshorn 1.00 – 4.00 p.m. with Betty McIntosh.

Fairly quiet this afternoon. Weather still unusually warm and pleasant. Even get people coming in to get out of the sun! Difference from last year when they were dodging wind and rain. Two of our visitors were men who worked in the Planning Department and were impressed with the work done by the University in the refurbishment of both the Ramshorn and the Barony. These particular men were very knowledgeable about the past and the future of Glasgow. They had come in on their lunch break and hurried back to their office to send some of their interested colleagues to see for themselves.

### Thursday 24 August 1995.

Contacted by University to take part in the Elderhostel programme. This group from U.S.A. had arrived in Glasgow the previous evening and our task was to walk them round the city centre to familiarise them with their surroundings, point out Banks, Post Offices, Shopping Facilities, the City Chambers and George Square and generally reassure them that it was safe to do so. I only "lost" one man – his wife said someone had told him about a particular whisky and where to get a good deal, and so he had gone to "the liquor store".

## Saturday 16 September 1995.

This was "Doors Open Day" in Glasgow when buildings not usually open to the public can be seen. Last year both the Barony and Ramshorn were open for the first time and it went like a fair. Groups of between 30 and 40 at a time were shown around the Graveyard. By the time I got there at 1.00 p.m. the guides on the morning duty had almost lost their voices. The visitors were all very interested and appreciative. This year it was decided to open the Royal College Building and the Strathclyde Business School in addition to the Ramshorn and Barony and I volunteered for the Business School. As this building is off the beaten track we did not have to deal with the same numbers as Barony and Ramshorn. Several of our visitors were former students who were greatly impressed with what had been done with what they remembered as a very run down area and particularly appreciated the landscaped garden. This is a completely new building and when asked if it provided what was needed for the people who used it were assured by a member of staff that it did and that "it worked for them". I really volunteered to be on duty there as I had seen it start from scratch and every time I passed wondered what it was like inside. Today was our last day on duty until next spring.

## Personal Feelings about the Guiding.

While the refurbishment of the Ramshorn and the Barony Hall was being tackled, the University offered a class on the background of these buildings with a view to providing a Volunteer Guide force in the future. I applied and did the first course. The research and historical notes were produced by Norman Barr and gave us a clear picture of how things had been since these buildings came into being and what Glasgow was like before them. Building on the basis of these notes we were able to do additional reading as suggested and the Guides themselves were very good at passing on any relevant information that came their way.

We were also greatly helped by Jenny Laurie on presentation. If you are not in the habit of addressing public gatherings it can be very daunting to find all faces turned towards you awaiting words of wisdom or knowledge. Like everything else, it becomes easier with practice. Even your last tour in the afternoon's spell of duty can be much better than your first as you can bring in additional information brought up by previous visitors that day. For example former member of the congregations of both churches are a fund on information and anecdotes.

The Volunteer Guides have also formed a club that holds monthly meetings where we can all get together and exchange information. We have speakers and recently had someone who had been involved in the storing of the Ramshorn windows during World War II when they were removed, boxed and stored in the Crypt to avoid bomb damage. When they were replaced after the war it must have been like making up a gigantic jigsaw puzzle. We even learnt that some of the windows had been inadvertently switched!

Lastly, I have always enjoyed reading books with a historical background and it's good to see how they "tie-in" with the facts. There are so many familiar names on the stones in the Ramshorn Church Graveyard – all those real Glasgow characters, just waiting for someone to tell their stories.

## *Kathleen Chapman; Sileby, Leics.*

*Kathleen lives in Sileby where she shares a house with a friend and a cat called Rosie.*

*Kathleen enjoys cooking and drawing and has won an art competition. She was also commissioned to produce a work for a local housing trust. She enjoys shopping for clothes.*

## My Direy of Learning

### Cooking and Washing

When the time came for doing our programme, rota for churs. Me and Nick take it in turns to cook, meals, washing pots is grate, its been programmed OK naw to share.

We naw have 3 keyworkers at Gleeb house, Mr Gegery Mrs McConal and Mrs Wesley, thy are there to suport are weaknes and to help me with my troubles, thay came to us after Carol Foster left, I find them very useful.

In the Year of Janurery 1995 One Year before 1995, the weather was very unusal we had a very bad PowerCut, and a case of snow came down bad, the Hostle was in candlelight, for some time, the most kind Resedent, was Ivon who stayed for sometime, the worst weather of Jan.

When the time we took Rosey Vets. She made A Terrable fuss because she was a bit skard to Have Her Jabs. So after thay had finisd her, its a lot of hard work to be a doctor or nurse.

I Like Animals Nick and Myself, Have a nice Pussy Called Rosey, shes Longhaired she Has Lots of Cuddles, from us both, I Like going shooping for nice things, I buy thinks Like ShowerGell, Pens, I Like Taps to Listen to, musics very relaxsing, I Like to Get My house nice and tidy. I am not a very messy Person and Like Things Going Smouthy.

### Groups and Crowds
### My Dairy about Groups

Well I think talking to one persons very much like nice convercason, Groups are Like being to Bossy, Crowds are Like rushing and shouting though citys and towns, thay make Me feel frittened.

It Has Been very hard Getting are Home togeather we Got Help from Gleeb House aad Caroline foster, My home has a very Good Support, We Go On Fridays in turn to Silbey Coop fore Grosrys

Whots Happead to Me since 1994 to the years going By, Well Iv been though Lives Wose, Happings, I Hade, a very changeble childhood as from a baby, to the age of 9 years old, I Can Remmber being a child getting what I wonted. I Class My Self as a Lovebly Little Child.

## My dos aad donts Living at this House

Nicks My friend Hes 51 year old, He Wont stop Drinking He smocks Lot of fags, Likes Vidos, Works at Whithades 5 days a week, The House is big We chose are nice furiute, its a addvance accommadaitson, and Iv Been there since 1992.

Many years past for Art Work I Liked doing My Learning, with Comuety Skills, the Adult Commuity College, Was One of My fabuluse itles to Anything, Getting On With Poeple isnt very Brain thinking, thay seen very odd at times, there was most times I liked was With My friends

Iv always had nice times together with them.

## My Direy off Learning 1995 from Life and Kindness to My Freinds and Family.

My Life begain in a upside down Life from Living with Mum and Dad Sisters Brothers, We didnt always like being togeather. Mostly sometimes, Dad was very ill at that time so We had to go along Being fine, from 1994 was a Lot for Me Cope with from Moveing in to Places to Live for My futhure,

Iv Been to very Good Lessons Like Longslade were was met with Sheon Cope who Lernt Me very Good teatching skills, We done being bravery Goups, florwer Araeing Like with using dryed flolews, skills are very usfull, to help you, went there untill Aprill, time, Rawlings Night School Last fore 2 years Course, I Got On very well with Gilly Wollonts,

## The day that Iv Had

Naw after so many days Iv Had thats Bad most days cover, My Calender, Ive often been in a rush and Been Clumsey and Brocken My Best itmes, Ive Gone out and ben out the rong shoes.

Rathbones employent College was most sucesesful to try. I past very well progress in my Books, Ronder, Chanal, was very Good with helping to acive My Ctivecutes I Passed them all.

I went to a Resedenchal, School for hard Behavey. Very well strolen. It was on the Barkshire side of Windsor Castle. I liked learning with my class,

My Part in Making My Ways to Happyness helping to Look Smart when Going Out with nece fork, makeing an atcivement at hard working, doing the right thing propply.

## Me and Moveing in and Advance House.

Ive had a quite time for managing to Live Here, setting up My Home was not very hard going. David Rollings is the Maneging Boss, for I think he works hard to I Pub hiss writings to words,

Pulieen Holland well Ive know Her since shes Been Comeing for My checks, I get On Well with her,

Ive enjoyed writing my direy on, the ways of my Life and probbles, its been lots of intresting ways how to get on with My friends, the things in My Direy are, my intrest on My feelings, and life. Makeing a Book of your own is a Good thing, Ive enyed it to.

Im 36 year old and Live in Sileby, I hope is Direys fine and you Like My Readings. its all I could do.

*(See facsimile, page 131)*

### Julie Smithson; Wakefield

*I am 35 years old with one son, Guy, who is 10 and I have one brother, Paul. Luckily I have an excellent relationship with my parents who have been very supportive and helpful in both my new home and my college life.*

*Guy and myself fled to a Women's Aid Refuge in Leeds in 1994 to escape a violent man who had ruined our lives. In 1995 we were given a new house by Leeds City Council and I began a course at Park Lane College. In 1996 I am starting an Access course and I hope to go to Leeds University in 1997 to do Environmental Studies.*

*At the moment, my life is wonderful; I have my confidence and self esteem and feel I can achieve anything.*

## How I came to be at Middleton Skills Centre

This was due to an unfortunate event in my life.

I was quite content after I divorced my husband in 1990. My son and myself lived in a nice 2 bedroomed house in Mirfield. I had a full-time job and supported us financially, we always had a car and enough money for the little extras.

The job was only in a factory, sewing, and although I always felt I was more capable than this, you tend to stay where the money is.

I have always been outgoing and fairly confident, until Jan 93 when I met my new partner. He was the person you only read about in the paper. By Nov 94, I had been beaten – all the time, not just occasionally, demoralised and turned into a quivering wreck. I ended up at Leeds Woman's Aid. I had no job, no car, no belongings, just myself and my son. Once we had pulled ourselves together and I realised we were going to make a completely new life for ourselves, I decided, I would no longer be 'just a machinist'. This was where the good life started.

The refuge was near Park Lane College. One day , I was walking past and impulsively decided to walk in. I felt a little silly as all the students looked so much younger. After speaking to a nice lady we decided as I had no qualifications that the 'Women into Work' course would be the best way to get started.

Although my confidence at this time was **nil**, I couldn't wait. In a way I had my violent ex-partner to thank for this – ironic isn't it.

## 25-9-95

My first day at Middleton Skills Centre.

As I did not know anyone on the course, I felt a little apprehensive. The first lesson I had was Psychology. It had begun the week before and I hadn't known so everyone was sat in the room already, as they knew it was an early class, having started at 9.30 a.m. rather than 10 a.m.

I settled into my seat and began to listen. I thought the rest of the class understood all the jargon and I must be one of the 'thick ones'! I found out later that I wasn't on my own, we were all as baffled.

There was no way I was going to participate in making comments, I didn't have the confidence to speak up. I decided I would just sit and listen and hoped I faded into the background so the teacher wouldn't pick me to answer any questions.

I sat at lunchtime with Wyn, everyone else seemed to go home. I felt I could chat with her, she didn't make me feel intimidated. Of course the fact that I did feel intimidated occasionally was no ones fault. It was just a reaction from the previous 2 years.

I felt slightly more at ease on Monday afternoon in New Opportunities. I understood what we were talking about. I still didn't join in as I felt I would be laughed at if I got something wrong.

## 27-9-95

Wednesday of my first week and I should be going to the Skills Centre for my Counselling lesson. I had been up all night with a migraine and no way could I get to College. I couldn't even focus. I felt so guilty. I phoned the Centre and explained and Maureen made me feel at ease by saying it couldn't be helped.

I thought I would have given the impression of someone who couldn't be bothered turning up, but really it was quite the contrary.

## 29-9-95

By the Friday of the first week my confidence had returned slightly. I went into English Workshop. There were only 4 of us. I had decided early on that I would like to take English GCSE. I asked Linda if this would be possible. She couldn't see a problem with that and made me an appointment at Park Lane main site to enrol on this course.

I felt at ease with Linda right from the start and hoped to have her for my tutor.

During my first weekend at home I spent a lot of time doing homework. I was glad of this, as at the moment I have no social life and it gives me something to do. Also I am enjoying it.

I am hoping to give education at least 2 years, and learn as much as possible.

We have been told of a Belgium trip in December. I can't see that it will be possible for me to go as I don't have any spare income to spend.

## 2-10-95

Monday again. Psychology was just as confusing, but I have now found that the other girls in the class feel just the same. Jerry's a difficult teacher to learn from as she talks so fast and it seems impossible to take notes. It seems the only option is to go out and buy the book she teaches from. This poses a bit of a problem if there is no money to pay for the book in the first place.

My confidence in general is definitely growing. I join in, in class and now make comments and suggestions, and don't feel embarrassed if I get it wrong.

This is definitely the best thing I have ever done and I wish I'd done it sooner.

## 4-10-95

On Wednesday I finally turned up for Counselling at 10 am. To find it had started at 9.30 am. I was about to turn around and go home when Cathy persuaded me to go in. It was terrible having to walk in when everyone was already there. Mary Smith was very nice. I explained I couldn't get a bus to get me there until 10 am. She said that was fine but I would miss quite a bit. I decided in future that I would walk, and therefore arrive on time.

Mary was kind enough to give me a lift to Leeds after the lesson. I had to enrol for my GCSE English that afternoon.

I arrived at Park Lane at 12.30 p.m. Nobody seemed to know where I was supposed to go. I spent 50 minutes, being passed from one dept to another. I had just given up hope when I decided to try once more. Luckily the lady I asked, took me to the right place and I was seen to. I walked out of the College at 2.45 p.m. I couldn't believe it had taken so long.

## 5-10-95

This is my second week in Computer Skills. I enjoy it more than I expected to. These days a lot of occupations call for someone who can use a computer, even if it is only basic. This was the main reason for wanting to take the subject. I had a vision of a person sitting all day, pressing keys and yawning with boredom.

Actually I find it very interesting and hope to stay on longer than the 10 weeks to take an exam.

## 6-10-95

I have just finished my second week. My confidence has grown tremendously. Although I'm not sure what I would like to do when I finish at college, I feel very ambitious. I want to learn as much as possible and pass as many exams as I can. I feel determined I will be something one day.

## 9-10-95

My weekends, at the moment, are spent looking forward to Mondays. In New Opportunities on Mon. afternoons we have been filling in JIIG-CALS. This is really interesting, it's amazing to see the job suggestions it comes up with. Most of mine I found I could possibly relate to in the future.

I am learning at the moment that my biggest problem is going to be further education. There are other courses I would like to enrol on but because they don't teach them at Middleton I would have to go to Park Lane main site. Unfortunately this is impossible as I have to be there for my son before and after school.

## 10-10-95

Supervisory Skills is a great lesson for teaching self confidence. If one begins college feeling useless and worthless, these feelings should soon be expelled as this lesson goes on. After putting our abilities in writing, it is easy to see just how much we are capable of. The list of skills and duties each of us does in just everyday life is endless.

We were asked to write a piece for homework titled 'What is a Supervisor'? I got great comments and 'Excellent' from my tutor. My confidence has just grown some more.

## 11-10-95

Counselling is very nerve-wracking. The first half of class is spent doing exercises or going through hand-outs. The second part is the hard part, well, I think so.

We are asked to counsel each other. As it will be a different person each week, it causes a lot of apprehension.

Of course we have all agreed to strictest confidentiality. This lesson wouldn't work if there was no trust, I think I will feel better when I get to know the other members of my class. A lot of them don't come to the Centre at any other time, this makes it harder to get to know them.

I have now got enough confidence to come to the Centre and join in! I participate in class, giving my views and opinions and no longer feel embarrassed if I get it wrong. I enjoy every class, even Computing Skills which I felt I would find boring. Once a week I get out of bed thinking 'Oh God, I don't want to go today.' This is for Counselling. I always feel apprehensive beforehand, but I am always pleased when I have taken part.

## 12-10-95

I have surprised myself in Computer Skills, both by how much I have achieved already and how much I am enjoying it.

I never expected to be Word Processing paragraphs and saving them on my own disk so soon.

I quite look forward to the lesson. Carol is great, and very patient, always managing to spend an equal amount of time between each of us.

## 13-10-95

Friday morning – support your studies. This has to be my favourite lesson. It could be because there are only a few of us, I'm not sure.

Linda is very helpful, and I think, tolerant at times. I am getting impatient waiting for my English GCSE to arrive.

I feel full of enthusiasm and can't wait to get started.

## 16-10-95

Psychology had a new meaning today. Until now the lesson has been very mind boggling. I speak for the whole class when I say today was the first time we felt as though we had learned anything. We had a stand in teacher and she made things much clearer. I went home and deciphered my notes quite quickly. This usually takes me most of my Monday evening.

## 16-10-95

The JIIG-CALS were interesting. I found I related to the jobs which the computer showed for me. The main problem is I would eventually like a career in something I have a real interest in. This way my heart would be in the job. I find anything to do with Craft, needlework, art, animals interesting. The JIIG-CAL showed this.

I particularly enjoy sewing and would be happy in a job which included this. My biggest interest though has to be animals. I would love to work with them, maybe an R.S.P.C.A. inspector, if I could cope with the hurt the animals go through.

As the weeks go on I feel more confident. I want to go on to further education next year and really have a go at doing something with my life. The unfortunate thing is getting from A to B seems to be a problem. Especially as I have no help with my 9 year old son. If I go into an Access course at Park Lane, I cannot get home in time for him.

At the moment I spend 2 hours, maybe more on homework. I am always pleased to be given some as I am eager to learn as much as possible, this is good. The only bad thing about it is that I have only been in my house 6 weeks and I find little spare time to decorate.

I am now walking to the centre on Wednesday mornings. I leave home at 8.30 and arrive at 9.30, by the time I get to class I am shattered. When the bad weather comes I will start getting the bus and arrive late at 10 am instead of 9.30.

I love walking, but at that time on a morning when its freezing cold and I've got a heavy bag to carry, I can't help wondering if it's all worth it. I just hope I can keep it up.

My English GCSE file arrived. I was looking through it when I got it home, I didn't understand much of it at all. I hope it will all become clearer as time goes on.

Although I want to pass everything possible this year and hopefully get certificates in other subjects, I really want to pass my two GCSEs in English and Psychology. If I can do this it will give me the confidence to do more courses.

We have been given a project to do for Supervisory Skills. We have 7 weeks in which to complete this. Julie Holliday, Wyn Howley and myself are working together. We have decided to work on 'Domestic Violence'. We are trying to find out how Women's Aids started, the difficulties which the women in charge faced then, while they were trying to get help and how things are now. Have things improved? How? I phoned Leeds Woman's Aid to ask for permission to interview their workers.

I have decided to go on the trip to Brussels, after originally not feeling that I would be able to. I am looking forward to it but am a bit apprehensive about the journey. I will be glad when we have landed!

I have started my English GCSE. The 12 foundation units at the beginning are to be done first. I find them a little puzzling and hope as time goes on, when I look back they will look easy.

The work in these units has answers to be written in the blank boxes. Unfortunately as I am writing my answers it is hard not to glance underneath. This is where they have printed their answers. I don't think they should be directly underneath, as it makes it hard not to peep!

## 24-10-95

I have just finished Computer Skills. I seem to be understanding this subject quite well. We have covered Word Processing briefly. I was given some work to do with the 'mouse' and drew a little man. I was quite pleased with myself as I never expected to be doing something like this so soon.

Carol's very good at splitting herself into about 6 different people and being with each student at all times!

I have just spent the day listening to my tape which was sent with my English GCSE. There is a play on the tape called 'The Ants'. I had to listen to the play, then answer the questions at the end. I found this quite easy to do, it was simple really, the answers were on the tape. I suppose it was just to get me used to comprehension.

It's now 4 weeks to the Brussels trip. Oh God! I'm really panicking about the ferry crossing. Sea sickness doesn't worry me, it's the sinking that does. I'm trying really hard to save some extra money to take. My parents have told me I mustn't take any presents home, but I will, after all they have been good enough to offer to look after Guy while I go on this trip and I think they will deserve something. Guy will definitely expect a pressie.

## 13-11-95

I'm afraid we as a class, have had to have a word with Jill about Jerry who teaches Psychology. I personally find her a lovely woman and I believe, so does the rest of the class. Unfortunately we are finding it very difficult to learn from her. She tends to talk extremely fast and it's difficult to take notes.

I feel that a few visual aids would help and if Jerry slowed down or left gaps between points, enabling us to get them down, this would be better.

### English

I have just completed an assignment about the 'Tollund man', this was for my English. I found it really interesting but parts of it were hard to comprehend. This is something I know I have to get used to.

I was asked to write 500 words about a photo of the Tollund man. I started with 100 and stretched them again and again until I had the right amount. I didn't think I would be able to do it. I enjoyed it though. I found it surprising as I would never think to read a book about the Bog People, now I want to.

I am now starting a biography. I have chosen my father to write about. I have already interviewed him.

I have just finished a piece of work which had to be stretched. Now it looks like I have to condense one. I have so much to write about and only 1000 word to do it in. This will be difficult.

The notes I had had to be shortened and shortened until I had my 1000 words. Lots of things about my dad's life had to be left out of the biography and I found this ever so frustrating.

Unfortunately I didn't do as well as I had hoped. I stupidly switched from 2nd to 3rd party while I was telling the story.

## 27-11-95

Today in Psychology, we were given homework. The answers were in the books we have been advised to buy. Luckily my father bought me the book which at £11 is quite expensive. I felt the homework was a good way of learning. The chapter had to be read and re-read until the answers were found. By this time, the information was learned.

The class is much more at ease now, as the learning is easier.

## 28-11-95

Today was our last lesson in Supervisory Skills and English for business. They were interesting subjects but I definitely think 10 weeks is long enough to cover everything. Although it would be great to start another course to fill the gap on Tuesdays, it will give me more time to concentrate on other subjects which are on-going.

## 30-11-95

Computers
I am quite looking forward to the introductory finishing. We are starting a CLAIT after Christmas and I think I will enjoy this.

So far we have learned, Word Processing, Graphs, Database and Spreadsheets, but only in small bits. It created enough interest to want to continue though, this I think was the purpose of the 10 weeks and it seems to have worked.

## 1-12-95

English

I was given some work by Lynda today about the Taming of the Shrew. I didn't know what to expect after the Twelfth Night, but it looks a little more understandable. You never know it may grow on me, but at the moment I just feel I will be glad to see the back of Shakespeare. It could be that I am looking too deep into something and making it more difficult than it is.

## 4-12-95

Psychology is definitely much better now. I think Jerry feels comfortable with us again now and we are learning from her now. I finally feel that this lesson is coming together. I understand what I am being taught and it's a great feeling as I never thought I would.

Tomorrow is Brussels!

Oh God!

## 5-12-95

I spent this morning packing, after seeing Guy off to school. My father took Wyn and myself to Park Lane College and being as punctual as he is we arrived there in plenty of time.

We left the college approx. 2 p.m. I've never been to Hull so it was a nice drive for me.

On arriving at Hull docks we were taken on a tour, it was explained to us how the import and export works and what goes in and out of the country. Although I didn't expect it to be interesting, it was.

We boarded the ferry and it was 1 hour before it actually set off. It was like waiting in a dentists to have a filling. I couldn't wait for tomorrow to come so it would all be over. Wyn and myself put our things in our cabin – which measured 5 x 6 ft, and had bunk beds. We then rushed down to the restaurant for our dinner. It was a carvery and as I don't eat meat I had to have the veg pie which I didn't really enjoy.

Later at about 9 p.m. we decided to go into the bar and listen to the band. By this time we started having gale force winds and we were rocking all over the place. Some of the girls were being sick. I didn't affect me in that sense, I just hoped we didn't sink.

After a sleepless night, we had breakfast and set off for the hotel.

As the ferry was late arriving in Zeebrugge, we were late getting to the hotel. We had exactly ½ hr to get our cases to our rooms and run around the streets trying to find somewhere to buy a sandwich.

At 1.30 we arrived at Grand Place to meet our Guide. He was a pleasant man who was filled with enthusiasm about his city. Unfortunately, because we hadn't had time to get changed into warm clothing, we were all so cold we didn't appreciate what he was telling us. We just couldn't wait for it to be over.

When we got back to the hotel – once again we had exactly ½ hr to get ready for the European Union. How the heck do you get a shower, wash your hair and get dressed up in formal clothing in that time?

It was a ridiculous day. We got to the Union just in time. A man called 'O'Neil' talked to us for some time. By this time all the lack of sleep and rushing about caught up with everyone. I kept seeing heads dropping then lifting back up, as people were trying to stay awake. Mine included. We joined Mike McGowan and listened to the Youth Awards. This I found very interesting – maybe because I have an interest in art, maybe I managed to stay awake because we were stood up. I had plenty of questions to ask and enjoyed the evening.

Later at 8.30 when the presentation was finished the evening was our own. A few of us had a drink in the hotel bar then went to bed. As usual I couldn't sleep. Our bedroom was right over the front of the hotel and there was too much noise.

## Thursday

The phone rang this morning. Half asleep I hadn't realised it was an early morning call, I picked it up and said 'Hello' and couldn't figure out why no one was answering me.

I felt like I hadn't gone to bed.

We had 4 talks today, they were all interesting, especially the one about the women's lobby.

I wanted to find out more about the 'Animal's Rights' but not knowing how 'politics' works, I felt I did not know what to ask.

Wyn and myself found an Indian restaurant and called in there for our tea.

## Friday

The group set off for Luxembourg this morning. It took 3 hrs to get there by coach.

On arriving, we were given a map and told we had 5 hrs free time.

We found the market. It was the most beautiful market I have ever seen. The stalls were wooden sheds – larger versions of Wendy houses. They sold loads of craft work and sweets. We bought sweets at one stall and the girl who was very pleasant and helpful, gave us all a free Nougat, which I thought was nice of her. I really enjoyed the day.

## Saturday

Our bags were packed bright and early this morning. We had breakfast and set off for Brugge.

I don't have the words to describe the beauty of this town.

It was like stepping back in time 1000 years. There were still cobbled streets, horse and carts, lots of people riding cycles and magnificent buildings which stretched up to the sky. On the contrary there were quaint little houses and shops.

I needed a week here to explore. 4 hrs was not enough. It is one place I will try to visit again.

After Brugge, we were back on the ferry for 5 p.m. and ready for some dinner.

I was praying we would have a smooth crossing and we did.

As I find it hard to sleep in strange, noisy places, I decided to join some of the other girls in the disco until the early hours of the morning.

It didn't matter, I could have an early night tonight.

## 11-12-95 Monday

Until now I have had a lift to college which has enabled me to get to Psychology on time as it starts at 9.30 am. Unfortunately Wyn has given up, as she finds it hard to understand.

I could get a bus but wouldn't arrive in class until 9.50 so I got up this morning at 7 am and decided to walk the 2 ½ miles to college.

I needn't have bothered as Jerry was late!

There were only 5 people in class. I think everyone's recovering from the trip.

## 12-12-95

I had arranged with Wyn for her to come to my house today so we could put our Supervisory Skills Project together, and prepare our talk which is tomorrow. When Wyn arrived, she said she wasn't going to do it and I had to do the talk on my own. I was already nervous, now I felt terrible, and a little annoyed that she would let me down like that.

I decided not to give the talk on my own.

## 13-12-95

This morning in Counselling, I was watched by two members of the class as I counselled another member. They were asked to fill in a score sheet for me, assessing my counselling skills.

I didn't do too bad. I got a lot of 4's which meant I was 'usually good at that skill'. I'm still not clear on this lesson though, because we don't have a lot of written work to do, it seems odd when there is no homework. I feel as though I should do something at home but I'm not sure what.

After class I went in the canteen to wait for Jill so I could tell her I was not giving my talk. As I spoke to the girls about it they were very supportive and encouraged me to give the talk on my own. Jill agreed that I should just talk about the part I had researched. This was 'Domestic Violence' and how it is dealt with nowadays.

I stood up and fastened my pie chart and bar graph to the wall then turned to face everyone. My legs suddenly started shaking. Luckily as I have the personal experience, I didn't need to read from my work as the others had done. After a couple of minutes I got into the swing of it and found it a quite enjoyable experience. I was quite pleased to find a few people had questions.

We were all given a certificate afterwards which was a nice surprise as I hadn't expected one.

I was so glad I had decided to stay and give my talk.

## 14-12-95

I had to miss Computers this morning as I had an appointment in Bradford. I found this very inconvenient as it was the first lesson of the CLAIT. I hate missing lessons like this. This means after Christmas I will be one step behind everyone else!

## 15-12-95

I handed my work, on the Taming of the Shrew, in, today. I had not done what it asked. Once Lynda had explained I realised where I had gone wrong. I wanted to do it again because I feel I must get the highest marks possible. I don't want C's and D's in any of the subjects I take. I don't feel that would be good enough.

## 19-12-95

The Women into Work Course has now finished.

I am continuing courses: English GCSE, Psychology GCSE, Computer CLAIT, Counselling 7 units.

I enjoyed the course immensely and I am really pleased I decided to go to College. My confidence is a lot better than it was and I feel very enthusiastic and ambitious, although I haven't really found a job I can aim for. Once or twice I have had an idea but find it impossible to get on the appropriate courses.

I will keep on trying and hopefully one day something will turn up. I am really grateful for being given this chance, without this course I wouldn't have known where to start.

## Charles Nicholson; East Midlands

*Charles Nicholson is the essentially necessary pen-name of a recently retired adult educator who has now become a mature student and a much more active member of his 'village' community near Leicester. After several years in industry selling steel products, then installing computerised systems 'CN' moved into the training and education scene, becoming an Area Organiser in the West Midlands before helping to set up the adult literacy campaign in the mid-70s., eventually staying on for twenty years with the leading voluntary organisation for adult learning in England and Wales.*

*He continues to enjoy a busy 'early retirement' – and recommends it.*

## SUNDAY

Expecting a busy week, as the "end of term" approaches, and more activities seen to be piling on top of each other. One thought for sure, less than 6 months into retirement, that whereas 25 hours per day weren't enough at work, eight days a week don't really give enough time for all the things you can now choose to do – even if there is the drawback of spending out all the while and not nearly as much money coming in; with the credit card account usually exceeding the pension income.

Stay on after morning Church for a short music practice for the players who'll be accompanying the choir at the Carol Concert. The occasional odd noise from the – mainly young – violinists – but the flute player rather good, and she's only 11.

Some more serious practice on own this afternoon, in attempt to retain place on back desk of second violins in the University orchestra; plus a bit of Spanish Level 2 homework; and, having almost caught up with post-card collection last month, an hour or so on the stamps, again making mental note NOT to join Philatelic Society, as they all sound too keen AND money has been known to change hands at their meetings.

## MONDAY

Usual, or at least fairly usual, early morning swim. Nearest sports hall/leisure centre 5.8 miles away, so does need a car – Bus absolutely impossible any time of the day. Changed, showered, and into water by 7.35 am, par for the course, and a pleasant 30 degrees, an improvement on the mere 29 degrees several of us grumbled about last week, and the extra warmth results in a few extra lengths, needed anyway to work off some of the weekend alcohol.

Back to a late post 9.00 am, breakfast – a healthy one, no fry-ups these days – and a steady morning and afternoon; a couple of letters written, preparatory scan of Xmas card list, practise the faster passages in the Verdi, revise the vocab. list for lesson 20 in the Spanish text book, token gesture towards helping with the lunch-time washing up, etc.

BUT, the highlight of Monday is the English Country Dancing group in the evening, 7.30-9.30pm; or thereabouts. Used to be a "class" in the regular programme of a local community school; then had to become an "associated club", and eventually, because of further red tape and excessive paperwork and registration regulations, and so on, the two tutors concerned, a husband and a wife team, made it their own show, hiring the church hall one night a week and taking many of their followers with them.

That was almost ten years ago. We've been going five, and are now established enough, and good enough, to be "reserves" on the "demonstration" team, when needed. The current group holds together well; payment on attendance, £1.50 for the two hours – which includes the usual coffee break; up to 30 couples, but more usually 20 couples, some 'singletons' pairing up as required, and overall leading to a variety of 'sets' and dances.

Most of the folk do it more than once a week – dancing, that is. Some do Scottish, others 'clogging', maybe a bit of 'Maypole'; there's even a Morris 'person'. However experienced they are, they're all very welcoming to new couples who turn up at any stage during the two term "session" in response to steady publicity; and this overall style emanates from the tutors themselves, highly regarded members of the local scene, who show great patience, have an easy going teaching style with a fair bit of background information about the dances and their historical development – all combined with a neat line in wit, banter and repartee plus a flash here and there of innuendo – this form of dancing is after all a contact sport.

## TUESDAY

Temptation to lie in after Monday evening dancing, but a determined effort to get to the pool for a quick 50 lengths – or was it just 40 lengths this time, even 35? Hot shower afterwards, luxurious.

Post arrives mid-morning, and includes early circular with advance information about various musical activities as far ahead as the summer at Knuston Hall, the residential adult education college in Northamptonshire; dates now fixed for string weekend, with flutes and recorders, late July; and for all instruments/ "small orchestra" one week Summer School, Sunday evening to Friday lunch-time mid-August. Make a note of both; exceptional value, and not too demanding a standard in previous 2/3 years.

Slightly unexpected late afternoon phone call from near neighbour Bill, also 'early retired' recently, for advice on the German language course he's starting, along with a few thousand others I'd guess, next February using the Open University Broadcasts. Wants to show me the "diagnostic test" he's just done, which seems to indicate he doesn't need to start at 'Beginners Level'. Agree, and he walks round in 10 mins, giving the bottle time to get up to room temperature.

Indeed, he has done quite well under test conditions, and in a way, that's as it should be. With a little school French, a long time back, but no formal German, he found himself in Stuttgart ten times for 5 days in his last two years at work when his company, almost the "jewel in the crown" of a large UK engineering group, was sold at a significant paper profit to a German industrial conglomerate. He didn't much like the upheaval and living out of a suit-case in expensive hotels – this export glamour/international business travel much over-rated – but it's given him a taste for non-technical German. Not bad at all on some of the grammar and a number of structures, and a bit of everyday vocabulary to back it up so I suggest he does aim for the higher level start, still a bit below 'O' Level – and as we open the second Gallo, just for a top up this time, I offer, in return for a couple of bottles of Scotch, to give him the benefit of my rather rusty degree German, and during January about half a dozen 30/40 minutes 'blitz' lessons to get him slightly better prepared for the February transmissions.

Fortunately Bill can walk back round the corner. I finish the red wine at dinner – only faggots and peas! – but some nice cheese afterwards. Almost fall asleep watching evening television. The penalty for this indulgence will be 10 extra lengths tomorrow.

## WEDNESDAY

Let myself off those extra lengths – and indeed any early morning swimming – because it's Wednesday, and that means 'Mature Movers' sort of aerobics at 10 o'clock, for an hour, followed by, and included in the subsidised price, as second "activity", most choosing swimming, with badminton or nipping off early to the local pub a close second equal.

In the September start to the session at the sports centre, there had been talk of mid-day 'circuit training' at a variety of standards on Tuesdays and/or Thursdays in addition to what was on offer in the evenings and across the weekend. However, despite the market research, not enough takers, a bit of a disappointment to some of the keen, young enthusiasts on the staff of the sports company now running the centre for the Local Authority. Not for me any more evenings out, or the crush in the changing rooms on Saturdays and Sundays – all these 'Jack the lad' types with their locker-room talk, and their flexing muscles, and less that half my age, and their strutting around arousing my sense of inadequacy as I realise I can't measure up to them in the way I used to – if I remember correctly.

SO, 'Mature Movers' on Wednesday it has to be – and an unusual and worthwhile group it is too – and a bargain at the price of £1.50 for the two hours/double activity, and a free cup of coffee in the indoor bowls lounge at the half-way point – or just £1.20 if you've got annual membership (individual, couple or family) of the Sports Centre anyway; and a free go in December if you've been every week throughout November. Numbers good as well; never seen less than 45, sometimes about 60. Generally aimed at the over 55 years of age, some nearer 50, but several over 65; quite a few widows. Everyone trying hard without overdoing it, even when a little obese. This week fifty-four, about 7 rows of about 8 'movers', taking up about half the hall. Fifty women, four men; two 'first-timers' this week, even so late in the term, but half a dozen who were at the start of the group over 18 months ago and who helped to spread the word about what fun it was and who regularly relate the way stiff joints could be heard cracking in the wide open space when just a few turned up in those early days.

The tutor, Jeannie, is marvellous, and adored by everyone; poetry in motion, in her multi-coloured leotard. Has all the certificates as well, and knows her stuff. Kitted out with a head-fitted radio mike, has the right hardware for the tapes and can make herself heard at the back of the hall as she prances about giving the lead from the table-top platform at the front. Keeps a careful eye on any newcomers. Spotted my frozen shoulder within 15 minutes of my first attendance. Reminds us frequently not to over-exert, just start to feel the stretch, then maybe push a little bit extra. Gives us a steady warm-up routine, an energetic middle half hour, then 10 minutes slow down, with "pelvic floor" exercises, for the men as well. Have been meaning to look that up in the book. Am I really built like that?

Short socialising coffee-break, then on to the swimming pool. Try to look casual as I show off my free-style, and practise a couple of racing turns. Respond to the request to help a couple of "mature ladies" with their back-stroke technique. Eat your heart out, Charles Atlas. Got publicly reprimanded and told to behave by my partner of 35 years and more, and mother of my children (grown-up), and warned I might not be allowed to do the Sainsbury's shopping again if I go on like this.

Just time to get a sandwich lunch and off to City Adult Education College for early afternoon Spanish class. This Level 2 has settled at a dozen participants, from the original 16. Most did some sort of 'Foundation' course last year, and can generally cope with the pronunciation, days of the week, months of the year, telling the time, numbers up to 100. We've signed up under the OCN/Open College Network System to help ourselves to a slightly subsidised fee and the institution to a few extra "points" in the eyes of funding sources, with the intention of building up a "portfolio" of work over the next 4/5 terms, then taking a GCSE type exam.

As can be expected from members of an afternoon class, some are already retired, or work part-time, mornings only. One is unemployed and has his sights on a good summer working in a Benidorm Bar, as recommended by his elder brother. The oldest member of the class, 68, still has some difficulty in putting together even a simple sentence with fully correct grammar and agreement of adjectives, but, after three holidays in Spain in the three years since his retirement from shop-floor sweeping duties in one of the city's knit-wear factories, he has a startling store of colloquial words and phrases, often entertainingly and maybe deliberately mispronounced. The tutor just about has the measure of the group, keeping a bit of pace going, in spite of having to cope with late arrivals, early departures, and the non-stop questioner, who again hasn't done the minimum amount of homework, as requested.

Much animated talk, in English, during the break about the possible excursion to Valencia for the firework festival in March; is it worth the money, and who will "share" with whom to avoid the 'single room' supplement? One or two quite exciting suggestions put forward.

Tutor scores a winner this week by inviting in for the second half a 21 year old from Gerona working as an "au-pair" to an academic family in "millionaires row" and a member of the tutor's "English as a Foreign Language" class. After a little hesitation, the questions start coming in moderately fluent Spanish, and Rosa sees the funny side of men almost three times her age asking her what she does in her "free time", and does she like going out for a drink, just so we can practise what we have been learning. Turns out to be a good revision session for the whole term.

Fully intend to spend part of evening making immediate start on final Spanish homework assignment of term. Disturbed however by agitated call from 'Neighbourhood Watch' co-ordinator. Two cases in the past five days of cars being stolen off drives in the early morning, one in next avenue, scarcely 10 houses away. Meeting with the "Community Bobby" next week. Feel very angry, and can't settle back to Spanish. Resort to crashing through the last movement of the Tchaikovsky. That doesn't really work either. Get a couple of cans and some crisps and watch the snooker instead.

## THURSDAY

The Thursday morning variation on the early swimming is yet another "class", to all intents and purposes, and thankfully at the slightly later start time of 8.00am. Sometimes unimaginatively called "The Old Codgers" when our 'critics' think we're out of earshot, our group of 10 'oldies' is mainly made up of those who can't quite make the "Veterans Swimming Team". As members of the 'Veterans Swimming Club' and in some cases members of the overall Centre Swimming Club, "The Dolphins" (sic!), we're given the free extra practice class as some sort of sop, in my view. But then I've taken things hard and have somewhat of a jaundiced outlook. Last year I'd just made the team, doing the back-stroke leg in the relay, on one occasion, and in a winning 'meet' when "they" moved the goal-posts, or rather changed the rules, lowering the qualifying age, making a 'veteran' anyone over 50, not 55. At 57, I couldn't compete with so many extra fit 51 year olds who crawled out of the wood work. As it is, the 'Vets Club' proper, scheduled for tomorrow, Friday, used to meet that day at 11.00am when I rejoined in September; but after what was an hour's quite tough practice, everyone would resort to the pub, drink at least three pints, and undo all the good, quite apart from spending a small fortune. So it was changed a few weeks back early November, to 2.30 in the afternoon. Ever since then, it's been known for one or two to turn up, if not paralytic, just a little too full of booze to be safe in a swimming pool. But, we all enjoy ourselves so much, especially as there are no children's school swimming lessons on a Friday afternoon.

But it is still only Thursday afternoon – so, family and business letters, another go at that Spanish, and some music practice.

Early light tea, and into town for short, sharp 30/45 minutes, subsidised fee, private violin lesson from member of University music department staff (almost a personal favour), prior to snatched coffee and currant bun in Student Union cafeteria, then full Orchestra rehearsal. Nearly all late teens/early twenties "conventional" students, a couple of post-grads., not many 'mature students', just me, one of the double bass players, one trombonist – and the conductor, a member of staff. Some of these 'youngsters' really very good; Junior Prom standard, and that sort of thing; Northern Youth Orchestra; Hampshire Schools County Orchestra, etc.; a cello case with stickers from festivals all over continental Europe. Several so good they don't think they need to come to every rehearsal. Two of the string players confessed to me they'd sight-read the (for me) almost impossible passages of the Schumann; no sweat.

But in both cases they were former leaders of School orchestras with regional reputations – whereas I just managed to struggle through Grade V, and that was almost 40 years ago – but coming back to violin playing after such a long gap was a part of the retirement planning – and it's already a special part of my life once more, even with so many other basic diversions around.

## FRIDAY

Friday swimming as already mentioned, now an afternoon event. Gives me a morning chance to clean the car, and do an hour in the garden.

As I settle down for mid-morning coffee, Jack and David of the 'Kabaret' group come round, unannounced – always welcome of course – with steam coming out of their ears. The comedy script, closely based on a version of 'Allo', 'Allo', with extra interlinked sketches, and which we'd sweated over in October and November, and which was to be given a fund-raising charity performance end January, "has been rejected out of hand by the Rector". My view is that the Rector has the final word on the situation. Most of any 'proceeds' were for the Church roof restoration, with a nominal 10% to go to the 'Youth Club Project' – and that gang aren't in anyone's good books at the moment as some of them were almost certainly responsible for setting fire to the recycling containers in the recreation ground car-park the other night. The way things are going at the moment I don't know where I'd find 6 – 10 evenings for rehearsals, final rehearsals, dress rehearsal and the show itself. So if the Rector wants to drop the idea – and lose maybe £500 into the bargain – that's up to him. I can always go elsewhere and play my violin or have another swim. Anyway, we can salvage some of what we've written and offer to do a fund-raising event for The Children's Society.

A bit puzzled to hear the Rector quoted as considering the triple-author script to be unnecessarily crude, "for what would mostly be a 'Church' audience". I thought we'd come up with some good music-hall type material – a bit vulgar here and there maybe, but within local limits. Perhaps he'd been upset by Dawn French's closing sequence joke about Adam and Eve in the latest episode of 'The Vicar of Dibley'. Also a bit miffed to learn that he felt my sketch about Hyacinth and Onslow and Daisy et al, just wasn't funny. It had everyone else in stitches. Still, I've had worse disappointments. A true adult learner will always bounce back – but I'll give the veterans swimming a miss this afternoon, anyway I know I am not in tomorrow's team – again.

The subject of the 'Kabaret' evening is not referred to when the Rector and I pass each other in the churchyard in the evening as I join a few other musicians for a short practice with the choir before the Carol Concert in a few days time.

## SATURDAY

Allowed to go out early for the Sainsbury's shopping after all.

On to the City College for 'Open meeting' with the Governors for benefit of the 15,000+ students. Scarcely 20 turn up. I felt the publicity had been less than useful, and told the Principal so, in the hearing of his Chair – but we're old sparring partners and have known each other on the circuit for well over 10 years; and anyway, on reflection, he agrees and is glad to see several mince pies and cups of coffee disappear, despite the poor turn out.

No probing questions from the floor – at least not about the "Curriculum", more on the new-style cafeteria service, generally satisfactory, and College promoted excursion trips, and educational visits; couldn't they be subsidised more; answer, "Sorry, no!"

Overall, College doing very well. With many institutions taking the chance to "opt out" or become 'incorporated', this group of Governors, who have influence in many areas, are at present more than happy to stay with an extremely supportive Local Education Authority.

Numerous afternoon bits and pieces, mainly odd jobs, catching up here and there, chatting to folk in local shop en route to pay paper bill, etc.

The "once a month" extra country dance, tickets sold this time by a couple of the 'Monday nighters' who know that they only stand a chance of convincing me if the venue is within 10 miles. After many years as a rep on the road, before I ended up in an education office, the less driving I have to do, the better – especially on a Saturday night.

This dance is in a junior school hall, just 4 miles along the ring road; proceeds to a water project in India, event promoted by local environmental campaign group. Some members identifiable by their long floppy skirts, open toed sandals, and numerous children in various states of casual turn-out, but all exceptionally well behaved. A "caller" with a touch of individuality, everyone has a good time and enjoys the fun dancing, over £250 raised for the cause.

I don't mind money being collected from me in this painless way – and I wouldn't volunteer to work for nothing in any part of India.

## SUNDAY

Looking back over these notes on a very full week, I realise again how fortunate I feel I am and how I have a lot going for me as I pursue a new career as an adult learner. I have the base of a wide circle of friends and acquaintances, residence in a pleasant and generally well resourced area with a valued post-code, many like-minded neighbours – plus an extended range of interests, nothing too consuming, built up over many years; and just enough money in retirement to indulge gently in a few of my own personal choices, clearly avoiding anything grossly extravagant or wasteful, aware that I can have a morning in a sports centre for the price of a pint of extra strength cider, especially after the Budget increase.

Above all perhaps there is the educational background. Able to jump through examination hoops at an early age and supported by a family with no tradition of formal education, I progressed through the system via a scholarship award route to obtain the best that public money could buy. Surely there was certain to be a lifelong interest in education, in its widest sense. I'm not at all surprised by the research which shows that those who have done well at school, who have benefited most from the formal system in early years, are much more likely to participate actively in forms of continuing education and training later in life; while those who got fed up with dull and boring lessons need a lot of convincing to try again.

There's a target for the advocates and providers during European Year of Lifelong Learning and as Adult Learners Week, May 96, approaches; to stimulate wider participation, for the benefit of our economic society, if not for personal development and fulfilment.

Still, let's not get too philosophical; a busy Sunday ahead, and no chance these days of going back to work for a rest tomorrow.

## Mary Gilmartin; Bradford

*Family, Faith and Friends are the fun and fulfilment in my life. Seven grandchildren (ages 2 to 17) living close-by, challenge daily my memory and knowledge, but most of all my stamina – I delight in the closeness of our relationship, from playing hopscotch to talking computers.*

*As parish secretary I am very much involved with my church, St Cuthbert's; I also hold office at local and diocesan level in the Union of Catholic Mothers, a national organisation committed to upholding the values of family life.*

*In addition, lifelong friendships and new ones at Bradford University enable me to pursue favourite pastimes – rambling and theatre.*

## LEARNING TO LEARN

*"The aim of Education is the knowledge not of facts but of values".* Dean Inge (1860-1954)
I think Mary may not wholly agree!

### Prologue

In the squelching, bloody mud of the village of Passchendaele and the trenches of Ypres, Thomas had survival on this mind rather than 'the future'. (He had started in the mill as a part-timer at the tender age of ten years). When Thomas returned, more than thrice wounded, to the 'land fit for heroes', he was adamant that no child of his would become 'mill fodder' as he had been 'machine gun fodder' but would be given a real chance of 'EDUCATION'. In time his sons would make their mark in the world and his daughters would marry and give him grandchildren. "Man proposes, God disposes" (Traditional Proverb).

### And Now

Let me properly introduce you to 'Mary', born in May, 1929, the fourth child in the family of five children with which Thomas and Anne were blessed.

She had a very happy childhood. The family were poor, but she was unaware of their poverty; after all, didn't they have a tablecloth when others in the street used only the bare, well-scrubbed table top. She was one of the 'young ones' and slept with two brothers, all in striped pyjamas, all in one bed and covered with warm blankets. The two 'older ones' lived in a different world. Father worked hard but took them on 'outings' and Mother found time to laugh amongst the continuous round of washing, ironing, mending and darning. She was always there when they came in from school and the smell of newly baked bread was in the air.

Schooldays were very happy, and although Mary was bright no thought was given to 'staying on', nor was the decision queried by the girl. At fourteen years of age she had a brief educational encounter with shorthand and typing and then sallied forth into the future, armed with her Certificates.

## But Then

She met her future husband and life seemed idyllic. They begot four children. When they were of an age to start school, Mary took part time work so she could always 'be there' for the children who also came home to 'the smell of newly baked bread'.

Mary's fantasies of learning haute cuisine or becoming the equivalent of Florence Nightingale in the field of Nursing were pushed to the back of her mind in the hurly-burly of family life. Her husband's palate was well suited to her Ragoût de Mouton et Pâte Cuite and she knew "The Home Doctor" from cover to cover in nursing her brood through all their childhood illnesses.

## Life Changed

Mary's beloved husband, Maurice, died and she had to become the real 'breadwinner'. At this stage a better education would have ensured a more financially secure future for her family. No time now to think of that. Bills had to be paid and bellies had to be filled.

She resumed her previous work as a Medical Secretary and over the next twenty years both in General Practice and at the Hospital, Mary regained a purpose to her life in her contact in equal measure with joy and sorrow in her work environment. Meantime, daughters and sons got married and grandchildren added a new, loving dimension to the domestic scene.

In June 1994 Mary retired and despite her family involvement with the newest little ones, she decided that at long last the time had come for her to be able to fulfil her secret ambition of becoming a student.

Thwarted by bureaucracy, Mary was unable to take 'O' Level English Literature until she could prove her literacy with the English language. The first obstacle was surmounted and then came a wonderful oasis of learning Literature with a superb tutor who brought to life the pages of the Classics and the work of Modern Writers too. With growing confidence Mary opted to take a Combined English Literature/Language Course at 'A' Level and, surprisingly, came upon prejudice – against age! Neither one of the Tutors could understand why Mary wanted to be on the Course; they were busy with the 'real students'. The mature student plodded on and gained moderate success, but her confidence had been dented.

Armed with the supposed knowledge that everyone, irrespective of age, is entitled to one Grant in their lifetime, Mary queued in similar circumstances as those afforded by the delicatessen counter of the local supermarket, only to be given a veto by Bradford Council. Back home, 'midst tears of utter frustration, a recently read quotation of Eleanor Roosevelt's came back into the would-be student's mind. "Remember always that you have not only the right to be an individual, you have an obligation to be one".

Her Taurean stubbornness came to the fore and in a trice Mary was on the telephone to Bradford University and in animated conversation with a friendly and knowledgeable member of staff. Had she heard of the Associate Student Scheme? Yes, she would probably be awarded a Bursary. (Much nicer word than charity, don't you think). Brochures would be posted to her, and so on. At last things were falling into place.

## But

On the first Tuesday, with her self-confidence down in her boots, it was with trepidation that Mary mounted the steps of the Centre for Continuing Education and had not the class been sited in a room immediately beyond the front door, "Learning to Learn" may have been minus one student from the outset.

As it was, the Tutor beamed "Hallo" at Mary and invited her into the room. Other would-be students looked back at Mary and behind their smiles she detected the same apprehension she was feeling. It was going to be alright.

## THE COURSE
## EDUCATIONAL: ENLIGHTENING: ENJOYABLE: ENTERTAINING:

It was much more than 'alright' for Mary. The Course was wonderful; mind-boggling in its approach to learning as she tried to let go of the old regimen under whose authoritative sternness she had been taught so many years ago. A new world had opened up and Mary was being led, step-by-step, week-by-week through the intricacies of this maze of new knowledge by a caring and understanding Tutor, who laughed with her students, yet retained their respect.

### Notes from Mary's Journal – (her immediate reaction after each session)

Liked informality and handouts (Two sides of the Brain, Assessment Criteria, the Learning Portfolio, Approaches to Studying) which helped to build up confidence in one's own ability to assimilate knowledge. Music was a nice but intriguing touch – wonderful that explanation was kept to the end of the session. Groupings helped us to get to know each other from the outset. I think I'm going to really enjoy this Course – I will learn – but it will be hard, though stimulating.

Forms – Forms – Questionnaires – made me think. Took away a little of my confidence and complacency, but really good discussion and friendly banter – we're getting to know each other (and Christine). Music continues, I'm beginning to appreciate the soothing nature of the Tutor's choice. Have I bitten off more than I can chew?

Fun today – I know Japanese – well, how to say 7 and 8 (shi-chi and hat-chi)! We're getting to know each other more and more and have become less worried about expressing ourselves. I'm learning <u>about myself</u>. I've never had time for an in-depth approach before. I'm enjoying the class, but still worrying about how to sort the wheat from the chaff with note-taking. I feel confident, however that with Christine's patience I will gain something from the Course.

I've learnt a lot about myself today; things I'll have to change to make me a better person. I've never had this opportunity before – perhaps I may have been a 'new person' much earlier in life. Again, the Tutor is so knowledgeable and makes learning a pleasure. I'm still worrying about note-taking. My problem is retaining knowledge, despite my enjoyment of the Course. Everyone seems to know a lot more than I do.

Very challenging today, but fun nevertheless. I enjoy puzzles and tests. There's quite a lot of back-chat between us – barriers are coming down. Visited the University Library for the first time – the size is overwhelming! The Librarian was 'laid back' physically as he talked in a rather monotonous tone about the intricacies of locating a book – heaven help those who have no computer skills. We've got a Questionnaire to complete and hand in to him before next Tuesday – I do hope I can find the answers, the task is a bit daunting. I'm really tired.

The Information Retrieval and Research Session was completed and handed in to the Librarian, but a Second Session would take longer because of family illness and home commitments. Later Energy Cycles were discussed in class. (Had the Tutor seen Mary's notes, she wondered). There were handouts and checklists on TIME, GOALS, PERSONAL LEARNING PROFILES, TIME BALANCE SHEETS, together with humorous drawings and captions which helped to drive home what was under discussion.

Helpful notes were given on Reading Techniques and Effective Reading. Tests were undertaken in Reading Skills and explanations given of The Reading Process, Difficult Reading and – wait for it – NOTETAKING EXERCISES – Mary's 'Achilles Heel'. She faced it head-on in attempting to summarise a piece of writing previously prepared by the Tutor. Learning in this area is slow for Mary, but she feels she is getting better.

What Tutors look for in Essays and A Guide to Understanding Essays, together with a list of Common Abbreviations were all very helpful. But the most helpful, instructive and enjoyable session was learning Brainstorming. Various subjects were used; Food, Holidays, Music. Mary was fascinated to see how far her train of thought twisted and turned as her brain cells stretched themselves and reached out on these trips.

In a separate session the Students were shown how to cope correctly with References and Bibliographies. Getting this part of it right is most important when it comes to the marking of essays and such.

On another occasion there was an isolated teaching period led by another Tutor, but in the presence of our own Tutor, in a different room on the University Campus. It was a question of lists and how to remember them. The students were split into two groups and given differing written instructions. It was an effective and unusual way of bringing home a point and giving the brain an extra little aide-memoire.

When it came to the final session of the Course, a full day on the University Campus, being advised on how to cope with Speaking in Public. Mary and all her classmates were rather shy about the individual video tapings. To get them into the right mood, the Tutor 'played' a few 'games' with them. In essence they were very instructive but the laughter that accompanied them belied their seriousness and did exactly what had been intended by the Tutor – everyone relaxed before the T.V. appearances! Criticism had to be constructive and there had to be no discussion about the content of each little 3-minute talk. Again laughter and good humour softened the criticism and by the afternoon session all those taking part were convinced they had found a new career in television.

At the very beginning of the Learning to Learn Course, the Tutor had told all the Students she needed to know where they were at. That is why I have given a short synopsis of Mary's life to help the reader appreciate what it meant for her to be accepted, first of all by the University, but particularly to have the opportunity of taking part in this Course. There is no doubt that her capacity for enjoyment in learning has increased a hundredfold, thereby underlining her determination to succeed in her quest for knowledge. To paraphrase Jonathan Swift, "May she live all the days of her life".

A Teacher Is …

*Someone who is wise …*
*Who cares about the students*
*And wears no disguise;*
*But is honest and open,*
*And shares from the heart,*
*Not just lessons from books,*
*But life where you are;*
*A teacher takes time*
*To help and tutor,*
*With english or math,*
*Or on a computer.*
*It's someone who's patient,*
*Even in stress;*
*Who never gives less*
*Than the very best!*

Rebecca Barlow Jordan © Kristone

## The Epilogue

Despite the ups-and-downs of a tight budget, all four of Mary's children stayed on at School until they were 16; two of them continuing to Further Education. She is very proud of their achievements. Perhaps, in retrospect, she **would** agree with Dean Inge.

How do I know this? Because **I am** Mary!

## Joy Ball; Nottingham

*Joy Ball lives in Nottinghamshire and is in her early fifties. She has been keeping a diary for eleven years, chronicling her busy life which includes a full-time job, savouring the pleasure of recent grandmotherhood and undertaking an Open University arts course, currently in her third year. Having completed a bilingual secretarial course after leaving school at eighteen, to launch into continuing education was equivalent to re-opening a door to infinite and more appreciated delights. On obtaining a degree, she intends to catch up on her previous hobbies which include philately and collecting old, illustrated poetry and children's books.*

These are extracts from my dairy so, inevitably, have several irrelevancies to the subject of adult learning. In copying it, I was interested to see the development from trivial entries to increasing references to the subjects being studied and my intense and enthusiastic feelings for them.

Extract from my 1994 diary covering one week, 23rd July to 29th – (Open University summer school, Arts foundation course, A102).

## 23 Saturday

I was awake at 5, not surprisingly. I tidied my desk. Looks like another fine day. I'm nervous. I had a quiet half hour hanging washing out and playing Patience over a cup of tea. We left very early. Geoff fussed round me like an old hen. He'd put a card in my case last night and this morning he gave me some new business cards he'd had printed. At Grantham, we had coffee and biscuits and, at 1919, my train drew in and I said cheerio. I somehow felt less nervous once the train drew out. I changed at Doncaster, the next train getting in 7 minutes after I arrived and on the same platform. Unusually for me, I was curt with a couple whom I thought were sitting in my reserved seat. I managed to finish my unit book. We arrived in Edinburgh at 1 and I found the platform for the Stirling train which left at 1.18. I took a taxi to the University which is set in beautiful grounds although the building itself is quite modern. I met several people who'd been on the train. I got the key to my room, which was utility as are most halls' rooms, dumped my bags and went down to register. I met up with a couple of women and we went for a walk in the grounds and up to an old castle-like building which we looked in and admired some Flemish panelling. We chatted furiously all the time until we had to go to the Logie Room (an auditorium) for an information meeting. I am in group B1 (about 14 people). Our tutorial after dinner would be music so the music tutor showed us where we'd meet and took the register. We had dinner, went upstairs for coffee then back to our music tutorial. Bill is Scottish and I found I had to listen hard to what he said. He had a dry humour and made the two hours go with a swing. We covered Handel, Penny Lane,

Ghost Town and a couple of Victorian songs. (He ended up miming to Gigli on the desk top! We all clapped). I managed a quick call home. We had an 'ice-breaker' in the bar. I chatted to loads of people but ended up going to another bar and disco with 37-year old Christine and a young divorced lad, Ross, until midnight. I came back, unpacked, prepared my papers for the next day and fell into bed.

## 24 Sunday

I kept waking and dozing, felt tired and thick-headed and decided I would not stay up late tonight. I got up about 6.30, showered, went over to breakfast, always talking to someone or other, put my name down for a library tour tomorrow. This was the start of what was to be a long day that seemed to span 2-3 days. Our first lecture was literature (poetry, in particular) with David. I volunteered to read some poetry on Wednesday evening (mad!). We did what I loved doing, analysing poetry, peeling off the layers. He was very good. Our next one was philosophy with Francis who really brought the course theories down to two sentences. I want to do the exam tomorrow before it all goes (essentialist and consequentialist). We stopped for lunch then on to art history with Ralph (not before I'd persuaded Christine to do the poem 'The Ruined Maid' by Thomas Hardy with me, using the combination of Yorkshire and Kent accents). Ralph was good and we had the third active lesson of the day. On to history and Clare. By this time, we were even more jaded and, although she was very good and made it interesting, she was not as jokey and lively as, say, Ralph or Bill, so we were pleased when she got on to asking questions and involving us actively so we could stir ourselves. We went straight to dinner although I wasn't terribly hungry. Christine gave me a couple of Disprins for a thick head. We dropped our bags off in our rooms and walked over to the theatre where we watched a video of 'Patience' by Gilbert and Sullivan. Bill gave a wonderful introductory performance. I hoped I wouldn't fall asleep as I was tired but I didn't, even though I wasn't impressed by G & S. We had to leave before the end as we'd bought tickets to enter a Trivia Quiz at 9.30. Four of us walked in completely the wrong direction and ended up late but we got in, partook and had a great laugh. There were prizes for the funniest answers if we didn't know the true ones and we did quite well in that (no prize though). We got back about midnight again.

## 25 Monday

I can't believe I've only been here less than 1.5 days. I was up at 6.10, showering. Actually, I feel better today than yesterday. It was too early for breakfast but I wandered over anyway. We started the first interdisciplinary tutorial which went on nearly all day. This was taken by Bill (the mad musician) and concerned moral values and social order in Victorian Britain. We divided into groups after he'd talked to us a while about what we think moral values are and had to read a passage from Golby. It was an extract from Samuel Smiles' book 'Self-Help' and our group had to deal with all aspects of liberalism (laissez-faire, individual and natural). The other two groups had to talk about work and the home. We went for coffee after we'd seen a film on Prince Albert. I had to dash at 12-30 to go on a library tour and, although it was interesting to see the library and how it worked, I couldn't imagine I'd be using its facilities. I met up with a woman I'd met on the first day and we had lunch together. We continued our moral session, saying what we'd concluded and finished mid-afternoon. We all then had options, three at 4.30 and three at 7.30 and it was a problem choosing which one we'd like to see. In the end, I chose our art history tutor's talk about genre painting and iconography. It was very good but I kept having to fight back waves of sleep. Christine and I went off and practised our poem then had dinner. We made our way over to the Logie theatre and listened to the course director, beautiful, elegant, clever Janet talk about J S Mill and his logical argument against subordination and exclusion of women. She put his arguments over clearly and none of us could believe they weren't accepted at the time. She concluded (her opinion, mind you) it was due to the fact it was the only way men could be sure their offspring were theirs. We wanted to carry on but we'd decided to see the first episode showing of BBC 2's 'Hard Times'. At 10, we went on to a downstairs' bar where we joined in a ceilidh. Christine and I danced then we all joined in the 'Dashing White Sergeant', Gay Gordons' etc. I was 'approached' with the line "What shampoo do you use?"! We went back noisily and had a coffee in the halls, making fools of ourselves with two of the tutors.

## 26 Tuesday

Bit later waking – 6.20. Shower was cold! It did wake me up though. Overcast and damp today, in fact, raining when I went over to breakfast. No-one was around so I decided to give Geoff a ring. I'd posted him a card. I dashed back in the rain to the halls, snatching an umbrella off mad Bill the musician. Our lecture today was on culture with Ralph. It was an excellent day. We dealt with emerging and residing ideologies, read passages on Dickens, Pre-Raphaelites, etc., and I seemed to be on top form today, my wit denoting a high spot (for me) of the lesson. Ralph admitted over coffee that we were a good group, lively and full of ideas. Ross, one of the lads, came in late and I think we all guessed why. Things got a bit noisy when Ralph left us to read so Ross and I went back after lunch when it was quiet and finished the texts. The afternoon session went well and, after tea, we all split up to do an option. Another girl, Ann, and I chose, erroneously, to go to the philosophy in art lecture and neither of us came away any the wiser. The chap was slow, unclear what he wanted of us, I felt, and consequently, our momentum fell to zero. Still, I suppose we must expect one bad one. It was back to the dining room (haggis for lunch) and another analysis of what we'd all done. Christine had, at some stage during the day, gone swimming. The next option wasn't one at all, it was our mad Bill and another Bill performing a 'Victorian' routine on the piano. They were an excellent double act, our Bill – the extrovert pianist (tautology, I know) enjoying himself totally. They played Chopin, Joplin, 'On the Road to Mandalay', 'The Maiden's Prayer', Handel and all the greats, interspersed with comical readings from our Summer School booklet. Then it was on to watch the second half of 'Hard Times' and, afterwards, a sit down with Christine and a Becks. Denise wanted us to go to the disco but we weren't inclined so went back to the halls. We sat and chatted with some of our group over coffee downstairs. I went up about 11.45.

## 27 Wednesday

Going to bed earlier didn't help! I just woke up earlier so I got up and showered (hot today). Still overcast. Sat next to Francis, the philosopher, and then Denise joined us.

Our subject today was religion and we had Clare who was interesting, if tortuous in her arguments and answers. It was fortunate she picked the 1851 religious census to discuss as that's what I specialised in when doing my TMA. Again, I seemed to talk a lot. I certainly have gained in confidence as I can now string quite convoluted sentences together without forgetting what I had just said and what I'm about to say. At coffee break, I organised some rubber gloves for our poetry reading tonight and posted off a card to Mum. The second session saw one of the lads missing and I was told he'd been taken ill with nerves after having read a passage out loud. Poor lad, what would he have been like reciting poetry? We broke for lunch and Clare, one of our girls, Hazel and I wandered up chatting about fossils and the human factor. The afternoon saw us piling into two coaches to go to the Kelvingrove art gallery in Glasgow. It felt like being let out of bounds. We saw Stirling castle standing out high against the sky. Christine and I may go up and visit it on Friday afternoon, although I doubt we'll have time, what with farewells and all. The gallery was an attractive red stone building dating back to our period. It housed paintings, sculpture, natural history museum and a military museum as well as oriental and Inuit clothes and tools and weapons. We had a look at several, specific paintings to compare and draw out all we could. It was tiring and I fell asleep on the way home. I had a quick look round the bookshop and then went to get changed and prepare the 'props' for our recital tonight (a bunch of feathers tied together with my housecoat belt and some rubber gloves and an introduction – that famous 'Yorkshire' poet, Tom Hardy etc.). After dinner, we all congregated and it began. We were the second to appear and so it was over quickly and painlessly, although I shook for a while afterwards. Everyone said we were brilliant. The rest was excellent, funny, sad, serious, foreign, sung. The bar afterwards for some girlie amusement.

## 28 Thursday

The shower was cold again so I 'washed down' at my sink. Bit thick-headed. Wandered over to breakfast and actually had porridge and kipper. Our lecture today was on representation of the people and was given by Francis. I, personally, had a brilliant time. Somehow, and without design or conscious decision, I had assumed the leading role of our group of five. Our subject for research was the reason why women didn't get the vote in the 19th Century. We read the given references all morning and had to draw up some preliminary idea before lunch. There was a sale of second-hand books so I naturally had to have a look. I bought three, surprise, surprise – one, an anthology of French verse with Paul Verlaine's 'Chanson d'Automne', an Arnold Bennett novel and a book of cartoons by someone called Siné (Maurice Sinet) Massacre. We continued our preparatory reading then drew our conclusions literally on an A2 sheet. Our drawing was brilliant, although I did it myself and say so. Our tutor was impressed. I did two large circles representing women and men divided by a Gothic wall (separative effect) with lots of names denoting those for and against the subject. The foundations of the wall were decidedly unstable with the undulations caused by such people as J S Mill and F Nightingale. I loved the exercise. We went through each one then finished that lecture for the day. I went to Francis's option lecture in the afternoon when he proved there was a difference between causation and determinism, therefore we have free will. I took down all the notes which, perhaps, was a distraction to his talk but I think I got his drift.

We had dinner then I went back to halls to freshen up before the 'Arts event' in Logie Theatre. It was so good. The talent amongst the students was outstanding. We had an actor, five good female singers, some poets, Janet outdid herself by adding singing to her immense store of talents. It was extremely funny and we laughed and clapped our way through it. We then had a drink in the main bar when Christine insisted on inviting the 'shampoo' man over. He told me what he did and I told him what Geoff did. He said he may know of some outlets for him so I gave him Geoff's card in spite of the fact it has our home number on it. I danced with mad Bill and discoed till 2.

## 29 Friday

Feel OK. We didn't need to be at the lecture until 9.15 instead of 8.45. Nice morning. I was surprised to see Denise eating a kipper for breakfast after her alcohol consumption of last night. We had David and his topic was town and country. Although we got through the various aspects of this quite well, I felt neither he or we went into depth at all, which was a shame as it left the subject in my view somewhat underdone and I felt fine and could have coped with it. We had to look at various passages and view them from various angles, i.e. their reliability as sources, whether a novel, poem or commentary, information on town and on country as seen by the Victorian, production and consumption angle and its value (status). As usual, the same ones chattered, said irrelevant things and generally disturbed the others. One made some minutely relevant statement but it had to be funny, a thing I was interested to reflect was something I used to do but had become a lot more serious this week. I do hope all I have become remains with me for ever as I like me like this. I expect it's going to be short-lived. David obviously wanted to wind down and we finished early. A few of us had a cup of tea after the inevitable photographs from Rosemary and Christine. We wandered, a little bemused, a touch shell-shocked after the great week, back to halls to deregister. I was sorry I'd missed Ross and Ann who'd left straight away. Just so I can refer back to everyone's names, I'll mention those not already mentioned on this page; David, Hazel, Daphne, Gillian, Anne, Stephen, Jane, Jean. Everything started to fall a bit flat when they'd all gone and I packed then went round to Christine's for a chat. We had dinner and were presented with a bottle of wine (McLaren) from a kind gentleman and then we got talking to two ladies, Rosemary and Betty. Rosemary is diabetic and we talked a lot about it then we walked to the management centre where she's staying and had some drinks and a really good, deep chat about things. They came back with us and we finished the evening with Stephen. The chap who'd presented the wine joined us in the foyer at halls and we chatted into the small, wee hours. We parted at the bottom of the stairs with a platonic kiss. Nice, appropriate way to finish summer school.

## NOTE

I decided to take an Open University arts course because of the immense interest I already had in art history, literature and music, and its requirement for commitment and application, things which were appropriate to the stage I had reached in my life. It has re-opened the door for me to a world of interest and fascination which has captured my imagination and broadened by views and reasoning power.

The Enlightenment was the subject of my second year of study which intensified my enthusiasm and highlighted my main areas of interest, which are religious philosophy and music; the latter discipline I shall be taking up next year. One of the highlights of this year's course was a 5 day study tour in Geneva in July, and, if it is of any interest for this exercise, I give below my diary entry for those days.

Extract from diary, Thursday 20th – 24th, study tour to Geneva to complement Open University second level course, 'The Enlightenment'.

## 20 Thursday

I woke up at 4.15 and again at 5.25. Felt a bit grotty after the wine last night. John dropped me off a bit sharpish at Terminal 2 as he had to be on the first tee at 7 and it was already 6.30. I booked in, went to the duty free then on to the departure lounge where I read the Independent, not for long as I was soon on board and we took off at 8.10. It was a 110 minute journey. I got chatting to two women next to me who were also on the same tour. It was already hot and humid when we arrived in Geneva. We came in over the lake, 60 miles long, the largest in Europe outside Russia, and saw the 'jet d'eau'. Brian Norman met us and took us to the Hotel du Lac. I met Rita with whom I'd be sharing a room. She's English but married and divorced an Italian and now lives in Rome. The hotel is on the 6th and 7th floors of a rather unsightly 60s building on the rue de Eaux-Vives, an area of Geneva on the left bank of the Rhone, pretty basic but clean and fairly comfortable. Rita and I walked to the jet d'eau which was amazing, reaching what must be 400 feet. We met the others at 2 and Brian took us along the lake side, stopping every so often to tell us a bit more about the history of Geneva, a walled city, old Roman town, through which Caesar passed on his way from Italy to France. We walked in the heat to Voltaire's temporary house, Les Délices, and looked at his letters and books, then stopped at the hotel next door which used to be his stables, for a cold drink and a lecture about the connections between Voltaire, Rousseau and Gibbon. It was very hot and we were all tired. We went back, stopping at the island to see Rousseau's statue then back for a welcome shower and a rest. We all went to dinner. I chatted to Rosemary (has her own stage make-up teaching school and knows Alan Rickman), Sue who works at NATO in Brussels and Rita. We were taken up into the old part of Geneva where one street is all 18th century houses and the next all 17th century. It was lovely. The churches were all Protestant as the reformation occurred overnight in Geneva and the Catholics disappeared for a long time. We saw a Lutheran church, the Protestant cathedral, Calvin's lecture house and Rousseau's birthplace, the Hôtel de Ville and heard about the attempt by Catholics to storm the walls in 1602. We passed a square next to the Palais de Justice and police station where all the university students meet for beers and entertainment. We learned about the additions to the cathedrals and the grandees in their townhouses. Brian, although quiet, was obviously enthusiastic about this part of the town which was certainly memorable. We walked back, hot and sticky. Claire had put a card in my case.

## 21 Friday

Woke about 6 o'clock (Genevan time). Breakfasted on the veranda with Rita. We met everyone at 9 outside the hotel and set off for the lake where we caught a little boat to cross the lake. From there, we made our way up to the station and caught a lovely, air-conditioned train to Lausanne. We passed Coppet, where we'll be going later in the tour, sunflower and sweet corn fields, the lake on our left and mountains, châteaux and vineyards on our right. 34 minutes later, we arrived and discovered what a steep town Lausanne was. We climbed steeply, on and off, stopping for little lectures in the shade of a tree and noting, at one point, that we were standing on the terrace of a property and site in which Gibbon lived out the last ten years of his life and finished the last chapters of 'The Decline…'. The house was called 'La Grotte' and was pulled down in the last century. We continued our climb across what Brian called the ravine until we came at last, hot, sticky and tired, to the pinnacle and centre of the defended, walled Cité and the cathedral (Protestant). It was a good viewing point. We went down 174 steps for lunch. I sat with Brian and had a sandwich and apricot tart and iced tea, then back up to the cathedral which was cool and impressive with big, grey vaults and beautiful stained glass windows. The organist was filling the place with sound. It was wonderful. We set off again, down to the metro and went on it to the lake side where we walked round to the Hôtel d'Angleterre (where Byron stayed) for iced tea and tartelettes au citron. As always, our conversation was lively. Back to the lake side to catch the boat back. We sat inside and out, trying to get some cooling breeze. We had quite a nice dinner on board, and I chatted with Rita, Kath, Eileen, Jan and another woman who had been quiet up to now but had some quite definite views. The boat called in on the French side at Evian and several other towns along the shores and we stopped at Geneva again and walked, hot and tired round the end of the lake to our hotel. We had a shower and Rita and I chatted until we were called for to go out for a drink. 7 of us sat outside by the English Gardens and listened to a Portuguese/West African band play non-stop for about three-quarters of an hour. They were very good. We reminisced over the old days and had a good laugh. Jan is a DCI in the police force and has taken my address as she wants to know how I find the music course next year.

## 22 Saturday

It was a little fresher this morning but not much. I showered and we had breakfast, as yesterday. We all met up again at 9, although we still had to wait for people. I have a growing likeness for Jan, the DCI from Birmingham. We walked up to a shady, flat, quiet area in between Calvin's school and the Museum of Geneva where we all sat around a fountain and trough of that lively, ice cold water (things we found everywhere we went) in the dappled sunlight and listened to Brian tell us about the life of Rousseau. I must say, not only was it interesting but I was very aware of the idyllic circumstance in which I found myself. I took some notes which I hope will be relevant to my course, although I doubted they'd be of much use. We wandered to the museum/art gallery and Brian took us directly to the 18th century part and showed us paintings by de Latour and Liotard, particularly the one of Rousseau himself. We were left to wander by ourselves and I was particularly struck by some Monet paintings which I'd not seen before and by someone I'd vaguely heard of called Hodder or Hoddle. At 11.30, we descended and went across to the Hôtel de Ville again and into Maison Tavel, up several flights until we came to an ancient and huge model of old Geneva as it was in Rousseau's time. We then broke for lunch, although I did pop into the Hôtel de Ville to see the mounting, inside carriageway which took horses and carriages to the top, about 4-5 stories. I joined Sue (from Belgium, NATO) for lunch which was salad and two large glasses of cold lemon tea. We joined the others, went down and caught the bus out to France and Ferney-Voltaire. It's a lovely, old, small château with a wonderful view across the countryside with a mountain backdrop. It's a bit in need of repair, is inhabited by a family since mid-19th century and only two rooms were on show with the remains of Voltaire's collection, paintings, etc. We sat outside and Brian told us about the fight for causes Voltaire had and of his generosity, schools, churches, dowries, etc. It was beginning to cloud over and, by the time we got to the village for refreshment, the heavens opened but it didn't last long. I got some chocolates to take back to work. We caught the bus back on which I talked avidly with Jan. We went straight to the cathedral and listened to an organ recital. I felt I needed to understand Bach's fugues more as, after the first initial thrill of the great organ sending its noise out to wrap around the stones and pillars, it got too much and I began to feel sleepy. Gradually, the crowd disappeared through C P E Bach, a 'romantic' German composer whose name I missed and the last but best rendition of a piece by Liszt. I walked back with Sue, got showered, tried to ring home but got no reply, went on a trolley to Carrouge, a restored 18th century suburb where we had a delightful time in a restaurant, 'La Bourse'. Brian shared our table and he was an interesting dinner companion. I'm afraid I talked too much as usual but I did enjoy our conversation which stayed mainly with food and drink but did wander into the realms of government and its leaders (members of the Oxford Union which Brian belonged to whilst there). It was a bit expensive but we didn't mind that. When we got back, 8 of us went for a coffee.

## 23 Sunday

We had some disturbance about 2. Someone was loud but, I think, using the telephone. Woke again at 6.45 and, after breakfast, we all bought a picnic lunch from a patisserie and set off once more to the English gardens and a little, secluded pergola under the trees for a further lecture on Voltaire. It was greatly cooler and there was a very strong wind. We all queued to embark a paddle steamer which was to take us to Coppet, an old restored village along the northern edge of the lake where the château belonging to Mr and Mrs Necker was situated. They gave birth to Mme de Stäel, a renowned woman of conversation and writing who was a friend of Voltaire. We found the wind was strong but not cold as we got off the boat and assembled under a huge plane tree in a field to listen to further lectures on and readings from Voltaire. He certainly was a remarkable man. I've decided I need to get his Philosophical Dictionary and I must try to find more time to dedicate to reading. We wandered round the village and ended up sitting near the lake to eat our picnic. We bought an ice cream and walked back up the hill to the château which was again, picturesque. We entered by the carriageway arch into an enclosed courtyard with two round towers at two corners. The procession of students followed the recorded English tape around each room which held relics of great salon days and portraits of the family. Afterwards, Jan the DCI, Jan the redhead and I put on our swimming costumes and made our way to a secluded edge of the great lake and bathed and sunbathed. It was strange to be swimming in what appeared to the eye to be sea and yet was unsalted. We weren't as buoyant. However, the water was warm and we were glad we'd done it. We assembled at the ferry port and caught the boat back to Geneva. Brian explained to me where the post office was as I wanted to buy some stamps. We showered and changed and followed Brian to the old part of town to a lovely 17th century restaurant where I had gazpacho and moules. It was a lovely meal and, as ever, the conversation was sparkling. We went straight back afterwards and fell into bed. We are all in agreement this has been a wonderfully organised tour and we've all enjoyed it immensely.

## 24 Monday

Awoke at 6.45 and Rita and I went to buy Brian a card on which I got everyone to write a message of thanks. At 9, we set off on our studies for the last time, making for the university. We saw the modern (early 20th century) wall of sculptures. In the centre stood 4 huge statues of Calvin, Bege, Knox and another whose name I cannot remember. It was a (late) tribute and acknowledgement of the Protestant church in Geneva. Turning to the university, we sat on the steps to one of the entrances and listened to Brian read a section on the life of Gibbon, showing his background research before his grand tour and subsequent writing of the 'Decline and Fall of the Roman Empire'. After the appropriate group photograph, we went into the university for refreshments and it was here, in the students' cafeteria that I made a very short speech of thanks and presented Brian with his card. He appeared very pleased. We went on to the Salle de Rousseau and museum which were very interesting places. I took down some of his own manuscript, the beginning of Chapter 3 of his Social Contract. This intimacy with the past certainly brings long-dead people very much alive again. We then broke from our studies for the last time and were allowed to go our own ways until 4. Rita and I set off towards the bus station and Hôtel de Poste (which is possibly one of the grandest buildings in Geneva), passing the opera house which was very much on the lines of the Paris Opéra. (Indeed, when I commented on this earlier in the week, Brian confirmed they had had the same architect.) I bought some Swiss stamps, not as many as I would have liked but got three 1961 ones. Rita and I then wandered around the cuckoo clock shops; actual cuckoo clocks are very expensive so I got just one little clockwork one with a boy and girl kissing. We wandered to the English Gardens for lunch and then walked round the old Cité again, ending up footsore and weary, having our last French ice cream. We all met at 4 (although Rita and Sue had gone) and took the bus to the airport. Jamie met me at Heathrow and I said my farewells, especially to Jan. Back at John and Betty's house, she and I stayed up until 2.30 debating theology, religion and philosophy. I must admit, I enjoyed voicing Voltaire's and Rousseau's views as if they were my own and receiving the credit.

*Beginners' Drawing Course;
Newcastle-under-Lyme*

## Phil Morris

Before the evening class I had not attempted any drawing. After a few weeks the encouragement of the tutor and the friendly atmosphere had everyone producing presentable first attempts. Over the following term as techniques improved and new methods discussed all agreed that we must carry on and try other ideas.

Anyone can sketch with the right instruction, so why not have a go, it's great fun.

## Peggy Wardell

I've always liked drawing – in fact, I have an A-level in Art, so it may sound rather odd when I say I've never learned to draw, but, whenever I looked at drawings by great artists, I felt I didn't know how, or where, to begin.

I was attracted by the prospect of learning from scratch. When I heard we were going to learn "how to sharpen a pencil", I felt convinced this was the class for me. I'm very satisfied with this course.

Leave behind your ideas about the mysteries of art, and come prepared to learn. The rest is easy, because you'll enjoy the direct, positive approach.

I'm really looking forward to using by new drawing techniques, now I have the confidence to do all those drawings I wanted to do before, but didn't know how to begin. I'm also looking forward to learning how to use paints. The class is a highlight of the week. The company is great, the teaching is truly inspirational.

Pick up a pencil and come to the beginners' class – you won't be a beginner for long!

## Keith Riley, 46 yrs of age

Before attending the class I had not drawn anything seriously, since leaving school.

I was attracted to the class by the words "Beginners' Drawing". I felt that I would not be out of my depth with other beginners and would not feel too embarrassed at my failures.

I have kept going to the classes because of the new techniques I am learning and the friendly, club-like atmosphere. The course has more than lived up to my expectations and I recommend it to anyone taking that first step in art. I hope to carry on next year with a beginners' painting course.

I have developed an appreciation of basic drawing techniques, composition, tonal value, perspective which I only took for granted previously. The course has been fun, interesting and has introduced me to a hobby and group of friends that I hope will last for a long time to come.

## Angela Wright

I would heartily recommend the Beginners' Drawing I for the following reasons.

The class has not assumed a particular level of drawing ability, but has worked at each individual's level and pace. The carefully graded sessions have covered the basic skill necessary before beginning to draw; and then has applied these techniques to a variety of subjects and projects. As well as the course being instructive and rewarding, a friendly atmosphere has developed over the 2 terms, making the class an enjoyable evening out. I hope to continue the Class, by joining Beginners' Drawing II, a new course which is a development of Beginners' Drawing I.

## Jane

I hadn't really attempted any drawing at all since pre-'O' level art classes at school. I have long wanted to be able to draw but the prospect of launching into a complete scene or composition was too daunting. I decided to look for a suitable evening class. I chose the Beginners' Drawing Course at Newcastle College because it was local and more importantly the only art class entitled 'Beginners'. The classes are informal and relaxed, and they have progressed through the basic concepts at a slow-enough-for-me-to-understand rate! I find also that I can now analyse the elements and style of paintings and drawings in a way that I just wasn't able to before and this has added considerably to my understanding and enjoyment of art.

I hope to enrol for the follow-on drawing course, having enjoyed and gained from the classes that I managed to attend.

## Barrie Wardell – TO ANY WOULD-BE ARTIST

I started with the Drawing Class last year. I have always wanted to be able to draw and have even been to evening classes in the past – but all to no avail. I just did not make any progress. When I saw the Beginners' Class advertised I was interested, and when I saw it would – START FROM THE BEGINNING – why! I joined.

Over the succeeding months I have attended the class sharing in the progress of others as our drawing skill improved. At the same time enjoying the company of a group who had an interest in the world around them.

Months on from the first drawing session I can now look back with satisfaction. While I do not possess the ability to become a great artist or draftsman my pencil does now do more of what I ask. The shapes which I produce now approximate to that which I see.

My sadness is that I was not able to join a class such as this years ago.

IF you would like to draw.
IF the idea of shape stirs your imagination.
IF you want to understand perspective.
IF you do not know how to begin.
Then join the Beginners' Drawing Class, it's easier than you think.

While I would recommend the course, be warned you will only get out what you put in. At times you will find it frustrating, some drawings just do not look right. So – you start again, with professional guidance. The important thing is that YOU WILL GET BETTER WITH EACH DRAWING.

I will be going to painting class next year. Armed with an understanding of form and perspective and above all greater confidence. I am looking forward to a new challenge.

For me, like the other members of the group, the drawing classes have become a night in the week to look forward to. It has been both stimulating and rewarding. I have met some nice people – and the teacher is not too bad really, though he does make you work.

## Dave Barker

I am forty seven years old. I have always been interested in drawing and decided to join the class to improve my skills, with the hope of picking up some useful tips from the professionals.

The class quickly became a social group and any apprehensions I or other members had soon disappeared. This was entirely due to the relaxed manner and exuberant personality of the tutor.

The variety of exercises we have covered kept my interest going, turning up week after week during the winter months. I feel that I have learned both to tackle drawing and also gained a general appreciation of art from portraits and design to landscapes and perspective.

The course has lived up to and exceeded my expectations. The atmosphere has been friendly throughout and I recommend that anyone with an inclination to draw should enrol on this course.

## Gloria Dayson

I am a member of Robert Wantling's 'Drawing for Beginners' Class. Until joining the class I had not had a formal art lesson and knew nothing of drawing techniques. I always thought that on retirement I would like to try to paint so I joined the Water Colour Class in the College of the Third Age in Newcastle, which was where I learned of Robert's classes.

His excellent teaching method and support and encouragement for an absolute beginner has made the classes exciting and the resulting work, for me, surprisingly good.

The friendly atmosphere and good humour make the classes fun and I look forward to each week.

Learning to draw has made me more aware of my environment, increased my appreciation of Art and enriched my retirement.

## Sue Dyson; Poynton, Cheshire

*I'm a housewife in my (very!) late thirties, born in Yorkshire and resident in Cheshire for the last sixteen years. I trained as a teacher of Mathematics but have taken "time out" from employment to care for my two young children.*

*Although my days are centred around the kids, I still manage to find time for my own hobbies which include music, cross-stitch, badminton and bridge. I revel in the mental stimulus of a cryptic crossword – the more obscure the better! I also enjoy participating in church activities, especially bellringing.*

## Sue's Diary

This diary runs from Tuesday 21st November to Monday 27th November 1995 and is written with the help of my husband, Pete, and the hindrance of my two children, Matthew and Rebecca. I haven't tried to cover all my activities, but have picked out a few highlights – it was a very busy week!

## Tuesday

Tuesday evening – and Badminton 3, my Adult Education course. This is supposed to be my relaxation of the week, but Phil, the tutor has other ideas. He demonstrates a particular service – I stand back and mutter under my breath about it looking easy, and then make a pig's ear of it! "Try again" he says. I try, and fail. "And again" – the shuttle actually goes over the net. "Once again" – a success!

In a game situation however the theory goes for a ball of chalk and all my bad faults are overtly apparent. Phil has tried many differing teaching styles, from quiet chastisement to a not so gentle rollicking. He now just shakes his head in disbelief as I make the same mistake time after time. Still, practise makes perfect (I hope!).

## Wednesday

An exhausting day – toddler group, shopping, washing & ironing, school runs. Am thankful that I have a restful, if thought-provoking evening. For the last eight weeks I've been attending a course called Landmarks (it's sometimes know as Alpha) run by St. George's Church. In the comfort of someone's home about two dozen people meet to learn about the Christian faith. We start with worship – lively singing and quiet prayer – and then listen to a short talk, tonight on "Does God Heal Today?" There's plenty of time to voice opinions and to ask searching questions both in a small group situation and on a one-to-one basis. Because the group consists of Christians of varying maturity of faith and also "Inquirers" the discussions are intellectually stimulating. A definite highlight of the week.

## Thursday

I am certain that the most difficult learning process is the understanding of the English language. Rebecca (aged 21 months) has a limited vocabulary consisting of "Me, mine, Daddy, juice, teddy" and "car". Anything else is a "da" but her powers of communication are amazing. Matthew (5 ¼) has an excellent grasp of the language, but his conversational skills leave a lot to be desired:

"Mum, do you know what?"

"No, what?"

"I watched a video at school and do you know what?"

"No, what?"

"It was about castles, and do you know what?"

"No, what" – Need I say more?

Teaching him to read has heightened my awareness of the idiosyncrasies of our language. He's learned how to spell out difficult words, or split then into recognisable syllables. Today he met NOW HERE for the first time. Try explaining to a five year old the difference between NO WHERE and NOW HERE (his interpretation). I'm certainly learning alongside him.

## Friday

Bellringing's tonight – yes I'm one of those campanologists who have the audacity to wake up the residents of Poynton at some unearthly hour on a Sunday morning.

Practice starts with handling lessons on a one to one basis for the raw recruits – it's quite a skill coping with 7 cwt of Bell metal and 50 ft of rope (we haven't gone metric yet!). The first part of my evening is spent memorising a method – I've written part of it out – I have to learn the pattern of the line, rather than the numerical order of the Bells. Now to put it into practise, and chaos ensues. "STAND" shouts our Bower captain (that means stop) and he explains our mistakes. Ringing is very much a team effort and we are only as good as our weakest member. We have to practise regularly to achieve a satisfactory standard and the mental agility required far surpasses any physical effort. I'm still very much a learner. After all, I've only been ringing for twenty years!

## Saturday

Spent today catching up on those mundane household tasks that I should have done earlier instead of writing the diary! Also had to cope with an exploding light bulb and a leaking hot water pipe.

Am now sat comatose in front of the television catching up on the week's viewing – thank goodness for the video recorder!

## Sunday

Matthew requested that I help with a computer "game" they do in school. It's called Dread Dragon Droom (I think). He demonstrates the direction keys and lets me have a go. Why do I keep crashing into trees? Matthew's turn – he's now entering the fairies' house. Hmm – looks like we've got to solve a co-ordinate problem. Hastily trying to recall "O" level maths in order to explain – no need, Matthew has worked it out for himself. I must learn that the best way for my children to develop is to let them think.

Flushed with our (well – Matthew's) triumph over the dragon, I decide to write today's diary using the w.p. Am very rusty!

## Monday

| | |
|---|---|
| 09.00 | Big day for me. Am piloting an aeroplane for the first time. |
| | Last minute revision from booklet. |
| 10.00 | Drive Rebecca to Grandma's. Am now nervous – don't want to make a fool of myself. Weather looks dubious – could be a rough ride – hope I don't need the sicky bag! |
| | Arrive at Woodford Aerodrome Pete meets me – he's accompanying me as a passenger. Go through security check. |
| 11.00 | Meet my instructor who takes us on board. Runs through the controls – there's more lights than at Blackpool! Am desperately trying to concentrate. My mind flashes back twenty years, to when I learnt to drive a car. It's much easier when you're young. |
| 11.30 | Take-off, and I have the controls. What an exhilarating feeling. Daren't stop to admire the views – am having to listen to every word of advice. It's physically much harder than I imagined. |
| 12.00 | Time to land – hands start sweating. Try to turn and over- compensate. Runway zooms into sight – too quickly. We're going to crash! Panic over. My instructor switches the simulator off! (you didn't think I was really flying?) A marvellous experience. We have a couple more "flights" around Hong Kong and I begin to get the feel of the controls. Krypton Factor here I come!! |

| *Janet Knight; Hassocks, W. Sussex* |
| :---: |

## Introduction

The diary covers the building of a bridge. This was my first practical experience of bridge construction. I have taken and passed H.O.T. Highway Technology which has a section which covers the construction of a bridge in its most basic form

My role as a development Control Inspector is to ensure that the bridge is built to the drawings submitted to West Sussex County Council and that all material and workmanship are to W.S.C.C. specifications.

This particular development was approx 1000 meters of carriageway construction, two roundabouts and a structure to be used as an over bridge and an underpass.

The contract was for 22 weeks, apart from the construction I was involved and took an active part in:

Setting up a road closure.
Traffic Management.
Liaison with the general public.
Liaison with County – district councillors.
Liaison and close working with the local traffic Police, Fire and Ambulance services.

The road and footway construction was no problem, for me the bridge was probably one of the biggest learning points of my career.

Photograph 1 (page 133) shows the depth of the cutting to be excavated. The old road can be seen, and the made up ground on which it had been constructed.

The excavation work gave me no problems, a point of interest and learning was how the old road had been constructed, to its approach to the bridge over the A24.

During excavation into the deep blue clay water became a problem seeping through the clay layers. As the work progressed more pumps were brought in. Then came the problem of dispersing the water pumped away.

When the excavation was completed preparation for the blinding layer was carried out and the blinding concrete was poured. The work progressed well. Our only problem, as is so often, is the weather conditions and on this particular day it was heat, the sun was drying the concrete out far too quickly. (See photograph 2, page 133).

The next procedure was the steel work. This is where my learning was to begin as I had no practical experience at all, and working with men who were very experienced and competent it was only a few minutes before my inexperience was very obvious. As the only woman on site and having been so confident in questioning and correcting all work carried out up to this time, our working relationship took a very downhill turn.

I had to continue as best as one can with the theory of the work to be carried out locked away in your head. I had drawings and diagrams to follow but when the smallest problem arose I felt very inadequate to deal with it.

I personally was very surprised how quickly your self confidence can go. For several days I would have done anything rather than measure reinforced steel and check ties for both quantity and quality. The bantering and quite obvious misuse of steel became almost unbearable. This is the time I can quite honestly say being an adult learner has its problems. I am sure when you are younger you can cope with the feeling of being inadequate. It just seems part of your learning as other people see you. It seemed to me that everyone's attitude was that if you didn't know by now then it was too late to learn. I think this attitude to learning made me even more determined to carry on and do my best to get it right.

Steel was dropped down to the work area to be correctly positioned for the concrete to be poured. This would be the foundation for the road/carriage to pass through the underpass.

Each length must be correctly positioned for steel fixing, and then joined with a wire tie. All the wire ends must be removed from the floor base or corrosion of the metal ties starts to take place within the concrete, and can eventually lead to concrete cancer.

The delivery points were checked for safety and efficiency.

Before the concrete is poured, each lorry load has to be tested for rejection or use. For every load a cube test is also carried out. This is carried out in the lab to find the crushing strength of the concrete.

A turning point to my learning came when the steel fixing of the first wing wall started. Still far from confident, I could not help feeling that something was wrong, and no one was going to tell me or even discuss it with me.

I checked and double checked the drawings with the steel that had been constructed but common sense kept telling me that steel was missing and that the drawing was incorrect. I dug out all my old books and spent to 3am one morning trying to find the problem. So I sought the advice of one of the West Sussex County Council engineers. I can remember feeling a total failure at having to do this, but what knowledge I had told me steel was missing.

Following my request to visit the site, he arrived later that day. He was very helpful and encouraging; numerous phone calls took place from the site office following his inspection of the bridge, plus a meeting the next morning with the design engineer. Then he announced that the drawing had to be corrected and that the design engineer had made a miscalculation and a considerable amount of steel had to be added. The relief was unbelievable.

Together we approached the senior steel fixer (who I might add had given me so much grief). We told him of the changes and amendments to the drawing. To my amazement from this point his attitude towards me changed and from here on I never stopped learning from him and those who worked closely with him, mainly the shuttering contractor. What I learnt cannot be written down. It would take too long and so much was method and management.

Photograph 3 (page 133) shows the young man whom working with had been so hard, then a complete turn round to a person I shall never forget learning so much from.

In photograph 4 (page 133) the steel fixing has been carried out and the shuttering put up ready for pouring the wing wall concrete.

In four more weeks, the over road will be constructed; the black material laid on the underpass road; the verges and banks battened, top soiled and seeded. In no time the area will look as though it has never been changed, but I will be able to look back at this job as being the one I learnt the most from in the shortest time and a great boost to my career. The learning may have been hard at times but I can now look back and know it is all worthwhile

*The cover from Kathleen Chapman's diary (page 85)*

*Pages from Bob Smith's diary (page 41)*

*A selection of photographs from Janet Knight's diary (page 128)*

**Photograph 1**
This photograph shows the depth of the cutting to be excavated. The old road can be seen, and the made up ground on which it had been constructed.

**Photograph 2**
Our only problem, as is so often, is the weather conditions and on this particular day it was heat, the sun was drying the concrete out far too quickly.

**Photograph 3**
The young man whom working with had been so hard, then a complete turn round to a person I shall never forget learning so much from.

**Photograph 4**
The steel fixing has been carried out and the shuttering put up ready for pouring the wing wall concrete.

The diary of

# Hayley Morris

commenced

friday 3rd November, 1995.

*The cover from Hayley Morris's diary (page 75)*

I AM A FIFTIES CHILD WHO WASTED OPPORTUNITIES AT ART COLLEGE BECAUSE I WAS TOO BUSY WORKING AT BECOMING A TRENDY LLO SOMETHING. I HAVE AND WILL AWAYS OBSERVE CREATE AND SKETCH, IT IS IN MY SOUL. AND NOW I'M STEALING TIME FOR MYSELF TO TRY AND UNDERSTAND WHAT PICASSO WAS ABOUT.

THIS COURSE AFX PROMISES TO KICK ME ONTO A JOURNEY WHERE I WILL LEARN TO PAINT— PROPERLY. BUT STILL TURNER LEAVES COLD.

DRAWING AND OBSERVATION WERE OUR FIRST PROJECTS BUT WE WERE SOON INTO COLLAGE AS YOU'VE NEVER SEEN IT. 'CAN'T SEE THAT HANGING IN MY LIVING ROOM. WE HAVE SINCE WORKED THROUGH SEVERAL PROJECTS COVERING DRAWING, COLLAGE, PRINTMAKING AND ESSAY WRITING. (HATE IT!)

ON THE FIRST DAY I SAW LOTS OF OPEN FACES BUT FORGOT EVERYONES NAME AFTER INTRODUCTION. BY WEEKS 2 AND 3 SEVERAL WOMEN HAD DECIDED IT WASN'T FOR THEM.

IT IS NOW THE 8TH MONTH OF THE COURSE AND WE HAVE LOST SOME ON THE WAY BUT MY JOURNEY CONTINUES. I STILL DON'T GET IT WITH TURNER BUT I WILL EVENTUALLY. I KNOW.

SOMETIMES I FEEL REVEALING YOUR SOUL, TO OTHERS, WHICH THIS COURSE DOES, CAN LEAVE YOU VULNERABLE. RECENTLY I FOUND STRETCHING MYSELF TO CLASS, JOB AND FAMILY MADE ME TOO TRANSPARENT AND THOUGHT ABOUT GIVING UP. BUT WITH MY USUAL DEEP AND MEANINGFUL REASONING DECIDED 'FUCK IT. I KNOW EVERYONES NAME NOW. WHY LEAVE?

LYN SMITH

*Lyn Smith's diary; Access for Women into Art, Kent*

*Participants in the 'Moving Out' project used creative writing and drawing to make an installation to direct cyclists on a new cycle path.*

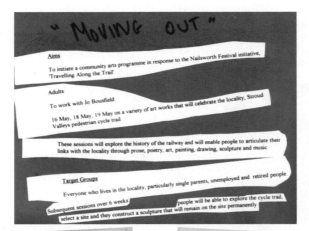

"MOVING OUT"

Aims

To initiate a community arts programme in response to the Nailsworth Festival initiative, 'Travelling Along the Trail'

Adults

To work with Jo Bousfield

16 May, 18 May, 19 May on a variety of art works that will celebrate the locality, Stroud Valleys pedestrian cycle trail

These sessions will explore the history of the railway and will enable people to articulate their links with the locality through prose, poetry, art, painting, drawing, sculpture and music

Target Groups

Everyone who lives in the locality, particularly single parents, unemployed and retired people

Subsequent sessions over 6 weeks          people will be able to explore the cycle trail, select a site and they construct a sculpture that will remain on the site permanently

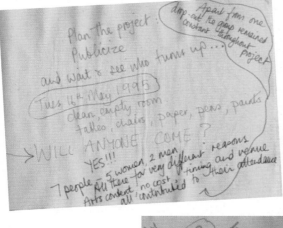

Plan the project:
Publicize
and wait to see who turns up....

Apart from one drop-out the group remained constant throughout the project

Tues 16th May 1995
clean, empty room
tables, chairs, paper, pens, paints
→ WILL ANYONE COME?
YES!!!
7 people — 5 women, 2 men
All there for very different reasons
Arts context 'no cost' timing and venue
all contributed to their attendance

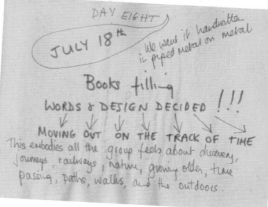

DAY EIGHT
JULY 18th
We wore it handwritten it piped metal on metal

Books filling
WORDS & DESIGN DECIDED !!!
↓ ↓ ↓ ↓ ↓ ↓
MOVING OUT ON THE TRACK OF TIME
This embodies all the group feels about discovery, journeys, railways, nature, growing older, time passing, paths, walks, and the outdoors.

DAY TEN
OCTOBER
TOM MAKES THE METAL SENTENCES
DAY ELEVEN NOVEMBER
THEY ARE DELIVERED TO Maggie

Moving out

*The finished installation, moving from shadow into sunlight*

on the track of

moving out

time

*The finished installation, moving from shadow into sunlight*

*A selection of pages and photographs from the 'Moving Out' project diary; Stroud (also facing page)*

**The DIARY**

**Friday:**

It's my A.F.W.I.A. course today. I was under the impression I'd be making pretty artifacts before I started the course, the sort of thing my mother would like! I suppose it's exactly what it's called – Access for Women into Art. It covers a lot of aspects, I would describe it as a crash introductory course. The week we made an attempt at lino-cuts, and I decided 'this is for me', and bought spare linoleum for all the work I promised myself I would do at home, never actually materialised. But it's fun

and at times a challenge. I find I work better when there's some pressure to have work ready, and with some of the new concepts I have had to consider, it's an extra bonus that 'it' is ready, but that I am also pleased with the result. It has introduced me to various ways of working which left to my own devices I would never have attempted. It's also introduced me to an awareness of modern art, this I have feelings about. I can now appreciate what an artist is trying to portray, but I find a lot of modern work is only suitable for large spaces such as galleries, it's not the type of work I'd want surrounding me at home. The way I work in future will have a different approach to pre-course work, I don't feel so intimidated and feel I'm over one hurdle at least.

*The cover from Trish Spence's diary; Access for Women into Art, Kent*

# Part Two:
# Adults Learning

*In this second part of the book, extracts from the diaries of adult learners submitted to NIACE are arranged by themes, and have been selected to illustrate different aspects of adults' experience of learning and education.*

*The first section concerns the various motivations which bring people to participate in both informal learning and formal education. The second section highlights the challenges which some adults have to overcome in order to make the most of education. The third section evokes the diverse nature of adults' learning experiences – what it's actually like to learn by yourself or in a group – and the final section celebrates the achievements of adult learners and considers the impact of that learning upon individuals, families and communities.*

*Within each section italicised text introduces sets of extracts which relate to a common issue. Of course, the experiences of adult learners don't fit neatly into categories, and you will see that individual extracts often relate to several overlapping issues.*

# MOTIVATIONS

*Adults have diverse motivations for engaging in active learning or participating in formal educational opportunities. Often there are several, overlapping factors which impel us to take the learning initiative; sometimes we discover new motivations – and new things about ourselves – as we get involved in learning. Underlying many adults' decision to join a group or take a course is a desire – not always fully articulated – to change oneself in some way, to become a different sort of person.*

**For many adult learners, memories of prior education, and particularly of schooling, are significant. Among the diarists school is sometimes recalled as a missed opportunity or with a sense of failure. Coming back into education as an adult may trigger memories of schooling, often evoking a contrast between learning at school and with adults. While some mature students are wary of formal education, they may also want to make up for missed opportunities.**

… I have rather painful memories round number work. When I was in Junior School, if you got under 5/10 for mental arithmetic you got the cane. Even cheating – i.e. my friend and I swapping answers – we still only got under 5/10 and even now I can see the red weals on my hand and see myself licking my wounds like a poor little animal.

Even at the Grammar School maths was badly taught – we had a different teacher every year compared with English where I had the same teacher from the second year to the second year sixth and achieved highly in this subject whereas I only got 10% in "O" level maths. Added to this the maths teachers never seemed to relate to the pupils very adequately. Two weeks ago I went to Sir Jonathan North School and enrolled in the numeracy class which is very informal. You have an assessment and work at your own pace. At the moment I am working on metrication and have learned at least one important fact – 1oz = 30 gm! If I only achieve conversion from pounds and ounces to gm and Kg, etc. I shall consider a good job done. Wednesday evening I am going to a GCSE maths class. For the first time in my life I quite enjoy the lessons (I have had two so far). The teacher, Pete, makes something of a game of it, and his enthusiasm for the subject is infectious. He says his objective at the moment is to get us thinking in numbers.

*(Kathleen Ferrelly; Leicester; Psychology, Computing and GCSE Maths)*

My senior school was solely for young ladies. Mary Boon School situated in West London was famous for turning out young ladies of distinction. It was a trade college offering the ordinary academic subjects plus dressmaking, tailoring, millinery, embroidery and upholstery. They also boasted a first class art department.

My first choice was dressmaking, unfortunately, there were not enough places on the course so I opted for my second choice which was millinery.

I did quite well in my trade subject but was only just average academically. Looking back now I feel that if I had had more encouragement both at home and at school I would have done extremely well.

When I left school I applied my trade for only one year. It was badly paid and the apprenticeship I was offered did not materialise.

By the time I was 21 years old I knew that I needed to get back into education. I gained employment in an office as a general office clerk. This job gave me the confidence I needed to join an evening course at Pitman's College. I studied shorthand and typing and did well.

I needed to bring the aforementioned clearly to mind before I could answer the question:

Is adult learning for me?

The answer has got to be 'yes' because only further education can put right the mistakes of the past …

… I decided to take the course covering general English. This will cover letter writing, essay writing, and appreciation of various types of writing. A certificate may be gained which is based on coursework. I am hoping that this course will give me self-confidence. I intend to enjoy learning from now on. I am 53 years old and THIS IS ONLY THE FIRST STEP IN ADULT EDUCATION.

*(Anne Kissane; Crawley; English)*

Brian is a 43 year old slightly Balding individual with an imposing stature dressed conservatively. He is so to speak a rough diamond, but years of business have left him battle scarred. He is more than capable of handling himself in any business confrontation. Brian had learnt the hard way street wise. He has a very inquiring mind and is forever looking to a more lucrative financially beneficial future. He is ready to move as market forces dictate, into varying areas of business.

Thus Brian's next move is Education, he sees this as being a changing world ever moving forward with technology, he will attempt anything to realise his ambitions. His only regret is that he never took advantage of education as a child. This he intends to put right by being a mature student at the Huntingdon regional college, by going on a course called Access, which will enable him to eventually gain a Degree. His subject is Business Law. His first challenge is to obtain some academic qualifications for the universities to accept him.

*(Brian Gray; Cambridgeshire; Access – Business Law)*

13 October: My daughter's 11th Wedding Anniversary. Had an ordinary night's sleep and up in good time to pick up Doreen and her spinning wheel. A lovely autumn ride to Wheathampstead. My learning was more consolidating than new information. We saw some fascinating ideas for weaving and I hope I can join a new class in 1996 to explore these. Frances is a brilliant teacher in that she moves one on by encouragement – a great need of many learners and in my school days in short supply. I vividly recall two occasions when this happened to me. The first came to mind when I saw a card of Turner's "Fighting Temeraire" in the village Post Office. At primary school I wrote an essay on this picture and the poem by Sir Henry Newbolt and the teacher praised it in front of the class – at ten years old I was very happy. While writing I have recalled one earlier instance. In a gloomy classroom in the 1930s when I would have been about eight years old we were being taught about 'cave dwellers' and I drew a family outside its cave home. The teacher commended this as very detailed and this is one of the things that encouraged my life-long interest in history. Now to the time when I was in secondary school I had an English teacher who was very frugal with high marks who on a couple of occasions very highly commended my work. This did a little to counteract the adverse effect of the previous teacher on that subject who had managed to turn an avid reader into one who rarely picked up a book unless required to do so for homework. I never did get back my enthusiasm for 'literature' but turned to non fiction which I still prefer.

*(Joy Tomkins; St Albans; Spinning)*

*A significant life change is often a catalyst for adult learners, just as, in turn, education can sometimes help people to make sense of change or may lead to new directions in life. For some diarists a serious illness, bereavement or disability was a triggering factor, requiring new activities or aspirations. Women, in particular, often write that as their children grew up they wanted a new identity and sense of purpose, to 'be myself again', and that education was a way forward. Sometimes family and friends were supportive, sometimes not.*

### Monday September 11th

I started college feeling very nervous, the entrance hall was full of young school leavers. All that was in my mind, fear, was I going to make a fool of myself …

### Wednesday September 13th

My husband I love him dearly, but he can be a pain in the backside at times, keeps saying "Why do you want to do it?", he can't understand I want to be myself again …

### Monday September 18th

I feel proud of myself for getting through the first week. My family said I wouldn't last a week and here I am starting my second.

Numeracy today, hated maths at school, but now I find it's not so bad if I take my time and think about it. Our class is great, we all get on really well and help each other.

### Tuesday September 19th

Tutorial – never knew what that meant till I started college, but it's a great way to express any fears you have about the college. Our tutor is really good at her job, she gives you lots of confidence and that makes me want to go on, when I have had a not so good day …

### Wednesday September 20th

My family don't laugh at me now and even my husband has started to take me seriously.

After years of looking after my family I am now able to think about things that I want to think about and not what my family wants.

College has opened new doors for me and put me on a new road.

*(Margaret Whiting; Peterlee, County Durham; Adult Basic Education)*

Cocooned in motherhood when my children were small, I had been happy to dedicate my days to them. As they progressed to school, I too felt the need for learning re-awaken within me.

I had a feeling of emptiness that only intellectual growth would fulfil. I began to question my life, my choices, who I had become. I fitted the mould of wife and mother, but I wanted a new identity, with a sense of purpose, not the negative labels I had attached to myself along the way.

For a time, the fear of failure (or the knowledge that I would fail), outweighed any motivation I might have towards self-improvement. At last I took the plunge and decided to add another ball to my juggling act. This one was labelled 'night classes'. This was my first real introduction to life as a mature student. It was not always easy dragging myself out on dark evenings in all weathers. Living as I do, outside a little village tucked below the fells, Carlisle is not always the easiest place to get to.

I realised during these classes, that I was not alone in my self-doubts. We would take a coffee break half-way through the class, and sit round a table together, discussing various problems: – Could we manage the work? Would we pass the exams? What were our next steps? It was reassuring to know that I was not alone in my fears. Here were other women, who like myself, had for years been overcome by babies, shopping and housework. So remote from academic study, so tired had we become, that we could do no more in the evenings than slump onto the sofa and submerge in 'soap'. But children get older, night feeds stop, they progress to school, and my life became unfulfilled. I realised I was extremely bored, nothing stimulated me.

So these night classes satisfied a huge part of me. My appetite for intellectual growth whetted, I realised I did not want to stop there. I wanted a career, something that I could feel was worthwhile; something to be proud of ...

*(Female; Carlisle; Access Initiative for Mature Students)*

## Sunday

My week of enjoyable learning starts at 9 a.m. with the arrival of the Sunday Express and the "Classic" Crossword. I checked last week's solution, and then with a cup of tea and a small pile of reference books I begin the "work". It is very exciting, and whereas my dear husband died some years ago I found Sunday mornings very difficult, now I can't wait to get stuck in and solve the clues. I'm delighted when there are questions on Shakespeare, but panicky when I read "name the genus of the plant ..." Oh! dear, I will need some help on that one.

After lunch myself and two pals, we all live in Grangeway, don our Sunday best and Maude drives us into Wilmslow and to the meeting of the Widows' Social Group. There, every other Sunday, some 35 of us enjoy a varied programme set up for us by a wonderful Chairman – Betty Harding – who is also the Secretary. What I've learned from the speakers at these meetings is phenomenal. Apart from "visiting" umpteen countries abroad, I've experienced, through them, the heart break of the plight of Romanian orphans, and the happiness of listening to stirring brass band music, and what happens to you when you present yourself at Buckingham Palace for your OBE. Oh! yes, there is still a lot to learn from other peoples' lives – king people – ordinary people who make me feel humble.

## Wednesday

Up with the dawn – struggle into leotard, joggers and flat shoes and puff my way to Handworth Tennis Club – in November? Yes! Under the expert, caring eye of Ann Ford I am learning to listen to my body and keep fit. It is absolutely wonderful what has happened to me since I joined the "Over 50s" keep fit or music and movement – over 6 years ago. I've been on keep-fit holidays in Southport, Rhodes, Italy and I'm off again in 1996. I've learned how to share a room with a more or less stranger, and to enjoy a holiday without my husband of nearly 50 years marriage. A tall order. Wonderful people became my friends and we laughed our way through ...

*(Marjorie Foy; Wilmslow; Keep Fit for 50s)*


1745 hrs:   Well, I've managed to cram yet more food into my stomach and I am now joined by Liz, our receptionist on our way to the Royal School for the Deaf for our sign language class. This is always good fun, but it isn't easy transforming yourself into an extrovert at such short notice. Shyness just doesn't go hand in hand with such a visible skill.

2000 hrs:   Home at last! Terry has been an absolute angel and cooked his own dinner which means I can spend some extra time with our homeworking children before I start mine.

2115 hrs:   Yet another load of grass-stained, gravy-splattered biroed garments are shoved into the washing machine, yet another stack from the dryer is distributed between the family cupboards and the ironing pile, and another eternal cycle begins! I've often wondered if I have the cleanest family in Exeter or the grubbiest! We've managed to squeeze in half an hour of sign language practise. We make a game of it and call it our "secret code", but it camouflages the sadder reasons that make it necessary. You see, we discovered this week that my thirteen year old daughter has hearing difficulties. She has been tragically unfortunate as she has inherited my deafness. We are optimistic as I was already profoundly deaf at her age and so far, she has lost only 25% of her hearing. Luckily, she has also inherited my stubbornness and determination to succeed in life, so with the right support and attitude, the sky's the limit.

*(Sandra Moore; Exeter; Sign Language, and Training and Development NVQ)*


1995 – this was to be the year when it all came together. I was going to be rid of this ghost once and for all. It had haunted me for the last 2 years, engulfing me in its powers. It almost won – I nearly died, February last year, in fact. Anorexia nervosa was my ghost. I was studying the second year of my HNC in Business and Finance. The only things that kept me going were the love of my family and close friends and the help and support of my tutors at Merthyr College, who never gave up on me, even though I had almost given up on myself.

I prayed for a second chance as I was threatened with drips, injections and blood transfusions. Everyone had said – it was so simple – a good meal, that's all.

I had the chance I longed for and the first lesson I learnt was life was too precious to throw away.

I continued with my studies and also undertook a Women's Returner Course in order to prepare me for return to my employment as Clerical Officer with the South Wales Constabulary. I met some special people on that course – life long friends. Women from various walks of life had come together – I soon learnt that my problems were little ones and appreciated the fact that I was there to listen and help others for a change.

*(Linda Birch; Merthyr Tydfil; HNC in Business and Finance, and Women Returners Course)*

**For many diarists, employment is a significant motivating factor. After being made redundant at one workplace, education and training provides a route to new work, and a chance to overcome shattered self-confidence. Others see education as a way out of a boring or dead-end job, or as the chance to gain new skills and attain promotion. Though employment may be a primary motivation, often education is also used as a way of changing other aspects of a person's life and identity.**

My name is Frances Gilbert. I am a wife and mother who is unable to go out to work as I have a severely disabled young adult son living at home. I therefore have been a home typist for some years and recently the firm provided me with a computer. I can type in the letters and print them out but apart from that I am "computer illiterate".

For tasks such as graphs needed for reports, my boss has to travel to the London office as I am yet unable to do these on the computer I have at home. It is an excellent computer and once I have the knowledge and skills to be able to perform the tasks she needs completed, I will be able to use the computer to much more avail which will save my boss from travelling to London unnecessarily; give me a far more fulfilled occupation and be satisfying to both of us! I would obviously be putting in longer hours of work which will give me a better wage as at present my hours are quite small because I am only able to type the letters.

As a child at school I was a distracted student – (unfortunately), and now realise – after only a week on the IT Course how much fun – and how absorbing and satisfying – learning actually is! I have enjoyed this first week at 'college' more than I could have imagined and am finding the studies challenging and adventurous. I am also enjoying meeting other students around my own age group and realising I could have the potential to learn all the computing skills I need to be better employed in my present home work. I actually feel liberated!

*(Frances Gilbert; Information Technology)*

For various reasons I was out of work and losing interest in the world around me. More concern was expressed around the home than was really necessary. Trauma had come and gone and getting back into reality seemed a long way off. I had seen the advert for 'Women into Work' but in my state of mind had not registered what it entailed. So I showed the leaflet to my daughter. Sitting there while she read it, I was soon being bullied into enrolling for the course, and being told it would do me good. I agreed and forms were sent for. When the forms arrived, I felt compelled to fill in where necessary, sign and post back. It wasn't long before a letter arrived, inviting me for an interview on 8 August 1995. I had something to look forward to … At the interview I was accepted … The door to the next path in my life was open.

*(Joan Chadwick; Leeds; Women into Work)*

In my wildest dreams I never once considered the possibility of returning to learning after ten years of working. If somebody had said to me even five years ago that I would be attending Carlisle College doing an Access Course I would have laughed. It certainly has not been an easy thing for me to do. I have battled against feelings of lack of confidence and insecurity along with feelings of yearning and a need for fulfilment. I have thought back to when I was at school and wondered whether I am capable of learning again after a break of what seems like an aeon. I know that many thousands of people do it every year and succeed, but I never thought that I would be one of them.

When I was fifteen I was constantly reminded by teachers, family and friends of how important it was to work hard and pass my exams. Like any young, impressionable person I don't really think that information actually sunk in. Although I thought at the time that I worked hard, looking back, I know I didn't work quite hard enough.

I found employment within one month of leaving school and never looked back, until about two years ago. My job was starting to bore me, mainly because it was too repetitive. Promotion was out of the question because the company I worked for was too small and any other jobs I was interested in were no good, either due to my lack of experience or being unqualified. I was stuck in a rut. Over those last two years I spoke to many people who had gone to College for various different things and many had been older than me. I began to realise that education wasn't just for children, so why couldn't I have a second chance?

*(Female; Carlisle College; Access Initiative for Mature Students)*


I returned to adult learning five years ago. I started with a word processing/electronics course. I then advanced to a CMS course which is a Certificate for Mature Students which included Psychology, Sociology, History, English Literature, Urban Studies and Maths. At this stage I knew I had become addicted to studying. My next move was onto a full time management degree course, in which I am now in my final year. The reason I decided to return to study was to work towards a job with responsibility, instead of jobs that I found were dead end.

The courses have not been easy, but I have learned new skills and also about my strengths and weaknesses. There were times when I felt I could not go on as the courses have been very intense, but with the help and support from my special friends I have stuck at it.

*(Jane Meah; Bradford; Management Degree)*


In May of 1995 I changed my job within the company I work for. For the last three years I have worked as a Laboratory Technician making pharmaceuticals to a catalogue specification. This work is done as a scheduled manufacturing operation.

I am now a Scheduler in the Materials Management Department and use computer software packages to plan the production processes within the confines of the schedule which projects the expected sales so that processes are planned using lead times, shelf lives and scales ensuring products remain in stock.

I am receiving on site training to gain new skills using the office systems. In addition to my normal job I have been nominated as a contact for people experiencing problems both with existing and new software packages. Initially I dealt with people within my own department but I have been requested to assist people in other areas of the company. This has also led to responsibilities related to hardware setup and configuration.

In September I approached my Department Manager with a request to study 'A' Level Computer Studies at evening classes over a one year period. The company has agreed to pay the course fees, examination costs and provided a £40 book allowance. The course will give me an understanding of computer programming and covers topics such as explanations of hardware, software package use, applications of computers and new product design. There is probably not a lot of chance for progression within the company just doing a Scheduler's job but other responsibilities and knowledge may mean developing key areas of new skills.

*(Kevin Gregory; Cardiff; 'A' Level Computer Studies and workplace training)*

As a family man, bordering on 50 years, facing up to the reality of losing not only a job, but the trade that had been for so many people a skill, that had me undergo a five year apprenticeship, college, night school, various courses and retraining on many different and upgraded pieces of equipment, only to find all this more or less finished was sad for me, and also worrying to say the least.

When looking for new work in the same field in the newspapers I was to find a new slant to the wording of such a post "NOBODY OVER 30 YEARS NEED APPLY!", to say it didn't do much for my ego is an understatement …

Unemployed, standing in line at the Job Centre was a prospect I thought I would never come up against.

As dramatic as it might sound, the reality of it hit me like a bombshell, as it did with some of my colleagues, I later was to find, for we did keep in touch by phone …

Having been a student of the Start Course has for me been a lifechanging experience, it has opened avenues for me that are honestly beyond any possibilities that I thought I may have had …

Although the recession did focus my mind on change regarding employment, I was already feeling somewhat 'stuck in a rut', possibly because the changing face of technology, my job was changing, the craft that I originally started with was now becoming very impersonal.

With the introductory reading of the Start Course came the thought that at the grand age of (then) 49 years, could I seriously make that transition from computers into working with supporting and caring for others. It's one thing to think it possible, but to put it into practice – that's quite a different prospect.

Within our church life, my wife and I had attended what was a support group for the bereaved. We would separately go to a bereaved's house where we would support them as best we could in their grief.

Through our church we were taught the use of empathy, the use of body language, also listening skills – these skills and more were needed when supporting the bereaved.

Although as an experience it was certainly a testing one, but I also found it fulfilling. I think it must have been in this role that the thought of a possibility of working in a caring capacity could be a positive one …

*(Doug Preston; Chelmsford; Start Course)*

**While some of the diarists are using education to improve their employment prospects, others are learning so that they will be better equipped for voluntary work in the community which may or may not also open up employment opportunities.**

I feel the main reason why most people join a Course such as this is because they would like to help people by listening to their stories, and I think this applies to me also.

My special interest at this stage is in Cancer support as three years ago I had the diagnosis myself. I am glad to say that since receiving the operation and treatment I have a good prognosis. The various cancer organisations prefer to have counsellors who have "lived with" the disease for at least two years. However, formal qualifications are not a stipulation, I just feel I would like to learn as much about the subject of counselling as possible to make sure I don't do any harm through ignorance. I am not even sure at this stage how much help I could be other than be just someone who listens and who has been there and knows exactly how it feels to be told they have cancer, and how this knowledge changes our lives. Maybe with some counselling skills I will be in a position to help people adjust to their lives.

*(Maxine Bancalari; Norwich; Counselling)*

I am starting a course on Hairdressing. Can't stop at home doing nothing all day. So I am looking forward to going to learn something new to keep my brain active. I was three weeks late in starting. I thought perhaps my tutor would give me a quick run through to that which I had missed. But no! I have to look it up myself. Just what I needed to start me off. Can't let these youngsters beat me to it.

My first day I did some blow drying on a dummy head of hair. I thought I did it all right – I enjoyed it so much, but there is always room for improvement.

When I have learnt everything to do it the right way and finish the course, I would like to be able to go round the people who are unable to do their own hair. I visit stroke victims and am a Trustee Visitor for Mencap.

*(Grace Fielder, age 79; Mid-Kent; Hairdressing for Mature Students)*

**Some diarists explain that they have joined adult education classes in order to obtain useful skills.**

I joined my French evening class last September after a family camping holiday for one month in France when I had found communicating even on a very simple basis, extremely frustrating and very hard work. I had it seemed packed everything essential to a good holiday except the peanut butter and the language!

I am, therefore, determined that my next holiday in France will at least be a little easier and that I won't be walking around the supermarkets and shops looking like a Una Stubbs with her team in tow!

I have three children, who, I am sure, have joined every after school activity available, and who all play different instruments which of course need to be practised daily. I work full time at my local school as an ancillary in the mornings and secretary in the afternoons, am Clerk to the Governing Body there and Treasurer to the Parent Association. I am currently working on a Diploma course connected with early education and lastly, of course, there is the Avon round.

*(Angela Pinnell; Brighton; French)*

It was whilst I was still at school that I started attending Evening Institute classes run by the Local Education Authority. Thanks to my maths teacher, I had started to learn practical bee-keeping as an extra-curriculum activity. Wanting to know more, I joined evening classes on 'The Anatomy and Physiology of the Honey Bee'. The tuition was first class and I became the youngest member of the local club to pass the British Bee-keepers' Association examinations. My delight at this was probably the initial inspiration for undertaking future courses.

In my third year of attendance it was a matter of cycling ten miles in the 'blackout' – war had been declared. Many times I sped home during an air raid and following one close encounter with some shrapnel (from one of our own anti-aircraft guns), decided to wear a tin hat. On several occasions the classes, held near the city centre, had to be continued in the cellar of the building or in the boiler room because of the air raid taking place 'up above'. Numerous times we emerged to see the sky glowing red from the fires dotted all about us, yet classes never closed down.

It was at this time that I started attending lectures on 'Air Navigation', 'Meteorology', 'Theory of Flight' and supplementary classes on 'Radio with Morse Code', 'First Aid' and important to me at the time, 'Accountancy', which latter I fancied as a career.

Following an eventful four years as RAF aircrew, I had changed my mind about accountancy and with further studies behind me, eventually joined the teaching profession...

Well, here I am, now retired and in my seventies but still attending four classes a week. In this day and age I feel it behoves everyone to know something about computers and their uses. Tried teaching myself at home from books for four months, then I decided to join my 'Information Technology' (IT), 'Desk Top Publishing' (DTP), and 'Word Processing' (WP) courses. At least now I can talk to my twelve year old Godson!

*(Geoff Meeks; Birmingham; Beekeeping, Information Technology and other courses)*

My week starts with Wednesday. Wednesday evening is the highlight of my week.

I love the feeling of belonging to this throng of people hurrying, with so much purpose and pleasure, through the darkness to the brightly lit school, with all its courses.

I left school aged fifteen, having hated every minute of schooling.

Creative writing is my subject. I want to write.

At the end of the evening we linger, unwilling to leave.

Thursday afternoon I go to a creative writing course in Market Harborough, and on Friday I go to a painting course. The rest of the week I prepare work for the following sessions.

I have to juggle my job around these new commitments.

My discovery of adult education has awakened a hunger for learning that I never knew I had. For me it will be my pension scheme, it has to be!

*(Sheila McKinnon; Brigstock; Creative Writing and Painting)*

**Many diarists explain that a tentative first try at adult education has 'awakened a hunger for learning', which may be fired by the thrill of mental and physical stimulation and new skills, or by the companionship and pleasure of learning with a group.**

I decided to attempt the City and Guilds Flower Arranging course in September 1994 to add a new interest to my life (and escape for a few hours a week from demanding children). As I'd recently taken GCSE Maths at night school I decided that I would like to try something more creative. This course seemed ideal as I enjoy working with natural materials. Little did I realise how involved the course would be – although each aspect of it is challenging ...

All in all this course is so interesting that it changes your life. County walks take on a whole new dimension – equipped with secateurs, plastic bags etc. Families find foliage soaking in the bath, roses drying in the microwave and flowers hanging upside down poised over people's heads like the sword of Damocles whilst eating at the dining table (cleared of notes, oasis, cut up plastic bags and preserved plant material).

I feel that I will have gained valuable knowledge from this course and made new, interesting friendships with people who are just as obsessive about flower arranging as I am.

*(Rosalie Darlington; Warrington; Flower Arranging)*

I have always been interested in articles made using enamelling techniques and used to buy a few pieces, so when I discovered there was a class teaching enamelling I was naturally keen to join. As well as learning how to make specific pieces and use the kiln – which could not be done at home – the classes are very friendly and interesting and extremely well taught.

I look forward to going every week as, as well as my wish to learn, I also joined to meet new people. Living on my own as I do now, I find going to adult education classes (I go to three, enamelling, pottery and short mat bowls) gives me a reason for getting out of the house – not having to spend much money after the initial outlay – the café is very reasonable with good food. I can also meet different people for a friendly chat. Another reason is the fact that the classes I go to are all in the daytime, as opposed to the old time "Evening Classes", which means I do not have to go out at night – which at my age (60) is very important.

*(Audrey Wythe; Croydon; Enamelling, Pottery and Short Mat Bowls)*

My name is Frank Pololi. I am a retired caterer and ex-local government employee. I have lived in Croydon since 1940, and have attended courses for the last 20 years (painting, pewter and enamelling).

### 21/11/95
I attend my classes to learn new skills, to keep my mind active, to meet people and improve my social life. I very much enjoyed the pewter classes with Bonnie Mackintosh, and also her enamelling classes. I find her a very good and dedicated teacher, always willing to help and offer advice. I look forward to many more years attendance to her classes.

*(Frank Pololi; Croydon; Enamelling)*

# CHALLENGES

*There are many obstacles in the path of adults who want to participate in lifelong learning opportunities. The writers for this book have all, to a greater or lesser extent, overcome some of these obstacles, and the section title 'Challenges' is intended to emphasise both a sense of possibility and the struggle often involved. But of course, for many adults the obstacles are sometimes just too daunting or too difficult. One of the strongest themes to emerge from the diaries is that lifelong learning requires a deep-rooted learning culture – embedded in institutions and workplaces, in homes and communities, and in our hearts and minds – which will support people to overcome the obstacles preventing access to, or participation in, adult education.*

*As one diarist explains, life gets in the way of learning. Adult learners, especially women with young children, frequently have to juggle exhausting combinations of work, family and study responsibilities. The practical and moral support of family and friends (and of an educational institution) can make all the difference, and their hostility or opposition can be an extra, even impossible, burden.*

It was a big decision for me to go to college again as it's been ten years since I last did anything in the academic line.

I don't think I would have enrolled if my husband hadn't pushed me to as he knows I have always meant to get around to this. But life got in the way. What with starting a twilight shift job and my shift starting at five o'clock, all the courses started on a night so it was impossible to start anything.

Also bringing up a young family I didn't have time to think about what I wanted as they take up all your energy and your every waking thought.

As I rushed about getting everyone ready so that we can all go out together (which is like a military manoeuvre) I don't have time to think. But on the bus to college after such frantic activity I started worrying about the class. Would it be full of fresh-faced kids just left school and would I have to compete with them or would I be able to do the work and could I remember how to do anything at all.

The class wasn't so bad, it was all people like me and all ages, afterward I realised it was my own perspective that frightened me.

*(Maureen Fradgley; Peterlee, County Durham; Adult Basic Education)*

**Wednesday**
Usual jobs to do concerning the house, family and pets which means my whole day is taken up working and I am unable to study.

Early to bed to read Dangerous Liaisons.

**Thursday**
Begin my essay on Hume which needs to be with my tutor by Tuesday. I find essay writing rather difficult and very time consuming but it has to be done, and my tutor will gain an insight into my understanding of the course and will offer help and advice where she feels it appropriate.

Work until 4.00, then take the dog out for a walk and then have to prepare dinner etc. Feel I have a headache coming – great!!!

**Friday**
Continue to work on essay from 10.00 until 1.00. I commented on the hours I have worked to my daughter who has been doing her GCSEs. She feels what I'm doing is a waste of time and perhaps she is right but I do enjoy learning. To continue my studying I find I will need to organise my days very carefully so as not to disturb the family's routine.

I have rather been taken up with studying and doing my essay and the house is in a mess and my husband wasn't very pleased this morning when there was no clean shirt. I was also a bit late with tea tonight and we ended up with tuna and salad.

Essay still in progress and by the time I have finished it would have taken me 24 hours collecting facts, organising these into a reasonable essay and then typing it up.

Tutorial tomorrow which I'm looking forward to as it helps to learn that everyone is having problems and it's not just me.

*(Christine Durrant; Norwich; Open University BA)*

On the home front, asking for help is something quite new and difficult for me. For years I have managed to resolve problems alone, being an independent creature, but to try and maintain reasonable order and sanity and reach the end of the course, I have had to change my attitude. It has been a pleasant surprise to discover that people like helping!

Fellow students on the course have had to cope with resentment or even envy from family and friends and are almost having to fight for the right to study. Luckily I have not had to deal with these obstacles.

*(Female; Carlisle; Access Initiative for Mature Students)*

Even though I made my decision to enter further education I still had some doubts as it is impossible to know whether or not one will succeed. I realised that I would be gambling with my own self-esteem and that my friends may judge me on the outcome. I am particularly aware of the interests of my former workmates who in the majority supported me, but I have a gut feeling that one or two are slightly envious of me and resent the fact that I am getting the chance to better myself. I am conscious of my associates keeping a watchful eye on my progress and at first this concerned me but now I am not letting it affect me and am trying to turn my thoughts onto more positive matters.

*(Male; Carlisle; Access Initiative for Mature Students)*

### Sunday 15 May 1994

Began to transfer my work on NVQ II over in preparation to start on my portfolio for NVQ III.

Spent about three hours doing this at my kitchen table after doing the week's ironing. My husband is not very happy about my working at home on this qualification but as I have set myself a target of 5 weeks to get this done, which will leave my assessor just one week to go through everything with a fine tooth comb before the verifier comes. I just hope that he will get through the strain of my doing this in my own time at home.

### Week Commencing 30 May 1994

Monday of this week is Spring Bank Holiday and I have taken the rest of the week off as annual leave in order to work on my portfolio work.

Over the past two weeks I have spent approx. 2-3 hours each evening and extra hours over the weekend working on my portfolio but have not had any time at work to manage to gather any evidence or writing up. Therefore this week I am going to start and number my evidence, cross reference everything in the plastic wallets, make a list of outstanding evidence required, draft letters to send out for letters of verification and look at the silver book.

### Mid Week

I feel that I am now beginning to get somewhere with the work in hand – making a comprehensive list of what I had done and what I still had to do has helped immensely.

My husband is still struggling with me working at home, I knew he would. Although he is diabetic and has a heart problem it is his mental health problem which is causing the trouble. Any form of stress, including my just working like this at home can affect his health so I am having to tread very carefully at present.

### 15 June 1994

Today I am using a flexi day to go through my work with a fine tooth comb to make sure I have covered every aspect required and to read through all the statements I finished two days ago in my silver book.

Yesterday I had to go to the doctors for my blood test results – a scan is now to be arranged with the hospital and I have been told that they are testing for cancer of the liver as I have some enzyme deficiency with my liver. This has now been hanging over me since 3rd May before I started my work on my present period of portfolio building, and some days I feel drained. Although I must admit that some days I am too tired from my stint at work and the writing I am doing at home each night, and over the weekends, to think about my health problem. This has probably been a good thing as I might have become as depressed as my husband gets if I did.

### 17 June 1994

Well, today was the day that I handed in my two folders of evidence and my silver book to the assessor for her to take away and look at. All the work is now behind me – just the worry of have I done enough in the time I allocated myself to achieve the qualification that I want?

### Week Commencing 20 June 1994

Sue telephoned this week to say everything is OK and Linda, the other assessor has gone through my files as well as Sue Bird at Newark and Sherwood College, and they say I will have passed.

Went for my scan at the hospital again on Friday – was told on the spot that I have gallstones – but now have to wait again for the results on my liver problem. I am now more worried over this than my studying and if anything goes wrong when the verifier calls next Wednesday and I am told that I have to gather extra evidence or do a particular unit again I shall feel absolutely devastated as I think at this stage I would not be able to carry on with this.

Probably this is just nerves and external pressures coming to bear but that is just how I feel at present.

**29 June 1994**

The day – arrived at work excited but anxious at the same time. As we were all on standby and could be called to see the verifier I was apprehensive but in the end had so much work that I blotted this out until we were all called en-bloc to say that we all achieved NVQ Level III in Business Administration.

I came out of that room on a high after all the compliments we received from the verifier for the standards of everyone's work. I must admit I felt extra pleased with my result as I had achieved the equivalent of 2 'A' Levels in just five weeks.

Now I am going to take a well earned rest from studying for a while but having done most of my studying as an adult I do not suppose it will be too long before I take up the pen again.

*(Sylvia Mendham; Mansfield; Business Administration and Customer Service Level III NVQs)*


I went along to enrol at my first lesson, where I encountered a real drawback. A financial one, I would have to pay my own course fees, but would I dare tell my husband how much? I knew for certain he'd think it an extortionate amount for me to cough up out of my meagre wages. However I duly signed the cheque and walking away thought "I must pass after forking that out". My eldest son volunteered a dictionary as his support to me and proffered kindly his library ticket for future use. The tables were turned, whereas I'd always been his mentor, here he was encouraging me. He was probably remembering how often he had turned to me when in difficulty.

Another problem was posed when, after two weeks into the course, my boss announced a change in my hours at work. I was in a quandary, I relied on this income but I'd already committed myself for at the very least every Monday afternoon. I surprised myself by pushing my qualms to one side and announcing that I would not be available during my allocated study afternoon. My assertiveness has paid off so far as I've been granted Monday as my "day off".

*(Female; Carlisle; Access Initiative for Mature Students)*


I joined the English Course in November 1994, I heard about the Course through a friend who at the time was already attending the course at Nine Acres County Primary School … Although I have a young child, it hasn't stopped me from attending the group. I can leave my child on the play bus for the two hours that I attend the course. The play bus charges just 50p and it's worth every penny and my child loves playing on the bus. I can honestly say I enjoy every bit of the English course. The theoretical and the practical work are both rewarding.

*(Theresa Williams; English)*


So in 1990 I went along to one of the open days and I did find the ideal course for me, linking into my hobby. This was the City and Guilds creative studies part 1, which includes design, pattern drafting and garment production.

After passing this part time course, I was allowed the chance, which I couldn't miss, to enrol full time onto the second year of the BTEC National Diploma in fashion design.

In many ways this was similar to my previous course, but a lot more intense, concentrating more on the industrial as opposed to the personal aspect of fashion design. Visual studies, drawing skills, knitwear, computer and business studies and a little French were just some of the many projects to complete and many deadlines to meet. I must admit that there were times I did find a bit difficult, balancing my parental responsibilities with my studies and course work, but I did learn to manage my time quite well. I was the eldest of all the students on the course at the time, but this didn't seem to matter as I got along with them all very well. I was also the only one with two children, and as I had previously arranged with my tutors, I was allowed to arrive at college a half hour late and leave two hours early every day to allow myself time to take and pick up the children from school. So I did have quite a lot of lost time to catch up on at home, plus the homework given. I did also take care of my friend's children after school until she arrived home from work. So you could say that I was extremely busy. I did sometimes have a bit of a problem when I needed to be in college and the children were on holiday from school, but this was solved by Mum and Dad who offered to look after them for me.

*(Tina Robinson; Cheshire; BTEC National Diploma in Fashion)*

**Though many adult learners struggle with the unfamiliar words and concepts which confront them in a new course of learning, people for whom English is not a first language face particular challenges, both in learning how to live in a foreign society and in using the education which might help with that task.**

### Tuesday
Last Tuesday I went to my college. We do some practice about the adjective. We put the word in sentences and we talked about the Language, Accent, Dialect. It was very easy. I enjoyed this class. I like to practice my English more.

### Thursday
Last Thursday I went to learn driving. I went to Leyton area. I learnt driving. When I sit in the car, I put the seat belt on, I check my mirror, I start the car, I give the signal to get the car ready to move. The driving is very hard for me because I can't speak English good. When my teacher talked with me I can't understand her quickly that's why the driving is hard for me. I feel confused on this day.

### Saturday
I'm teaching my children before going to school. My children will be very good. My children can now understand reading, writing and speaking. I know it is hard for me because every day I learnt to them about one hour but I feel happy when I visit The Arabic Teacher. She tell my children were very good.

*(Hanadi Jardali; Tower Hamlets, London; English for Speakers of Other Languages)*

I am currently employed as a community interpreter, so I need to expand my understanding of the terminology used by the health and social services, the Home Office and the housing department. A short trip to Holland made me realise the difficulty and frustration that so many non-English speakers experience in this country, and I do feel for them. We all want to understand and be understood, we all want to communicate with our public and we desire to be heard. Many Sudanese clients who seek interpreting help say they understand well but their tongues feel heavy.

I have always gained enjoyment from writing. Improving my writing skills will make me feel more confident when I expose my hidden feelings, thoughts and ideas. I have never regarded writing as a chore. During my school years, I thrilled in writing the compositions and précis which were part of our curriculum. The more I practise learning the craft, the more I find it pleasurable, satisfying and effective.

I first resorted to writing in my teenage years. It was a means of silently communicating my feelings, particularly the hurts. It helped me to unload tons of burdens. In the past I had always kept my writing under cover, no other creature could access my diary. Recently, I took courage to my side and revealed my hidden face to an adult education tutor from a local community college.

To my surprise she was impressed by my writing and was interested in seeing more. Like my maths teacher, she has offered guidelines and steps to encourage me further. My desk is loaded with dictionaries and encyclopaedias, reading and writing aids which I had never the time nor the opportunity to devour before.

This country is a fertile soil for learning. There is no age limit to ambition, and where there is a will, there is a way. There are unlimited opportunities for adult education and post graduate studies.

The writer with the big vocabulary can write fluently and precisely. A wide vocabulary is essential in creative writing. One can understand other people's ideas and express one's own.

I have learnt to expand my word power by reading more widely and responsively than my medical textbooks. I included in my reading task magazines, newspapers, literature, which I buy from bookstores such as the WH Smiths. I also borrow books every week from libraries. I had a very embarrassing and intimidating experience once because I kept a valuable book worth 40 POUNDS for only one day after it was due back. The librarian threatened to charge me ten pounds for failing to comply with library regulations about which I knew nothing.

Life in Sudan had been simple and flexible whereas here it is rough on our skin. But we must press on. Learning is not without many fears and distastes. When I am confronted with a horrifying situation in this country, it drags me down to earth and I feel that I want to explode at my irritant, for it triggers all the fears of the past. But "patience is a virtue, to learn try it if you can, seldom in a woman, but never in a man" as a nun once told me. Through patience I try hard to be tolerant. As refugees we have to live in two places at the same time. How much of our own culture and past must we abandon and how much of this culture and learning habits are worth imitating?

*(Rosemary Yonathan; Portslade, East Sussex; English)*

***Diarists with disabilities explain how their educational options are sometimes limited by physical barriers and by stereotypes about what people with disabilities can achieve. They emphasise the importance of equal opportunities and show what is possible with appropriate support from educational institutions and other students.***

I am 34, totally deafened for 10 years, partially sighted and have severe arthritis. Having had to abandon ambitions to be a professional musician, I started typewriting classes with Croydon CETS in January 1993. Before then I had done very little for several years. I was lucky to find a fine teacher, the classes went well and gave me a new direction to go in. I first began using computers that September at the Ashburton Centre. I have since taken several exams in Word Processing (WordPerfect 5.1 for DOS) and Computer Literacy (Microsoft Office), and I bought my own computer in September 1994, so I had more experience than others on the course, particularly in Word Processing.

I came on the course because I am now beginning to want a job to make use of the skills I have been learning. I wanted to see if I had any chance. I wanted to increase my knowledge of Word for Windows and Excel, and it was something to do and enjoy, get me out of the house.

As I am totally deaf and not the best of lip readers, the only way of communicating with me was by writing or typing to me. Because of this and my other problems, many special arrangements were made. These included providing a learner support assistant, Florentina, who had recently completed the course, to assist with communication and give me any other help I might need. The computer next to mine was kept free for Florentina to type to me, and the tutors always took the time and trouble to type explanations.

*(Jackie Aggett; Coulsdon, Surrey; Training for Work – Information Technology)*

At the advanced age of 81 I can look back on about 30 years of some degree of learning. I learnt a considerable amount of German from television and radio, and then at local evening classes.

I also took up drawing and painting classes, and, later, pottery.

Unfortunately, about five years ago my eyesight deteriorated, leading to registration as partially sighted, and subsequently as blind.

Painting became quite impossible but ever since then I have persevered to the best of my ability with pottery, with the aid and encouragement of the Royal Forest of Dean College of Further Education.

Since my eyesight began to fail several years ago, my activities, both mental and physical, have been severely curtailed. I live alone and have no family of my own and so have to rely on some degree of help. I have a home help for two odd hours a week and an occasional gardener. I also have three meals-on-wheels each week, but have to cope with all other meals as best I can. Everything I do, of course, takes much longer than it previously did.

I am unable to do many of the things I used to enjoy, such as walking, gardening, sewing and crossword puzzles. I listen to quizzes on radio and television and "read" many

RNIB talking books. I have to have help with form-filling and financial problems, and frequently have difficulty in finding ways of tackling things. However, I am determined not to give in, but to keep on trying.

*(Vera Moon; Drybrook, Forest of Dean; Pottery)*

We are a mixed class, the young students working hard to get to university, but we also have quite a number of adult students, who, like myself are making the effort to increase the quality of their knowledge, at both Advanced and GCSE levels. We are a happy group of students helping each other. The young and adult students go out of their way to help me because of my disabilities, they in turn ferry me to and from college because I am not mobile.

*(Doreen Whitehouse; Dudley; Archaeology)*

A few years ago I joined Anastasia's class, "Yoga for those with a Disability" with a younger friend who was recommended to do so by her Therapist, as she began to suffer from Asthma. Even though my friend recovered sufficiently to attend a more active Yoga class, I stayed on as I found Anastasia's class most beneficial and it is so nice to have such a friendly atmosphere, which is immediately apparent when joining. Undoubtedly all thanks must go to Anastasia who brings this warmth of friendship to the class and the caring approach she displays to everyone.

Anastasia offers during her classes, time for individual tuition, based on the amount of movement each class member has – some younger ones come in wheelchairs and have to be lifted on to the floor and older class members come back after hip or knee operations and improve their mobility. Encouragement is given to everyone and we are inspired by Anastasia to do the best we can with the bodies we have. She is a very active person and we are interested to hear about the Workshops she has attended, whether it is drama, dance, or even laughter as we can all learn something from these sessions.

Last year the class was very thrilled to receive an Award in connection with 'Outstanding Adult Learners' as we were able to say how our progress had been achieved.

I particularly found tremendous support from the class during this past year, as last December I had the sudden shock of my Husband's death – the one thing I did not want to give up was Yoga, as I knew each week I would be amongst friends.

*(Rae Kozary; New Malden, Surrey; Yoga for those with a Disability)*

In the run up to the exam I was feeling very nervous because there seemed to be a lot more material to get through. Out of the seven blocks I studied I had to revise block seven as well as three other blocks. Even though I started my revision in mid August I still felt rushed and because of this I felt the revision was not as effective as it should have been. The exam was on 24 October and although I had done many exams before this was a new experience for me. For a start I took the exam at home and second I was dictating my answers to someone. Once the exam got underway I felt very relaxed. I managed to write an essay for each answer, but I will have to wait until my exam results come through to see how I have done.

Apart from getting an education I have also gained confidence in myself, which I think has helped me become a better person. As far as the future is concerned I do not like to think too far ahead. I just take my studies one step at a time. However, one thing I do know is I do not want my studying to go to waste. I want to use it to help others and in a way I suppose I am already doing this by just studying, because myself and others like me are helping to change stereotypes about what people with disabilities can achieve.

*(Lorraine Hayward; Widnes; Open University Social Sciences)*

**Other people's stereotypes can be one of the greatest challenges for prospective adult learners, who may need to overcome the perception that, for example, they are too old or too stupid to learn, or that education is for other people.**

We were all talking about the adult basic workshop at Bournville College. We all came to the conclusion that most of us are drop outs of the early days of our education. People think we are stupid, we are brighter than that. We had to get through the system by hiding that we had difficulty with our education.

*(Doreen Stowe; Birmingham; Moving On)*

Today has been a very exciting but nerve-racking day. I had to have a test called the Bangor Test, it's supposed to find out if I'm dyslexic. I was really frightened about it, I couldn't stop shaking. I wanted them to tell me that I am dyslexic.

Jane did the test, when she had finished she said the words I wanted to hear. Some people might not understand why I'm so pleased to know I have dyslexia, but it's easy to explain, having dyslexia means I have an explanation, I'm not just stupid.

*(Debbie Brooke; Peterlee, County Durham; Adult Basic Education)*

I express to a fellow student fears that at my age I should be standing down to allow younger students a place as I believe there is a waiting list. She is encouraging in her immediate defence of my place in class. "Goodness me, don't even think of it, you are of great historical value"!!

*(Pauline Henderson, aged 72; Cheltenham; Creative Writing)*

*As the following diary extracts show, some people find it difficult to afford the expense of adult education, while others struggle to get to educational venues from homes in rural or isolated areas. Government and institutional policies can help – or hinder – efforts to overcome the barriers of cost and distance.*

My name is Eliane and I am 55. I joined the adult education when I lost my job due to ill health. I have always been interested in art; it was my best subject in school, but many things in life do not always permit you to pursue what you like best. And I fill those few hours a week, when suddenly you've got vacant time and you rediscover that you've got a place in your life for those skills, with courses that adults like me – and older – could afford to attend. I love to see people of all ages with different backgrounds happy to learn to do beautiful things. I will be very sad if they (government/council) stop funding these projects.

I have learned pewterwork modelling and now enamelling. I enjoy meeting people who have similar interests, and also doing something in my own space, keeping your mind alive. It is important to keep craft alive in a world so mechanised, to see old and young getting interested again, to be creative.

I would like to learn more, but sadly money, or the lack of it, is often a stumbling block.

*(Eliane Boyet; Croydon; Enamelling)*

In Norwich we are fortunate in having a splendid college of further education called Wensum Lodge. For three years running I attended Summer Schools there, 1991, 92 and 93 – two on painting and one on marbling.

Also enjoyed courses on "Psychology and You" at Wensum Lodge and Attleborough High School.

Now that my friend has no car, getting to Norwich is a problem, the buses seldom fit in with times of classes. Also adds to costs.

*(Rebecca Hilton; Norfolk; Women's Institute and various courses)*

Up at a reasonable hour to go to the airport to meet fellow students from Jersey, who have flown over for a Saturday morning tutorial. Only two have come over due to costs of flying and time constraints but it's nice to meet up again and compare notes. In the car on the way to the study centre we find out how far ahead or behind we are. It's comforting to realise we are not out on a limb but others are going through the intense bouts of concentrated work necessary for degree level study.

The day ends with a journey to the airport, with promises to keep in touch over the coming year. As a distance learner it can feel lonely, studying on your own day after day. It's important to meet fellow students for feedback, moral support and just to feel no one is alone. The tutorial provides all of this support and spurs us on to continue the work.

*(Sarah Guilbert; Guernsey; Open University Introduction to Psychology)*

Received Guide to Courses from National Extension College. Have decided to do their Creative Writing package. Although I would have liked to do the Health and Social Welfare, it cost almost £500, far too expensive for me. It would have been different if I were just starting out in my working life.

*(Lesley Barber; Wells, Somerset; Creative Writing and Bible Study)*

Financially, I found things a bit difficult at times, but there again I do anyway, as the children are always in constant need of something, and I'm only in receipt of income support benefit. But I was lucky enough to find a sponsor for my final collection, which otherwise I am sure could have cost me a total fortune, as I was in need of 16 metres of velvet fabric. So I must thank Drivers Fabrics of Stalybridge for this. Also, due to my personal circumstances of being a lone parent I was fortunate enough to have my educational fees paid for me by the education department, and I did also receive a grant from Tameside College, all of which I will always be grateful for.

*(Tina Robinson; Cheshire; BTEC National Diploma in Fashion)*

*As well as directly affecting adult students through fee levels, policy and funding pressures influence how well an institution can offer educational opportunities for adults. A 'week in the life of a tutor' of English for Speakers of Other Languages (ESOL) evokes the challenges from an adult educator's point of view, and their impact on adult students. The diary of a member of the University of the Third Age notes that current education policy is driving some people away from institutional adult education.*

### Monday 4 December

The demands of last week – an ESOL Presentation of Awards Ceremony to co-ordinate and a very frustrating day doing pre-Inspection 'consultation' exercise – left me listless and down with a virus.

I set a task for the students, that I felt they could manage independently, which was based on our normal Monday activity – NEWS – use the papers, radio and TV to see what has been happening nationally (Princess Diana) and internationally (the strikes in France).

### Tuesday 5 December

Asked the Head of ESOL to get the students to finish off a reader we've been using and answer the questions at the back of it. Not what I'd have done with them, but the best I could come up with, given the circumstances. It's always difficult to find things for our ESOL students to do on their own – cover is a rare luxury. Adult women have usually had to put all their energies and management skills into operation just to get to class – no cover always means letting them down.

## Wednesday 6 December

Returned to college to find the usual packed post tray.

Numbers had dropped to 6 (I usually get about 15 adult women students). We are under pressure to keep up attendance figures, so absence sends the attendance figures plummeting down and the guilt feelings plummeting up.

The students were relieved to see me back. We spent a pleasant two hours doing spelling work – I am trying to build up confidence by working on spelling patterns and a strategy for practising spellings; playing a game which reinforces the different soundings of -ed endings in the past tense. I think the students enjoyed that and it did seem to focus them on the different pronunciation patterns. We ended with a look at a few snippets I'd put together from the papers of Monday and Tuesday about Princess Di and her late-night visits to hospital patients, and the French strikes and their context. We discussed the importance of strikes and opposition and Diana's need for a new role. The students said that they'd found my presentation of the papers' contents useful and it had helped them understand it better. I hope so.

## Thursday 7 December

We've swapped rooms with another teacher on Thursdays (he needed better access for a disabled student on that day), so it's up to the cold roof-top classroom, tottering up a rickety set of wet and icy wooden stairs. The students don't much like going up there – they get cold and wet but recognised the need to make the swap. It took a while for the students to settle down to choosing spellings for their LOOK-COVER-CHECK sheets. Then, as part of our work on language histories, we discussed the role of mother tongue teaching in schools. Most students thought it was essential to provide it for their children – on a practical and a socio-cultural level. One student raised the point that more British people involved in the 'caring' professions should make the effort to learn their languages. I felt an abysmal, personal failure – speaking only one or two words of Bengali and nothing of the other students' languages. I have been offered the chance to be taught one word of Bengali per lesson by the Bangladeshi students… should I avail myself of this golden opportunity?

## Friday 8 December

The tutor of another group has had the day off to get married, my boss is going to cover the class from 11.00 so I have to dart between two classes for the first half hour. Luckily my students settle down to their spelling work and a worksheet on prepositions of time easily and quickly. We re-cap the story we have been reading and I go over some essential vocab – character, plot etc., and then the students settle down again to do a review of the book. They want to borrow the book over the weekend to finish the work. I agree, despite the fact that the books are really meant for classroom use only. I am thankful that we have come to the end of the week and that next week is the last week of term. I am looking forward to a holiday but not looking forward to returning to a term that will be full to bursting point with Inspection-hype.

*(Marilyn Hayward; Tower Hamlets, London;*
*English for Speakers of Other Languages tutor)*

Another morning sorting books left me very tired, so I was glad to go to my poetry group meeting and have a pleasant afternoon sitting down in comfort. This is a group run under the U3A, one of the best ideas anyone ever had. The University of the Third Age is for people over 50 who wish to learn from each other. There is a wealth of talent and knowledge about and one could be at classes every day if one had nothing else to do. I go to two – poetry, monthly and creative writing, fortnightly.

There are, naturally, more orthodox courses in Norwich, run by the council, the WEA and the University. But these are very expensive. Also, now that we are retired, once a week comes round too quickly and we like more time to go out and about. There is also an ominous new tendency in official courses, to lead to qualifications. Classes which do not are under threat and this is the most appalling thing which could happen to adult education. There are no jobs to be had, so what is the point of these qualifications? Let people learn for the sheer fun of it! That is true education, and the country needs educated people, those whose motives for learning are not just mercenary!!

*(Mary McLean; Norwich; Poetry and Creative Writing)*

# LEARNING EXPERIENCES

*Many of the diaries evoke in vivid detail the experience of being an adult learner; what people like and what they don't like about adult education; how we learn; the nature of independent learning or the value of the group and its tutor or facilitator; and how adults <u>feel</u> about learning and education.*

*Much adult learning happens outside of formal education, in the process of everyday social life. The following extracts describe such 'serendipitous' learning. They also refer to cultural resources such as the radio, local libraries or clubs and societies, which people use for independent learning. Sometimes serendipitous or independent learning is inspired by – or is a catalyst for – participation in formal education classes, and the extent and diversity of any one adult's learning can be quite remarkable.*

### Sunday 28 October

We invited Grampa's sister Posie to lunch today – had turkey and all the trimmings. When she went home, my brother-in-law insisted she take a large quantity of yellow pear-shaped fruit which were lying in the front lawn. I had never seen these before, and didn't know how they should be used. Apparently they are quinces, a relative of the pear family but rather dry and tough and not to be eaten raw. They should be sliced thinly and used with apples in pie, or else used to make marmalade. They smell lovely – a sort of mixture of lemon and pear.

### Tuesday 30 October

Went to a pub quiz with my family and a friend from Australia tonight. I learned all sorts of things – that Australian rules football has 18 players. We got that wrong despite having an Australian on our team. I learned that Claudius was poisoned by his wife Agrippina; that Bacchus' counterpoint in ancient mythology is Dionysius and that there are 16 quartos in a ream. I was pleased that some of the questions asked I could actually answer, but it was very revealing how much more most of the others in the room knew. Our team had 4 people with degrees – 2 with PhDs and a combined teaching experience of 85 years. But we came 7th out of 8 teams – most of the members of which had probably not been to college. I also learned how easy it is to forget again things you learn that you aren't particularly interested in.

*(Jean Day; Stockport; Bridge Tutor)*

I left school in July 1939, having learnt to enjoy history, art, English Lit, cookery, needlework and tennis.

I think we were taught very badly at Maths, I never really got the hang of it, but when my younger daughter was working for 11 plus, I bought a book called *Teach Yourself Maths*, and learnt more from it than in all my years at school.

I had acquired a taste for learning, an inquisitive mind, which I've never lost. Mother and I went to the Chain Library in Aylesbury, I remember her reading a novel by Ethel M. Dell to me when I had German measles, at the age of eleven, and was not allowed to read – I think she did a lot of skipping, and another by Warwick Deeping.

I developed a catholic taste in books, my father was a farmer, in the difficult thirties, Mother took lodgers to help to pay the rent and to send my brother and I to a good school. One such man worked in the County Offices, he was with us when Penguin started, he bought some, I read his when he was away at weekends, and when I had sixpence to spare I would buy one. When he left some hardbacks were discarded, including a book that I read so many times, *Death Comes to the Archbishop*, by Willa Cather – years later, I discovered the rest of her wonderful novels, and bought them one by one.

Very stupidly, I married too young, to a farmer, who despised learning, due sadly to the fact that he was not allowed to use the scholarship that he had won to Thame Grammar School, as he was needed on the farm. So he did not read, apart from farm journals.

At first, I subscribed to the Times book club which was in Elliston and Cavells shop in Oxford, the books went to and fro by bus, in a special bag.

In the early fifties, Thame found itself with a lovely new Public Library, the joy of my life, and I now I live less than five minutes walk from Attleborough Library, my lifeline.

I have always said that I was educated by the radio, mainly the old Home Service. When I lived near Buckingham, I went to WEA courses on English Lit and History, later in Aylesbury to Art classes and Woodwork. I have a very sturdy coffee table, of my own design, to prove it.

In 1968, I met and later we were married, John Buxton Hilton. I, at last, had found a soul mate, he had been a headmaster, was then an HMI, and was just about to publish his second suspense novel, and through the Crime Writers Association we met many writers. Though not my favourite form of fiction, I admired them for their dedication and very hard work, writing is a lonely profession. And when John had to retire early from the Inspectorate, for reasons of ill health, we moved to Norfolk, he became a tutor for the Open University. His subjects were French and German, he had little knowledge of 19th Century English Novels. That was remedied when he had to teach the subject for the OU. I had read most of the Classics, it was rewarding to see him getting so much pleasure from them.

John died in 1986, I had so much mental stimulation from him, so I did not need to go to classes, apart from one – metalwork, at Attleborough High School. I was the only woman taking the course, with nine men and four boys, when I asked for a reduction for being over 60 they said – No – but full marks for initiative!

I have been a member of the W.I., on and off, ever since I was sixteen, the movement teaches women to value themselves, as individuals, and as one of a group, to improve the lives of women all over the world.

As a committee member, secretary, president, I became more confident, able to get to my feet and speak in public at a moment's notice.

I have been to Denman College three times, on a painting course, Cordon-Bleu cooking and croquet, while on a special Norfolk Federation visit in July 1994. I have booked for November 1996 for Antiques and Family Heirlooms.

For about fifteen years I have been writing for Mass Observation, about three directives each year, we have to write mainly from our own experiences of life. I suppose it could be called Social Anthropology, I find it both amusing and satisfying that my descriptions of life in the past, and as I live now, can be used for research now and in the future.

*(Rebecca Hilton; Norfolk; Women's Institute)*

### Tuesday
This evening during English class, we were discussing where our names originated. Yeshwant was telling us how in India their names had to start with a certain letter for each star sign. All the names also mean something. When a baby is born, that child has his astral sign read for his future life.

### Wednesday
Dance class was a laugh tonight. We learnt four new dances but doing "Walkin' Wazi" my feet didn't seem to belong to me. They were everywhere except the right place. It was more complicated than some of the other dances we have learnt over the weeks.

### Thursday
At keep fit we had two new members. Both were men. All us girls know the routine, so we had to laugh at the men trying to keep up with us but I do applaud them for wanting to learn.

### Friday
I've started to decorate my son's bedroom. My husband always did the decorating but since we went our separate ways, I am now learning how to decorate with my son's help.

### Saturday
Had a rest day. I think I've done enough learning for this week. I do know, really, that we are always learning even if we don't realise we are.

### Sunday
Had eighteen people from the office round for a fondue evening. I have never cooked a fondue, so Paul, a colleague, said that as he hadn't either, we would learn together. We think we did a good job. Everyone enjoyed the evening so I think we can say it was a success.

### Monday
Was going to catch up with any outstanding homework but I seem to have misplaced a sheet of sentences I needed to do. I don't think it would have been much of a problem. I seem to cope with these sorts of questions. It's Tuesday tomorrow, so I'm off to class. It's becoming more enjoyable now. The class isn't too large but I think it's big enough. If it was larger, I don't know if we would have got on and learnt as much as we have. One thing for me, it has made reading different. I love reading but after talking about authors and the way they write and the words they use, I appreciate reading more.

*(Barbara Evans; Crawley; English, Dance and Keep Fit)*


### Thursday 25 January 1996
My car radio is tuned to Radio France in I believe the mistaken hope that by leaving it on I shall subliminally absorb the language. It does help with pronunciation but my lack of comprehension is a problem. One of my favourite programmes is a quiz that I occasionally catch at lunch times. I get a real buzz if I ever understand a question or an answer. In the event of a correct reply the quizmaster never fails to bellow 'Bien Sur' – marvellous.

Sophie is having tests every day at school. The results will determine which class she will be 'streamed' in next year. As usual I am summoned to talk to her while she has her evening bath. She has always wanted someone to talk to her from around the age of five – but I wonder how much longer this will go on. Anyway, tonight I lie on the floor and listen to her day. This afternoon she was videoed talking to a classmate in French. They had to ask each other personal information questions – names, birthdays etc. It was something she had practised and she was quite confident, but she said that the camera made them both babble too fast. I sympathised with her. At Christmas I did a similar exercise into a tape recorder with Pamela and dreaded ever having to hear it played back.

### Monday 20 January 1996

Sophie has stayed late at school rehearsing the part of a bored waitress in the school play, Bugsey Malone. She has lines to deliver in a thick Bronx accent and she practises them incessantly. As we drive back she tells me of her test results. In the three different French tests she has scored 81 out of 85. I would like to keep going with French to be on her level. It has been fun helping her practice for her oral test and her accent is considerably better than mine.

### Sunday 28 January 1996

It is hard to take time out of the weekend to study. Although I only started in September after many years of thinking I should make an effort to learn the language, I feel I am committed. It is easy to say it's too late, and at my age it is much harder to retain information but I have decided I will keep going to the end of the summer, and if I pass the tests go on to another year and try for the French 'O' Level I never took in 1963.

*(John Brown; Brighton; French)*


### Wednesday 7 June

Studying in the morning today.

2 p.m. Sat in on a Carers' Support Group meeting in the village. Felt a bit of an intruder because carers often have enormous problems, especially in rural areas, and they are diffident about sharing their concerns. The social worker who runs the group is often able to offer help and advice, and talking about problems eases the burden, so the group appreciate their monthly session together.

7.30 p.m. Committee meeting of a new WI – interesting because none of the committee has been a WI member before, so this is definitely a learning experience, although the President has been involved with other committee work previously. The women are looking for opportunities to make friends and learn new skills – to have time for themselves rather than just be involved with their work and families. Most of them have full time jobs, but they live in an urban area where neighbour contact is not easy.

### Thursday 8 June

1.30 p.m. Decorative and Fine Arts Society – time for a bit of culture. We meet monthly and usually have excellent speakers on a range of topics – today on Gillow – furniture maker.

Had a TV programme to watch this week – taped earlier (thank goodness for the video – although my programmes this year have been at 7.30 a.m. on Sundays, not too uncivilised). The programme was entitled "Zimbabwe – Health for All", looking at the way in which Zimbabwe's health care system has developed since independence in 1980.

### Saturday 10 June

OU Tutorial at Liverpool University – 2 hours, not very inspiring. I had hoped that tutorials this year would be an opportunity to discuss up to date developments in health care and disease – e.g. the spread of AIDS and the resurgence of TB and the dilemmas of NHS management. However, tutorials have been used simply to recap on the month's work and to give tips on answering the current Marked Tutor Assignment. Still, it's worth trying to attend because it is an opportunity to meet the tutor and some of the other students.

*(Mary Diggle; Cheshire; Open University – Social Sciences degree, Women's Institute and Decorative and Fine Arts Society)*

***Many of the diarists take courses through distance or correspondence education. Some are unable to attend regular meetings, others prefer a mode of learning which they can fit in and around the rest of their lives, and take more at their own pace. As the fifteen year old John Woodward suggests, not only adult learners can benefit from correspondence courses.***

I married a soldier which means I get to live in foreign countries and be part of a very special community; on the other hand it also means that I never seem to live in one place long enough to be able to complete long term projects. For this reason distance learning seemed the ideal option open to me and when the NEC introduced the PPA Diploma in Playgroup Practice it gave me the chance to gain the qualifications required to match my experience working in various playschools.

I am enjoying the return to education and I feel that as an adult learner you have more experience to put into your work. My tutor is a great support although it is sometimes frustrating only communicating by letter. My family, especially my husband, is very patient and encouraging although he is a mature correspondence student himself so appreciates that sometimes it can be difficult to get motivated.

Being a mum with two young children (age 4 and 18 months) studying time in the evenings seems to be pretty scarce (especially after the ironing etc.!!) My course is ideal in the way that you set your own targets for assignments and have a total of three years to complete the whole course. This means that you can work when you are really in the mood to learn and not under daily pressure. I can also put my course on hold completely if necessary for a couple of months – which I did recently while moving.

*(Jacqualine Lamb; Cyprus; PPA Diploma in Playgroup Practice)*

So far I have found my Psychology course interesting and challenging and enjoy it immensely. In many ways studying through a correspondence course has benefited me in ways that college cannot or is limited in doing so.

I am stricter and more disciplined about my study time. I have learnt how to analyse and understand things that I cannot at first understand through my own common sense as a teacher is not at hand to explain it to me. This requires extra concentration and patience.

I am very glad I chose to study Psychology, the course is fascinating, and also the manner in which the course is taught – through post, has also benefited me in ways I didn't think of previously.

*(Emma Pickles; NEC 'A' Level Psychology)*

### Monday

The nice thing about being educated at home is the flexibility. My sister and I did our Latin, French and German over breakfast and elevenses, and took a break halfway through maths to cook lunch. We did a bit of geography and history and then took the dog out before walking up the hill to our music theory teacher, Sue.

### Tuesday

We did some more language work and then moved onto our NEC Physics course. The dining table disappeared under lenses, lamps, prisms and spectra.

Mum cooked lunch while we wrote up our experiments. In the morning's post was my last assignment. On it my tutor had written nigh on a page of close written encouraging and helpful advice, which took me most of my lunch hour to read. They do not mark like this in school. Mum was deeply impressed. She can't afford the time for more than an encouraging word for most of her pupils.

### Wednesday

Mum's whole day off school, and our NEC Biology 'A' Level day. Our LEA Inspector was a bit fazed by me doing 'A' Level two years early and he couldn't cope at all with the idea of my sister following the course four years early. (Can't think why). We made some models of hexoses, amino acids, fatty acids and glycerol and mounted them on card. We take our time with this course. Mum is determined to be a thorough mentor.

### Friday

Liz and I went to Gran and Grandad's house which is a five minute walk. Gran teaches Liz how to ice cakes and Grandad helps me with my NEC GCSE Electronics course. He has a garage full of bits and bobs so we can usually do all sorts of practical work. He is nearly eighty-two but he used to work as an electronics engineer for the MOD, so he knows what he is talking about.

Life as a NEC student is much more interesting and offers a world more choice than school. You can study subjects that interest you, at your own pace and level. Exams can be taken when you are ready but there is no pressure. I don't think the NEC should think of itself as just for adult learners. It can make life easier for anybody.

*(John Woodward, age 15; NEC GCSE and 'A' Level courses.)*

***People who attend regular education classes often emphasise the positive contribution of the group experience. Though joining a new group can be an unnerving initiation, it can also provide camaraderie and support, and inspiration from diverse life experiences. There are, undoubtedly, bad group experiences in adult education classes, though few students have chosen to write about them.***

### Wednesday

Must brush up piece of writing for tonight's class. No time though. Real danger of the tedious routine chores yet again taking over the day. I will make time! Early on is best before the brain gets stultified with life's trivia.

Am sure I'd never have got down to doing this writing business were it not for the class. I'd just have idly dreamed as I have idly dreamed for years that one day I would write. Needless to say, one never does!

### Thursday

Excellent class last night. Despite being thin on the ground the writing produced was amazingly varied. In a group like this, one suddenly sees the endless possibilities – so many subjects to write on and ways to write. I drive home afterwards brimful of ideas and resolve to set more time aside for writing.

### Friday

Read piece from library book on how to write. Obviously some useful tips but rather a cold-blooded and clinical approach. It did not produce the same effect in me as the weekly class. No substitute for meeting other aspiring writers and hearing their work read and helpful comments from them on one's own.

*(Fiona Dale; Peterborough; Creative Writing and Life Drawing)*

Today is Tuesday, the day I attend Craft Class, and it is the highlight of my week. As a mature student, I have attended this class for the last twelve years, and each welcome session affords me ample opportunity for learning new techniques, and furthering an active interest in all that I see going on around me.

At present I am involved in toy-making, and with me are students of varied ages and mixed abilities engrossed in the tasks of making pelmets, bed-heads, quilting, caning chairs, upholstery work, and lamp shades, to name but a few.

There is a tremendous camaraderie amongst the students, and this warmth enhances our enjoyment of each session. There is a lovely sense of relaxation and pride of accomplishment, and, throughout, we never forget the real purpose of our attendance. We observe each other's progress, and are pleased when the projects in hand are completed, and throughout, the expertise of the tutors in charge, is freely and readily given.

I have only one complaint! I wish I had registered with this class, this particular one, many years ago! As a very elderly, mature student ... I can't afford to pass away ... just yet! ... you see – ... I have so many other planned projects in mind!

*(Annetta Owen; Wolverhampton; Craft)*

When I first went to college, I felt very apprehensive with me being a mature student. I didn't feel as if I belonged there with students younger than myself and wondered whether they would accept me being in the workshop, but I should not have worried.

As the days went by I got more confident and at ease with the other students and the tutor soon got me doing the stage 2 City and Guilds Wordpower certificate. As my spelling had improved, the tutor thought I was able to do the course well. I then went on to do the stage 3 course.

Tutors and students alike asked if I would become the student representative for the Open Learning Centre. This made me feel uneasy as I did not know what I was letting myself in for. I was then nominated to be student of the year, I was thrilled to be asked.

## WEDNESDAY:

In the workshop I gave a talk on horoscopes to some of the students. We all try and co-operate together as much as we can. So, when I have a talk to give, or a debate, other students who might be doing the SYOCF or Wordpower might listen to my talk, or report on it. This way, it seems like team work. It helps us all to get along together as well. Sometimes we talk about each other's writings as well as exchange ideas.

When I have finished some work, I was a little stuck, so I asked my tutor if she could give me some ideas as I had to speak about some experience by describing and reflecting upon it but would be acceptable to speak to the students about once I had written it.

We both found it very difficult as not many people have had shattering experiences. Anyway, we decided it would be something which would not upset any of the other students.

## THURSDAY:

I thought I would give a talk about my 2 children going to school and how I felt I was clock watching all the time.

So now I have to talk about the experience which I hope does not put them off having children of their own. I still have a child at school. I gave my talk and the students seemed interested.

## FRIDAY:

Today I had to evaluate a video as the tutors were more busy than usual, so as I had to evaluate a video for my course work, it was possible for me to see the film in the open learning workshop.

*(Angela Mary Atkin; Chesterfield; Wordpower)*

I have been teaching adults now for twelve years, near London and in Cheltenham, and I am constantly amazed by the richness of shared life experiences, and also by the writing talent. This reinforces my idea that anyone who really wants to write can do it – but it is up to the individual. Confidence can be built up by the group and by me, the tutor, but ultimately the commitment, discipline – and the drive to believe in the work and to send it on its way – has to come from the student. I believe that in adult education at its best it is the mix of people who might otherwise not have the opportunity socially to meet each other that gives such variety and richness. I have had in my classes all age groups (from 18 to 80), and all occupations – vicars, ex-policemen, teachers, fighter pilots, housewives, doctors, lawyers, the jobless, single young mothers, reformed prisoners … Computer experts, for some inexplicable reason, often turn out brilliant imaginative writing! And there are moments of sheer magic! An exercise in free writing – 'It was a terrible night for ballooning…' was misheard as 'It was a terrible night for the loony' and produced a marvellous piece of magical realism!

*(Jennie Farley; Cheltenham; Creative Writing Tutor)*

At first I found the lessons unnerving, mainly because I was in a room surrounded by strangers but now this problem has resolved itself. I found it didn't take me long to form new friendships and this has helped me to feel more settled and to realise that I am not the only one with self-doubts and worries about the future. I thought social problems may occur as I was under the impression that I would be doing the course with a bunch of middle-aged bores with whom I would have nothing in common but I couldn't have been more wrong. The students being of mixed ages works well as this means there are a lot of different points of view which can only help make the course more interesting and varied, especially in the discussions we have.

*(Female; Carlisle; Access Initiative for Mature Students)*

How wonderful it is to have found a class in which one can work hard at what one wants to do without having to make too much of an effort socially. I have belonged to Flower Clubs, Embroiderer's Guild, cooking courses, painting lessons etc. and have often found that the social considerations overshadow the original reasons for the class. In fact, students have seemed to be more interested in chatting to each other than in what is being taught or demonstrated.

*(Pauline Henderson; Cheltenham; Creative Writing)*

***Many diarists write about their tutors. They describe how good tutors inspire and guide learning, combining respect for the life experience which adults bring to their studies and positive affirmation for their efforts and achievements as mature students. One diarist, however, explains the negative impact of teachers who treat adult learners like children; indeed she wonders whether their attitude is even suitable for school students.***

Class started with the tutor handing back our first assignment, which she had asked us to hand in for her perusal. She had made a few comments on the each, and there on the bottom of the sheet was that word 'magic'. I am more proud of that word than if I had won an Olympic medal. I sit next to a man who is a bit of a lad, and he happened to glance across and read the comment, and shouted out – look what Doreen's says – but it was all in fun and we had a good natured tussle about it.

Class then commenced in earnest, and we went over the previous chapters and then read on. The characters in the plot are really coming to life, and the atmosphere created by the author. Our tutor has the happy knack of really lightening up the atmosphere, and even the students who aren't really keen on English are enjoying it. The class are really participating and contributing something – there is a real buzz in the classroom.

All too soon the class came to an end and the Course co-ordinator arrived to give us some information. "There is far too much hilarity in this classroom," she commented with a twinkle in her eye. Just goes to show, doesn't it! Really hard grind this Access Course.

One of the most marvellous things to come out of this course, is the wonderful support and encouragement I have had from my daughter, son and daughter-in-law. They are so proud of me just for enrolling. I feel so blessed and fortunate. I do have to put up with a bit of teasing from my husband, but even he has changed his schedule, so that I can have the car to get to class on a Thursday, when there is no bus available! That's real love for you!

*(Doreen Bullock; Cambridgeshire; Access Course)*

## Monday

Of course, we have all been talking, reading and writing since childhood but this tutor of ours leads us down untrodden paths and opens our ears to different nuances of our language and gently nourishes the embryo talent which lies within our group.

It is 9.30 p.m. and I am driving home from Poynton to Bollington. The windscreen wipers beat out a rhythm and my mind struggles to create a poem. The ideas that have been tossed around during the last two hours are simmering and rising to the surface of my consciousness like bubbles in boiling water – a whole choir of words ready to be born, ready to become a line, a stanza. The incessant tune of it all throbs in my ear. Driving the car becomes merely the occupation of a robot. The poem and giving birth to it are all that matter. I'll not sleep tonight unless some sort of order is created and the ink flows unchecked from my biro ready to be transposed on the computer tomorrow.

I park the car and enter a welcoming, cosy but silent room. No partner with willing ears to listen to my creation tonight – slip it into a drawer. It might ripen. He can listen and taste it tomorrow.

## Tuesday

Take out the writing. Handle it with care. Change a word here, a rhyme there. Remember what the tutor said. Give it an airing. Listen to this. What do you think. Yes, this is poetry – it doesn't have to rhyme. We even learned about haiku last night. Now that's beautiful. She's good, our tutor – makes us all feel like real writers.

*(Ann Clowes; Macclesfield; Creative Writing)*

The tutors have as many different personalities as there are days in the month. Most love their subject and are in their prime when teaching – Sue (WP), Mary, the same age as myself but always displaying an enthusiasm for what she teaches. Angela (DTP), always helpful, probably writing some applications for 'Word 8' even before it's published. Dave who crawls around inside computers and Steve, problem solver extraordinaire – each of his fingers acts like a magic wand when it comes to programming. The Reflexology tutor who tries to kid us that using lavender oil is 'as an antiseptic' when maybe it's really because of the odour emanating from thirty bare feet!?!

There are those who obviously are in the teaching profession, or have been, and continue to demand a group of adults to 'pay attention' or 'hurry up' or 'get on with it'. Inevitably we have the tutors who are easily diverted and will happily spend time discussing other topics – from babies to clothes, from cars to politics, from restaurants and theatres to TV programmes, in fact anything to avoid looking at Jack's maths or Jimmy's soldering. Such diversions, planned or otherwise, can give a welcome relief from the heavier subject in hand.

Some tutors disappear during the tea break whilst others mix with (or should I say 'tolerate'?) the students.

Teaching techniques vary, as one would expect in those from all walks of life. There are the tutors who write diagonally on the blackboard; those whose writing demands taking a telescope to the lesson. There are some who religiously mark every piece of work meticulously and those who never bother until a fortnight before the examination. Some will hand out duplicated notes at every lesson and others consider it unnecessary; luckily mine produce some useful informative documents. Some will display brightly coloured charts and diagrams and others trust the students have good imaginations. Many will teach the class as a group whilst a number will flit around the room in an endeavour to give every student individual attention. There are those who give huge amounts of homework and never collect it or collect it and never hand it back, whilst others leave it entirely up to the student or even fail to mention it; fortunately my tutors set work and mark it when deemed desirable.

And dare I say it – those who are always ready in plenty of time and those who dash in at the last moment and demand 'What did I say we would go on to last week?' Yes, I know all about tutors – I was one of them!

No matter! Ultimately they all do their best for the students (otherwise would they have a class next year?) – standards have improved vastly over the last ten to fifteen years – and should there be an end of term get-together, they invariably socialise well with their groups. Long may they continue! Here's to education!

*(Geoff Meeks; Birmingham; Computing and other courses)*


It is so easy to get things out of proportion, which is why I have left it a day or two before writing up the events of Thursday. That day I had a busy time in town and didn't have time to go home to pick up my class things for the lesson at 3 p.m. I tried to explain this to the tutor who demanded to know where my computer etc. was as we had been given instructions to bring them the lesson before. She was very angry, and nearly bit my head off, as the saying goes.

Such intolerance, and the way she spoke to me in front of the other students was very humiliating. "She doesn't really want me there, was going out of her way to make things uncomfortable for me" passed through my mind. She had said in our walk in the park (only the previous day) that she didn't want me to answer questions she asked –

the other students at eighteen were very lazy and didn't want to think for themselves. My speaking up discouraged them. In this situation she was instigating fear through me – i.e. she, at 61 is no different from you at 18. "Well," I thought, "This is an interesting new role, but I don't think it is one I can go along with". With society being in the state it is – too many people and no jobs, the learning society would indeed be a useful one to nurture. But if this is the way to go about it, then it's not going to be popular with many people!

Several of us mature students were talking together and asking each other how we were getting on. I told them I was trying to write about my experiences as a mature student and thought our collective opinion might be useful to voice. The first fact that emerged was that each of us was frightened of being thought subversive or anti-establishment! Perhaps that is how the teachers view us, too. Potential trouble? But this is how our free, western society is supposed to be different from oppressive regimes. As a mature person we are supposed to be able to criticise, open our mouths and it should be a growing point. But the criticism has to be just. Some of the criticism I'd had of my essays, for instance, I felt wasn't just. What I'd been saying implicitly to the teacher on Thursday was "I'm older and I've got other commitments". And what she'd been saying was "Because you're different you irritate me. I'm going to make it so uncomfortable for you that you go away. Authoritarian, heavy-handed ways and frightened people. No wonder the mature students intake is a ticklish situation.

The last point that was raised seemed to create more feeling than any of the others. It was felt that there was NO RESPECT for older people. One chap said, "I cannot believe how much my initial confidence has been battered from me by being so insignificant". "Yes," I thought, "That's how I feel, too". I had achieved 'O' Level English Language and Literature and also 'A' Level and had always written. And yet I'd had a detrimental, derisory comment about my punctuation, in one essay. If a good reason can't be found to knock you, they knock you anyway, it seems. Perhaps knocking style is really a way of saying "We don't like your content". But we don't like to admit it. But the end-product that came across was what this man was saying – battered confidence; I feel insignificant; people do not respect me. It's permissible, is it, to feel this at 18, but not 60?

"We're here because we want to be. We're here voluntarily" is a far cry from most school-children and proclaims that the aims and objectives of mature students are different. One man implied that he'd come to get greater insight into the job he'd been doing and had raised a question relevant to this and was made to feel totally out of place because of it. Obviously another example of the teacher knowing less about the subject than the pupil did. It links up, too, with what I was saying about superficial knowledge. Insight isn't always valued. We wondered whether we were just there to "fill out" course places and create a need for more teachers and more money – in other words, who are we there for – us or them? If the answer is "them", it would explain why, for instance, we haven't been told what the usual difficulties experienced by mature students are so we can avoid these problems.

We wondered if some teachers were as inexperienced at teaching 16–19 year olds as they were at teaching mature students – would the problem be addressed with more importance and understanding? And we agreed that it is more difficult to mould mature students – we are all the sum of our experiences – we are moulded already, so a different basics is needed there. How important is the education of the mature student in comparison to the 16–19 year olds? What is it that the older students are hungry for? If it is pure knowledge, in certain subjects it would be helpful to have a grounding in basic subject terminology. One woman was struggling to do chemistry from scratch where the other pupils in her class all had experience of the subject.

Are we trying to use education to fill some more basic human need – a need to be together in groups and be more loving and creative "to fill the vacuum with stories"? (Joanna Trollope, *A Spanish Lover'*), as well as the more overt reason of better education, better job, more money.

*(Kathleen Ferrelly; Leicester; Computing, Psychology, GCSE Maths)*

After much encouragement from my husband, I began my course in Creative Writing in August. I hoped the course would give me the opportunity to prove that I had the ability to string a few words together although to write well would take more practice.

At school, I had constantly been told that I was not good at English and, was advised not to consider taking further education in any of the English subjects. Always the rebel and, determined to proved people wrong, I ignored all advice and entered for English Language 'O' Level early, passing with a grade B. I then took my English Literature during the following summer and achieved another grade B. It was extremely hard and other subjects, in which I had previously excelled, suffered but I still remember, with great satisfaction, the look on my teacher's face as the results were given.

I have always wanted to write; not for financial gain (although I wouldn't refuse if somebody offered me silly money to write a short story) but for pure enjoyment. I write for myself and rarely show my writing to others. To submit pieces of work to my tutor for criticism was, at first, extremely difficult but my tutor has provided support and encouragement together with criticism, so kindly suggested, I am now prepared to send things in even when I know they are not very good. I have happily submitted first drafts fully aware that they will be scribbled across but not once have I seen the phrase so often in my schoolbooks "must try harder".

I have had no verbal communication with my tutor to date, although his introductory letter said I could telephone him. However, with every assignment I submit I enclose a letter telling him of any problems I have had with a particular section and seeking advice. I find that he always responds; providing useful hints and tips and always with encouragement.

*(Sue Perrin; Eastleigh, Hampshire; NEC Creative Writing)*

Went to my U3A Creative Writing class this afternoon. A new member remarked to the class leader that he should not have to pay a share of the room hire, but he assured us he was not the teacher, but the co-ordinator. He does teach if the need arises but the class is not a systematic teaching of creative writing, merely a chance for us all to practice and learn from each other. The co-ordinator sets the assignments which are intended to spark off a story, poem or other piece. He has asked me to speak soon about the writing of poetry – that will need plenty of thought.

*(Mary McLean; Norwich; Poetry and Creative Writing)*

It has helped me because I can understand things that I couldn't understand before. I feel more confident in everything now and my English teachers are very good. I have never been with kind teachers like them. With them I can learn anything.

*(Harriet Birungi; Croydon; Springboard course)*

**The diaries evoke the processes and pleasures of adult learning, whether it happens during a weekly class or study trip, at a workplace or in everyday social life. They highlight how we actually learn – making new sense or developing new skills – and how that learning spills out into other parts of a life. For these adults, learning can be difficult or revolutionary, but it can also be exciting, stimulating and fun.**

This new venture is revolutionary, I have not studied for many years. My seat of education is becoming quite numb, my television viewing has been cut by over 50% but I can hear it in the background. Everything I read or watch is a major task. I am analysing nearly everything including statements made by my wife. I pick up mistakes made by other people when they write to me. I play better scrabble, at last I don't have to wait to pick out "s" letters.

I feel great even after one course. I know I am going to enjoy this new start.

*(John Heywood; Crawley; English)*

**20.9.95**
**Dear Diary**

I started my English course today. I was a bit apprehensive this morning about attending. I needn't have worried. Everybody was friendly. We all gave a brief talk about ourselves which was extremely interesting. In just a couple of hours I learnt a great deal. I have taken the first step towards my goal today and I feel confident that I will succeed.

**24.10.95**
**Dear Diary**

This morning at my English course we covered sentences. I was amazed at how much I have forgotten from school. For the last ten years or so, I have probably made no sense in any of my letters or written work. Hopefully now I will start making sense. Being in such a small group helps a great deal.

**31.10.95**
**Dear Diary**

Today, I have started yet another course. I decided that as I am coping quite well with English that I should go on to Maths as well. I am really pleased that I did. My tutor is excellent. He talks through everything and gives out handouts on the work we are covering, which is great for revision. I feel like a new person. In a few years' time I know I will achieve my goal.

## 1.11.95
## Dear Diary

We have been studying reading and appreciation today. Looking into a writer's thoughts and ideas by reading their work. I haven't ever really noticed different styles of writing before. This exercise today has made me more aware and I'm sure in future I will study other people's work more intently.

*(Claire Britton; Crawley; English and Maths)*


After a good night's sleep we awoke to the sight of the coastline. We managed a hurried breakfast before we finally docked at Hull. Then it was back on the coach and our return to Park Lane College at Leeds. It was Sunday morning and there was hardly any one about, we called a taxi to take us home. The end of a wonderful, fantastic, cultural, informative, busy, lively, enjoyable journey which I will never forget. Even if I had a choice I would still love to visit these places again, there is so much beauty within these cities. Their culture is more of religion and heritage than commercialisation. They are a warm and friendly people who could teach us many things.

*(Joan Chadwick; Leeds; Women into Work – study trip)*


## My Diary Day

On Thursday morning I get up at 8.00 a.m. get ready for college and have my breakfast. I prepare my flask of tea and take my packed lunch out of the fridge. I leave home at 9.00 a.m. and walk to college on my own. When I get to college, I meet the other students who are on the same course as me, in the canteen. At 9.30 a.m. we all go to our classroom. The course I am taking is French. My tutor's name is Barbara. I have learnt several so far:

    Bonjour monsieur – Hallo
    Café             – Coffee

At 12.00 midday, I leave the college and walk with my friend Alf to the Delos Centre and have my lunch. Afterwards we have a craft lesson. So far I have made a leather belt to keep my money in.

I get paid my wages at the end of the day. At the moment, I am saving up to go on holiday to Butlins with some friends and care workers. We have tea at home about 6.00 p.m. and help wash up afterwards. I watch Eastenders and The Bill. I then make some supper for myself, wash up and then get ready for bed. I go to bed around 10.30 p.m. really exhausted.

*(Eric Ratherwood; Wellingborough; Confidence and Assertiveness, French)*


On Monday I went to my English class. Our teacher Marilyn didn't come to the college because she was sick. Another teacher Kate came to our class and she gave us work writing three paragraphs about personal news, national news and international news.

She had another class. When she left our class, then we started song. We were all singing, Shahida also singing Urdu. We did fun just enjoyed our self. It was really fantastic time. We also worried for Marilyn because she was sick. We didn't know how she feeling. I said to God "Oh God you make feel her better". I hope she feel better and she will come to the college …

At home, my neighbours came to my home. They want to learn embroidery. Now I teach them and they are learning to do embroidery. They didn't pay me any money, they are learning free.

I'm happy about it. But in the future if I do teach it, I think I will charge for it. Because I need money …

I went to the college. English class was not that day because that day was our LOCF ceremony. So we were all going to the Theatre. College Principal and teachers gave us our certificate. After that some students said some things about college teachers and classes. And two people read poem that they wrote. Then Somali people started Somali music. It was interesting. I couldn't understand but I did enjoy it, it was really fantastic. Finally I sang a Bengali song and Anju also sang. Before music we drink and ate some food. Myself really enjoyed it a lot that time. My teacher Marilyn dressed up nicely. She looked wonderful. Marilyn gave me flower. It was really nice.

*(Shamima Aktar; Tower Hamlets, London; English for Speakers of Other Languages)*

## What I got out of the diary experience

Although it was time consuming, I think it has demonstrated to me what I have intuitively known (and preach almost every day in my role at work) but often don't formally record for myself – that every day brings potential for learning in every aspect of one's life, both in and out of work. This potential may not be realised, however, without conscious effort to capture the learning, often through putting time aside for reflection. I see myself as fortunate in this respect, in that the nature of my job is such that it is important that I do focus constantly on remaining up-to-date and open to new thinking and experiences.

The learning I have experienced, however, has, more often or not, been unstructured and unplanned; as likely to arise from a chance conversation as from work on a traditional educational course. Having said that, going back to formal education this year to do an MSc at Birkbeck College has provided a new dimension to the scope of learning, by getting me to:

a) read academic articles each week and so open my mind to new knowledge
b) take a new perspective on my experiences at work, past and present, and re-consider how I evaluate the impact of what I do
c) discuss what is being learned with others on my course

In this respect, despite a gap of 13 years from formal education, I have come to recognise that its value is not yet redundant, even at my advanced age! (34)

## Sunday 22 October

Read "People management" re articles on 'Business Process Re-engineering' and 'Organisational renewal'. The latter was interesting for its focus on the link between people and organisational structure – fast response, less bureaucracy etc. This had links to issues I had recently covered on my MSc course.

Later I joined my department's bi-annual Management conference – this one focused on our Business Plan for next year. Largely lecture update prior to dinner. Main messages related to the future of the business – interesting again as the issue of structure and responsiveness to change came up as a feature along with the issues of values. I reflected that I would have liked to have weaved more of this into my MD Framework had I known about the work that had been done. This therefore proved again the value of keeping abreast of what others are doing before getting too stuck in on your own work.

I had some interesting discussions over dinner re Scottish roots, local history and the education system, which had its moments – the nature of conversations with strangers being that you never know exactly where it may lead; sometimes nowhere and sometimes to some surprising stories. The after dinner "games" I didn't enjoy so much – group 'Pictionary'. I think I learned that I will tend to avoid the "risk" of an embarrassing failure, even though I believed I might be able to do the pictures better myself. Later I re-learned Bar billiards, which I re-discovered to be a not very interesting game!

*(Alistair Cumming; London; MSc, Organisational Behaviour)*

Diaries have been written for hundreds of years, some by famous people e.g. Samuel Pepys. Now I will attempt to write my diary, the easy and difficult times of being a mature student now that I am over sixty. I have experience of life to give me ideas, but usually feel too lazy to write them down. I left school in 1948, computers and wordprocessors unknown, I still lack confidence in using them.

BUT I DO LIKE LEARNING, and I enjoy every minute of the City and Guilds Wordpower course. I can work at my own pace, and the tutors always show an interest in my work. They give me lots of encouragement and help when I need it.

### Tuesday 19 September
Today the new term started for the Cyfle Arall course, and I made a start on Part two City and Guilds Wordpower. I still feel thrilled to bits with having passed Part one, my mind is full of ideas but writing them down so they make sense is the difficult part.

### Thursday 21 September
Went to the class yesterday, have to make the most of every minute because we now get only two hours per lesson instead of three hours. I feel as if I have only just started and it is time to stop. I will have to do more of the work at home.

*(Dorothy Gravell; Gwynedd; Cyfle Arall – Second Chance)*

I travel to France on holiday a lot and I want to learn French so that I can converse properly when I am there.

As an adult I decided to attend evening classes. I find that some nights after a hard day at work it is hard to concentrate on the class. It is also sometimes difficult to fit in quality time to devote to learning during the week.

I enjoy the classes very much but a lot is left to learning in your own time if you really want to progress. I also find that being an older student it takes longer for things to sink in and remember. I have tried writing everything repeatedly and this does help. I enjoy the classes more when we do role plays and actually speak. We have tapes of the course and these are also very helpful but again it is being strict in sitting down and listening to them.

*(Heather Lankshear; Brighton; Beginners French)*


My Pottery class begins at 7.30 p.m. until 9.30 p.m. every Monday at Wensum Lodge. It is the highlight of my week. I can't wait to get there to bring my ideas to life.

Juliet Barnes is our tutor, her outstanding feature, apart from her skill and knowledge, is her crooked index finger, probably formed to the shape it is from too many hours on the potter's wheel!

When I enter the class I already have my evening planned out, what I'm going to make, how to achieve the effect I want etc. Most evenings Juliet will give a talk on many aspects of pottery such as glazing, clay types, different techniques etc.

I must admit that I don't always want to listen, as my brain is on overdrive with ideas wanting to come to life. Quite often I think to myself "Oh hurry up and finish so I can get on". It's not until she has finished that I realise she has given us another valuable insight into the potter's craft.

My first pot that I made took about two weeks to make. I was really pleased with the finished result, until it was fired in the kiln and the bottom fell out. I was devastated to say the least! People in the class usually laugh at me when I arrive because I always bring a template or some cardboard cones etc. to work from.

From these templates I have made a house number plaque and a platform shoe vase. Unfortunately my idea didn't come off this week. I wanted to make a vase. I had made a cardboard cone and I wanted to roll out the clay and then pull it up at the edges, then place it in the cone so it would have a creased effect at the sides. Sadly this idea didn't materialise.

I looked like a demented Italian struggling with a giant pizza, in the end, in temper I tore the cone up and used the clay to make something else.

Never mind, I've got another idea and template ready for next week.

*(Kevin Lange; Norwich; Pottery)*

# ACHIEVEMENTS

*One lesson from the diaries is that adult learners – unlike some politicians – do not make neat distinctions between learning for interest and pleasure, and education for qualification and employment. Very often the learning of adults has multiple and even unexpected outcomes. What does come through many of the diaries is that alongside the achievement of new skills, stimulating ideas or employable qualifications, adult education often instils self-confidence and a sense of new options in life.*

**This first set of extracts highlights the combination of sociability, enjoyment, stimulation and skills which many adults achieve through education.**

On my first day I vividly recall arriving at Class with a horse under my arm … a rocking horse! He was decrepit, frayed and forlorn! He sagged badly in the middle where generations of smiling children had seated themselves and enjoyed thrilling imaginary gallops that ended with them still being stationary, in the same spot! To me, he seemed to be beyond repair, and fit only for a well-earned retirement in a distant equine Valhalla!

The skills I was taught, and acquired when I repaired him were too numerous to mention. I was so proud when I had finished him. He seemed to shine with the lustrous sheen of good health and his eyes flashed with evident pleasure. I was more than happy, it was me who was responsible for his metamorphosis! He was good enough for entry to any Rocking-Horse Grand National!

*(Annetta Owen; Wolverhampton; Craft)*

Hurriedly type up latest piece of writing for the class tonight. I wonder what the others have produced.

My daughters, now at University, are bemused at their mother's classes. I tell them that despite what they may think, their mother is still capable of intellectual growth and that it is not the case that all cerebral activity ceases at twenty-one or thereabouts. I tell them too, and this is absolutely so, that my appetite for learning something new has grown amazingly over the years. They yawn when I add that perhaps education is wasted on the young. That is not true, I know, but neither is it wasted on the not-so-young. I can certainly vouch for the truth of this.

*(Fiona Dale; Peterborough; Creative Writing and Life Drawing)*

I am a very mature student as I shall be 90 next year, but I am still attending and getting enormous pleasure from my studies.

I still work at "Advanced French", for which I received the award of "Outstanding Student of the Year" in 1994. I hope to continue there as long as I am able to take my full part in all our activities.

We are a class of about 24 – all ages and both sexes. We are fortunate in having an excellent teacher, who makes all our work stimulating, interesting, varied and enjoyable. We study French history and literature and contemporary events. Everyone is very friendly and co-operative and the standard is very high.

I have also attended classes in Spanish, Calligraphy and "How to enjoy your Retirement".

I shall never cease to be grateful for all the enjoyment and stimulation Adult Education can provide – even at approaching 90!

*(Margaret Prett: Sutton; French)*

**28.09.95**

I arrived at Coombe Cliff on Thursday 28 September 1995. I came with my Mum who is also starting today in the same class as me. We were both very nervous but were surprised to find a parking space easily. We walked up the stairs to our class and sat together and met all the other people in our group.

Both Mum and I really enjoyed ourselves and can't wait to go back next week.

**18.10.95**

I have settled in my class very well now. I feel more comfortable in asking questions and getting on by myself. Today I did some notes for a story, then wrote it in rough and typed it on the computer. I printed it out and checked it for spelling mistakes and when I had found them all I went back and corrected my mistakes. Then I had a nice story to take home.

**02.11.95**

I get muddled with words that sound similar but have a different spelling so I wrote some sentences using these words. I now know the difference between 'bought' and 'brought'.

Carol told me about the City and Guilds Certificate today. We talked about it and she explained what I would have to do. I am very interested and I am going to work hard towards getting it.

*(Emma; Croydon; Springboard Course)*

**14.11.1995**

I have been attending adult education classes for about three years. I retired from my job 4 years ago, and I wanted to do something worthwhile during the day.

I started as a student in enamelling, which I thoroughly enjoyed. I went on to do other courses – calligraphy, pewterwork. Today I helped another student in class. I support a student under the Integration and Support Scheme. I'm also attending another course at present, cookery, which is fun.

These classes have been very good for me. It's a good way of meeting people, and it's helped my confidence.

**21.11.95**

Cheryl, the student I am supporting, is making a brooch at the moment. Today we ground and washed the enamel, using a mortar and pestle. Cheryl then wet layed the enamel onto the brooch shape, using a quill. It was dried on top of the kiln, and then fired. We will continue using more colour next week and also adding bits of silver.

**5.12.95**

Today is our last lesson this term. Cheryl will be putting her final colours onto her brooch.

I enjoy coming to adult education classes very much. Although this class does not lead to any qualification, I think it is still very important. There are lots of people who are retired, and not unemployed, and I think they need to be considered as well.

I attend classes because I enjoy meeting people, and I think it's important to have outside interests away from home. I have also learnt a lot, and it has got me interested in all sorts of different arts and crafts.

*(Frances Withall; Croydon; Enamelling and Cookery)*


When I first started this course I was terrified to touch a computer for fear of making a fool of myself. My intention was to overcome this hurdle and learn some basic computing skills. After 12 weeks I feel I have achieved much more than I had expected. I have enjoyed most of the course, although I have found it a challenge at times. Many people have been surprised that I have continued, when it has been obvious to them that certain parts of the course have been a struggle. Hardly a week has gone by without me wondering whether to keep going or not, but as the weeks have passed by I have become more determined to stick with it, even when I have felt like screaming. Funnily enough now that the course has finished, I will be quite sorry that it has reached an end. Although I am anxious to do my best for each assignment, at the end of the day, pass or fail I am just pleased to have completed the course, it has been a worthwhile experience and good for my confidence. Now that the course is finished the obvious question I'm left with is:

Where do I go from here?

*(Genevieve Ball; Croydon; Information Technology)*


***'Where do I go from here?' is a common refrain among diarists who enter education to improve their employment prospects, and in doing so discover unexpected abilities and opportunities.***


To some, my achievements may be small, but for me I climbed a mountain and realised an ambition. The problem of redundancy is in a lot of cases not monetary, often the state will look after home and family. It is the feeling of failure, loss of self esteem that's the hard part. If, like me, you are over fifty, the outlook is more bleak, who wants to employ the older person?

There are now opportunities, GO BACK TO COLLEGE. Become a Mature Student, you will enjoy it, you will gain, if nothing else your self esteem will return. Meet people in the same situation as yourself, talk to them, study with them, share experiences. Who knows, you may be as fortunate as me and get a job out of it.

I am pleased that I can help other Mature Students coming into College, at least they can talk to someone who has been through the same problems as they are facing.

*(Stewart Hardie; Dorset; Further and Adult Education Teaching Certificate)*

I have decided to stay at college for a further 12 weeks in order to complete Business Administration Level 3, as I feel this will be advantageous. The course has been good for me, it has made my brain work again after all these years, I have more confidence in myself.

*(Jenny Jerome; Sittingbourne, Kent; Training for Work)*

Despite all the hard work it was worth it. I have enjoyed learning and I now want to do more computer courses. After 12 weeks I have my piece of paper that will say I have passed something.

*(Karen Piesley; Sittingbourne, Kent; Training for Work)*

I have gained full NVQ certification, so it's decision time. After some consideration I feel that I could do with more computer skills before putting them into a job, so I am going to enrol on further computer courses, then, hopefully, with the skills I have acquired on this course and my NVQ I will get a job.

*(Nina Brittain; Sittingbourne, Kent; Training for Work)*

I have decided to stay at college for a further 12 weeks to gain certification in Business Administration Level 3. This course has flung open the doors for me to know I am now capable of moulding a new career for myself. I have been fortunate to be part of a varied group of people (tutors and students) that have given me strength, encouragement and support. There have been parts of the course that have given me nightmares. The course has encouraged me to open my mind, expand my ideas. When I have completed Level 3 I feel this will give me even more valuable experience for my next job.

*(Dawn Inns; Sittingbourne, Kent; Training for Work)*

Even as a child I was illiterate and had to rely on my Mum and Dad. At school I was not very good. My brother was a lot cleverer than me but did nothing with it.

The jobs that I had were all labouring ones because I felt I was not clever enough to do anything else. I could not even fill in time sheets.

Some parts of my life were very rough and that was because I could not cope with not being able to read and write, especially after losing my parents.

I came to Sheffield to live in 1970 and got a job with Spear and Jackson. This was when I met Betty who took me in and has been both landlady and surrogate mother to me. Ken Waller turned my life round for me when he gave me that first job.

After a while they brought in time sheets and I panicked and decided to leave. That was when I admitted that I could not read and write. He found me a place at NACRO and I started to go there until they shut it down. After a couple of tries at other courses I arrived at College.

My life opened up. It was like a picture opening as I tried to do things I had never done before. I learnt Maths and English then I took up cooking which has now changed from a hobby to an obsession almost. I love cooking and watch all the cooking programmes on television as well as the educational ones. I gained an Award from the Sheffield College which was linked to the National Adult Learners' Week. This was presented to me by Joe Scarborough. I consider this to be my greatest achievement.

Since then I have just passed my exam with credit for the City and Guilds Cooks Certificate Course and am now taking the City and Guilds Cooks Professional Course. I am carrying on with a spelling workshop and hope in the future to do NVQ 2 in Catering. I owe my success in learning to Pauline Young and lots of other people at the Sheffield College.

*(James Harkins; Sheffield; Maths, English, and Cooks Professional Course)*

### October 6th

Wrote a CV for myself. I have never written a CV for myself before and I was afraid to do so as I know my Education was a shambles mainly because I never actually completed two years in any one school. As a family we constantly moved as the family increased in size! I was aware also of the number of jobs I have had – so easy through the sixties to 'job-hop'!; interlacing the gaps with as much foreign travel as I could. I feel surprisingly comfortable with what I now see has been my life – I feel it has given me a wide experience of living and people – it has been a good experience for me to have sat and thought about me and to realise I am not the failure I have thought I was.

### October 10th

Tuesday is our day for a lecture – I look forward to this: I find it stimulating and informative: seeing job adverts in ways I have not seen them before!

We looked at two adverts and endeavoured to draft a letter which would accompany our CV when applying for a particular post. At first sight the work looked very involved but as we realised our capabilities – felt it possible to apply. We worked with partners to draft the letter which was another interesting aspect – I would usually prefer to sit and ponder over a work on my own, make my own mistakes by myself! But sharing the task made me feel it is – different yes, but still enjoyable to work with someone else. So now I would feel more confident either way – working alone or with another. Each of us saw 'more' in a statement in an advert than just the words written and this helped us to build a better picture of the employment required. When we eventually shared what we had discovered and written with the other members of the group more and more seemed to come from the advert and gradually a very 'whole' picture of the job advertised emerged. I feel I would now look more 'closely' at advertisements for work and know better what I was applying for. I have learnt now that it is important to address each point made in the advert, whether I feel competent in that 'field' or not, e.g. if I had not actually accomplished one of the tasks asked for I could still mention it saying I am willing to learn. This aids my application if put through the 'grid' system.

*(Frances Gilbert; Information Technology)*

***Some diarists explain that adult education has 'changed my life' or even saved it. Learning has been a key to creating a 'very different person'.***

Monday afternoon is the writing group. This is very rewarding too. I like to think I have beaten those teachers of my youth who said I was a 'no hoper' who would never learn. I think I have achieved more in the last four years than I ever thought possible. The more I learn the more I want to learn.

### Tuesday 5 December 1995

Tuesday morning I usually do my shopping. But in the afternoon, I go to a ladies' group at the adult education centre in Middleton. We do various projects over the year. At the moment we are working with other ladies' groups on something for International Women's week 1996. We are making a very long tent. Each group is working on a panel for the roof. Our piece is wonderful. It starts with the sky then we have a crescent moon in silver and stars, going down to a beautiful sunset and mountains. A river runs down the mountains, we called it the 'river of life'. It is sewn in different materials in what is known as 'appliqué'. This is a relaxing day.

Starting to learn again after so many years changed my life, in some ways saved my life. When I have done some work I think it is very good. It gives me an excited feeling in the pit of my stomach like the feeling I got on Christmas Eve when I was young.

*(Pat Hewitt; Leeds; Word-processing, Writing, Appliqué and Astrology)*

Have now sent away for Open University pack. On Social Health and Welfare. At same time have been in touch with the National Extension College Cambridge. This is about a Creative Writing Course, priced at £165. I must say this appeals to me very much because I love writing. Their address was given to me by someone at Strode College.

Have been busy making pickles and chutney today, plus pickled eggs.

Wrote a very long letter to my former Doctor, who now lives in Lima, South America. He is very interested in what I do now, owing to the fact I'm a very different person these days.

All this just because I have gained so much more confidence since returning to school.

*(Lesley Barber; Wells, Somerset; Creative Writing and Bible Study)*

I knew without a doubt that returning to the working way of life without fulfilling my ambition in education would be a horrendous mistake.

Putting all my pessimism aside for the rest of the time preceding College, I entered my first class with slight apprehension. Succeeding this apprehension though, was an intense pride. I felt like screaming out, 'I've done it', but decided not to do so remembering that here I was in a strange environment, with perhaps, some strange people.

Sociology turned out to be a class of extremely friendly students, and I achieved a glowing feeling of belonging. Leaving College that night I realised that I wasn't just a mother, a daughter, a fiancee and a friend. Today, I had become a student, and the huge feeling of contentment came from knowing that I was studying for myself.

I cannot remember exactly what I did that first night home from college, but I'm certain I must have skipped around the living room whilst I polished.

*(Female; Carlisle College; Access Initiative for Mature Students)*


At long last I've finished my formal letter. Found out I can keep up with the class – I'm not as brain dead as I thought. The list we made about how we felt nervous, apprehensive, lacking confidence etc., seems to be fading. I now feel a lot more confident, and quite excited really. I feel better for coming. The group are very friendly, we have lots of laughs. I like being part of the group.

*(Pauline Peters; Peterlee, County Durham; Adult Basic Education)*


**For some of the diarists, one of the most satisfying outcomes of adult education is that they have developed the skills and confidence to teach others within their families and communities.**


**Monday**

As usual I went to school where I help. While I was listening to the readers, I realised where I was wrong in grammar, specially in commas. Before that I wasn't taking notice. Since I joined the Thomas Bennett I am thinking more about my spellings and grammar.

**Tuesday**

Today I went to the Thomas Bennett at 7 o'clock. We learnt how to use apostrophes. Before this lesson I was not putting them in the right place where they should be. Olive Huston, my tutor, explained it very clearly. We did some exercises just for practice. It was very helpful.

**Wednesday**

I went to Maidenbower, day centre. I am running a very small group of elderly ladies from Pakistan there. While I was teaching numbers to the old ladies, I realised in any age, people can learn. It was good experience for me. It is never too late to learn. The ladies wanted to learn numbers. At least then they could read the prices and dial the telephone numbers.

*(Bilques Khan; Crawley; English)*


I told my children the writer of the book – ERIC CARLE. I read the story of the Hungry Caterpillar to them, and they listened attentively and laughed whenever I demonstrated anything in the story. The story also teaches them the days of the week, category of fruits, colours and the development of the butterfly – from egg – caterpillar – butterfly.

I think the L.T. project has been very helpful in many ways for the parents and the children, because now we know how to teach our children and the desire to do it on daily basis unlike before. The children have developed a lot of Interest in Learning with the help of this course e.g. by bringing home different games and books, leaflets with rhymes, etc., every week.

It reduces the rate of ILLITERACY in the country amongst youngsters.

*(Cynthia Mbah; Swansea; Learning Together Project)*

My young son of 15 years is preparing to sit his mocks at the end of November. He had prepared question sheets for me to test him on. We enjoy this time together. He is able to assess his weak points and make up worksheets covering them. My son, Stephen, appreciates the time I spend with him. He feels that we both develop through learning together. Through entering back into the education system myself, I feel that I have a deeper understanding of the difficulties he is facing at the moment.

*(Anne Kissane; Crawley; English)*

### Saturday 24 June
"You don't need to take us round the Barony Hall, we worshipped here when it was a church and we know it well". So said the middle aged couple. I let them walk round for a time then asked them if they would tell me something of the building when they worshipped there. They were delighted and told me many interesting stories. Before they left I said to them "would you like to see what a good job they made of the restoration of Christ in Majesty" – a painting on a wall in a small side chapel which is hidden from view. They never realised there was such a painting. That's what a Guide is for.

### Tuesday 4 July
A day off from Guiding and a visit to the Strathclyde University Archivist to have a look at the old drawings of the Ramshorn Church – these are the originals by the Architect – Rickman. The drawings were made 100 years before I was born. It makes you proud to be part of a great city like Glasgow and you want to find out more about its history and pass it on.

### What has guiding given to me?
Before entering the Guides I had a known past (of preparation for life and my profession), a known present (consisting of work, bringing up a family and plenty of contact with friends in our mutual interests), but my future was the $3^{rd}$ age – what would it be?

The Guiding and all the learning which is associated with it has broadened my mind. My life is now full of work, bringing up a new family of interested visitors and contacts with new friends in our mutual interests. My future looks busy, no time to sit doing nothing, too many things to find out, and also so many friends to keep me looking forward to the future.

*(David Harvey; Glasgow; $3^{rd}$ Age Volunteer Heritage Guide)*

### 11 April 1995

It's now the Easter holidays and I have to say that I miss my weekly visits to the Learning Project. Every week I feel that I have made a little bit more progress. I no longer panic when my children ask me to help them with their homework or ask me if I know the meaning of a word. I bought them Junior Scrabble and Boggle so that we can play word games as a family. All these things are "normal" to me now and I don't feel embarrassed any more about my lack of basic literacy skills.

### 7 September 1995

I really feel a sense of achievement today. Tonight I attended my first tutor training session and am looking forward to learning the various methods of helping other people with learning difficulties to overcome their problems.

A year ago I would not have thought this possible. I am very pleased at the progress I have made with the Community Learning Project and cannot thank enough all the people who have helped me along the way.

### 30 October 1995

Today I completed the tutor training course and I am looking forward to being matched with my first student. I am very excited at the prospect and am enthusiastic at being able to help somebody else, as I have been helped myself. Having been on the "other side of the fence" I know the feelings of inadequacy and shame which are experienced by people who lack basic literacy skills. It doesn't matter what other skills or qualities you might have you are still viewed by some as being inferior to them. It's a sad fact of life that if you are not able to read, write and count to a certain standard you are socially disadvantaged and are definitely handicapped when it comes to applying for jobs. I hope that as well as having the necessary tutoring skills that my empathy and understanding will help my student feel at ease and a working relationship based on honesty and trust will quickly be established.

*(John Pearson; Glasgow; Basic Literacy and ABE tutor training)*

***On the facing page is a facsimile reproduction of a page from the group diary of students on a Springboard course in South Norwood, London, in which different voices evoke aspects of adult learning.***

# Springboard at South Norwood

## ......extracts from our diaries

I was apprehensive about coming and wondered whether I could cope with the work. Now I really enjoy coming. I learn something new every day and I've made new friends.

Group learning helps me to retain information more. After having some time off sick I still feel able to cope as everyone rallied round to fill me in on what I had missed.

I learnt about formatting and how to use bold, italics and underline.

Everyone encourages each other and we share our ideas.

Subtraction has always been a problem. I actually found out how to do it in one lesson.

I came with the idea that I wouldn't last the day because it would be like school. I was wrong!

Doing the Springboard course has given me more confidence in myself and my ability to communicate verbally and in writing.

I have always wanted to go back to some form of education. What with holding down a full time job, being a mother and wife, the years seemed to fly by. Springboard is a course consisting of English, maths and word processing. Within a moment I had decided that it was the course for me!

...another thing I have found useful is proof reading.....I told my daughter about the method I had learned. She thought this was a good idea and will be doing it this way from now on. I think the things I learn will also help my children.

After the first three days of Springboard I was totally exhausted! I am so pleased I have made the first step and look forward to the rest of the course.

I think doing this course is like being given a second chance.

My son asked his dad how to spell 'situation'. From the kitchen I shouted 'S I T U A T I O N'. My 9 year old said, 'Well done, mum'. I felt ten feet tall!

# Afterward: Working with the Diaries

Though this book is primarily aimed at adults interested in learning, we hope that it will also be used by adult education practitioners. Teachers and organisers in adult education programmes may gain insights from the diaries about the types of educational provision which seem to work well for adults, and about how best to recognise and tackle the many obstacles which get in the way of learners and learning. They should also take heart – at a difficult time within education – from the enthusiasm and commitment to learning expressed by the diarists, and in the evidence that adult education can change people's lives for the better.

Adult education researchers, too, should find much of value in the book and in the larger archive of diaries collected for the project, which NIACE plans to place at the Mass-Observation Archive in the University of Sussex where they will be available for research. This afterward notes some of the ways in which the diaries may be of use to researchers wishing to explore issues about adults' experiences of learning and education in more depth. We also highlight the limitations of the project: what the diaries may not be able to tell us about adult learning and education.

An historian recently commented that 'the present enthusiasm for life histories' among adult education researchers is in danger of 'obscuring the big picture and policy studies with fine, meaningless details' (Fieldhouse, 1996: 119). Our response is that life stories about people's learning – such as the diaries used in this book – are not 'fine, meaningless details', but rather can illuminate the lived experience of the institutions, structures and relationships of education. Personal accounts evoke the myriad, complex motivations for participation in learning; they record the factors which make it difficult for people to participate in and benefit from education, and how these factors change throughout people's lives; they reveal what forms and processes of education work, and sometimes don't work, for men and women; and they show what adults can get out of their learning, for themselves, their families and their communities.

Life stories about educational experiences can be particularly valuable because they situate learning alongside other aspects of people's lives. One person's story, or a set of personal accounts, will reveal the inter-connectedness between significant factors: for example, how learning in our everyday lives may connect with learning on a course; or how the particular opportunities and expectations for women learners may be influenced not only by their gender, but also by age, or economic circumstances, or ethnicity, and so on.

Learners' life stories can also help us to understand the personal significance and impact of particular educational policies or forms of provision. Indeed, the so-called 'big picture' is fine but meaningless without the stories of the lives within the picture. Better understanding of the actual experience of learning can, in turn, provide lessons for the people who develop policies about funding and priorities for adult education. Thus we hope that education policy makers will be another audience for this book, and that the diaries may help them to think about how policies might best serve the complicated situations and needs of diverse adult learners, as well as the demands of economy and state.

Life story projects are particularly useful in relation to relatively powerless social groups – for example, adults with learning difficulties or people for whom English is not a first language. These people's stories are not readily heard, and they may have little influence upon policy and provision which is developed to meet their educational and other needs (assuming that such policies are even considered important). In this sense, the 'Diary of 1000 Adult Learners' project is typical of a wider social and intellectual movement – represented in recent years by oral history groups and community writing projects, by advocacy campaigns or self help groups – which seeks to make such voices heard and influential, and to generate educational opportunities within voluntary groups and through the statutory sector which genuinely connect with people's lives and dreams.

There are problems in using life stories to research and understand adult learning and education. In the list of further readings we cite other writers who have discussed concerns about the reliability and representativeness of individual life stories (see, among others, West, 1996; Thomson, 1994). More specifically, we note here factors which prompted some people but not others to write diaries for NIACE, and which influenced the types of stories which were collected and used in the book.

Within the diaries there are significant silences and emphases about the British experience of adult learning. The NIACE publicity for the 'Diary of 1000 Adult Learners' project did not seek to confine diary writers to any particular types of education or styles of writing; individuals and groups were encouraged to express 'your views and experience ... in your own words, and tell us what is important to you' about learning. Yet the project was explicitly intended to celebrate NIACE's 75th anniversary and the 1996 European Year of Lifelong Learning. This had predictable consequences: people who liked learning, who were excited by its possibilities and pleasures, responded. There are few dissenting or critical voices amongst the diarists.

A NIACE press release was widely circulated in the media and it did reach and inspire a few diarists whose learning happens outside formal education. But most participants heard about the project because they were already on a NIACE mailing list (including people who had won Adult Learners' Week awards), or through the staff at the adult education organisation in which they study. Some institutions encouraged their students to write for the project. Thus we have large numbers of diaries sent in from Macclesfield College, Croydon Adult Education Service, Thomas Bennett Community School in Crawley and Park Lane College in Leeds. Individual tutors also promoted diary writing, especially when it could be usefully integrated within a course curriculum. For example, some Information Technology courses used the diary format as a way of practising new skills, whilst Creative Writing courses explored the imaginative use of the diary form. As part of their coursework, participants on 'Return to Learn' and 'Springboard to Work' courses are often asked to write autobiographically about their steps into and through education, and some of these writings were submitted for the NIACE project.

This is not to suggest that diaries were only received from large institutions. Adult education centres and further education colleges provided the most contributions, but diaries also cover learning in voluntary organisations such as the Women's Institute, the University of the Third Age and the Workers' Educational Association, and through distance learning institutions such as the Open University and National Extension College (including one diary from a fifteen year old taking NEC courses at home as an alternative to school). Apart from the Open University, there were only a couple of diaries from university students, and university continuing education departments are barely represented at all. Given that mature students now make up more than half the numbers in British higher education this is a surprising and significant absence, which may reflect poor dissemination of information about the project within higher education. It may also be that the label of 'adult learner', with its conventional identification with adult education evening classes, is not one which is readily used by university mature students or their institutions. Equally significant is the under-representation among the diarists of men and women who learn at work. Again, it may be that workplace learners and their employers and trainers did not hear about the project, or that they assumed that the project was just for people taking evening classes.

The project elicited fewer than the hoped for 1000 diaries. Including those students who contributed as part of a group diary, approximately 400 adults shared their learning experiences. The regional spread of diarists is uneven. NIACE is the organisation for adult learners in England and Wales only, and so did not set out to recruit diarists in Scotland and Northern Ireland. There are a few Scottish diaries, though none from Northern Ireland. More surprisingly, there are only a handful of diaries from Wales and the Southwest of England. Though adult education participation rates do vary throughout the country (see McGivney, 1990), this geographical imbalance amongst the diaries received may have had as much to do with the publicity and profile of the project in different regions.

The diaries do reflect the higher proportion of women, and particularly older women, in certain types of adult education such as 'liberal' or 'leisure' classes, though other factors may also be relevant here. Seventy per cent of the diarists are women. Seventy per cent of the women who stated their age are over fifty years of age, with twenty per cent over seventy. Of the male diarists who stated their age, slightly more than fifty per cent are over fifty years old, with twenty per cent being seventy years or more. It may be that some older adults have more time or inclination to write about their lives, though the hectic lifestyle of many third age participants is quite astonishing. The small number of diaries which focus on workplace learning helps to explain the under representation of men, and of younger adults. Furthermore, the evidence of other writing projects suggests that women are more likely than men to be comfortable with diary writing and similar types of autobiographical narrative.

The perceived need to use the written form may also partly explain the under representation of adults whose first language is not English, and of adults with learning disabilities. Yet the written form did not silence Adult Basic Education students, who wrote some of the most moving diaries. Clearly, they were motivated to write about how the acquisition of literacy skills had transformed their lives.

At a more individual level, the diarists themselves offer evidence about why and how they wrote. Sylvia Mendham from Mansfield, who had volunteered to coordinate a diary writing project with a group undertaking customer care training, records her 'struggle to get everyone's diary entries ... I have religiously done my own entries each month but have found getting other people to commit themselves to this task is extremely hard'. A man on a General English course explains why he had missed out a four week block in his diary: 'Having never kept a diary, because I feel it is incriminating and time consuming, I have just not bothered'. A woman taking several courses at a Leeds college agreed that it had been difficult to keep a regular diary, but also came to see that the process of autobiographical reflection made a valuable contribution to learning on the course and through everyday life:

*The month has ended and so has this diary. There was a point where keeping it was a hassle, another task to do and a deadline to meet. Reading it back though I realise that it is a useful thing to do. Time goes so fast and there is so much going on in my life that there is often not enough time to assimilate things. Keeping a diary helped me to keep track and think about the things that I am learning. It is something I might consider doing again at some point.*

In a similar vein Joy Tomkins, who was doing a Spinning course in St Albans, writes that 'now the table is cleared I will be more inclined to work at it':

*That will include typing this diary to send off to NIACE. I have much appreciated this challenge, or perhaps encouragement would be a better word, to take a look at how I dispose my time. I wonder if it has played a part in my getting some of the chaos tidied up. I certainly feel more relaxed at the moment.*

Project contributors interpreted their task as diarists – and the nature of a 'diary' – in different ways. Some diarists wrote a single narrative while others recorded their experiences day by day. Few diaries are a record of one complete week; many explore periods of particular learning such as a course or a summer school. Others draw on the experience of both childhood and adult life to make sense of and to frame their learning experiences. Some are written by individuals, others by groups who put their separate stories together or, in a few cases, who wrote a collective diary about a shared learning experience. Most of the diaries are written – by hand, typewriter or word processor – though many include illustrations and are lovingly presented, and a few, mainly from art classes, offer a visual account of learning.

'Learning' is also interpreted in different ways by the writers. Some define it as what happens on a structured course, but many people also record the learning that they achieve by the very fact of being alive. Thus, people write not only of their evening class or distance learning course, but also of books, television, arts festivals, family events and holidays.

In editing the diaries for publication we have sought to counteract some of the more obvious imbalances in the set of diaries. For example, we endeavoured to include diaries and extracts from all over Britain, including the less well represented regions, and some which recorded under-represented aspects of adult education such as learning at work. For Part A we tended to choose diaries which situated learning experiences within the rest of a life, rather than those which just recorded the details of a particular course.

The selection was also, inevitably, influenced by our own ideas about what is significant in the experience of adult learners, in part based upon our backgrounds in community and university education, and from sharing the story of many diarists who juggle competing demands of work, family and lifelong learning. The diaries both confirmed and surprised some of our preconceptions. We also wanted to make a book which would appeal to readers. Though we have certainly made selections which we think will engage the reader because of the way they are written or presented, above all we have chosen diaries and extracts which depict diverse experiences of learning, and which explore learning experiences in depth and with insight.

As we explain in the introduction, the structure of the book is intended to allow readers to follow the learning experiences of individual diarists in some detail, and then to embark on a more thematic reading of extracts which evoke issues about adult learning. After we had selected the full diaries and extracts we wanted to use in the book, we wrote to their authors for permission to publish. This was forthcoming in all cases, except for a few diarists whom we were unable to trace. In these cases where we were unable to obtain written consent we have still used extracts, working on the assumption that by submitting a diary to NIACE the author intended it to be used for publication. Arrangements have also been made to secure permission from the diarists for their writing to be lodged in an archive and made available to researchers.

We have kept our editing of the diaries to a bare minimum, correcting typographical errors and occasional spelling mistakes. Facsimile pages and colour copies are, of course, unchanged. We have tried not to alter the meaning of any extract by using it out of context.

Reading and editing the diaries was never an arduous task. It was a privilege and a pleasure to work with life stories that were brimming with interest and emotion, which taught us so much about adult learning, and which were written with humour, care and passion.

*Pam Coare and Alistair Thomson*

**NIACE will be collecting more diaries by adult learners and if you would like to be part of the project, or know someone else who might be interested, then contact NIACE at 21 De Montfort St, Leicester, LE1 7GE, phone 0116-255 1451. Researchers who would like to look at the diaries should also contact NIACE. The following publications offer further ideas about the life stories of adult learners and how they can be used by adult education researchers, practitioners and policy makers.**

## Further Reading

Armstrong, P. *Qualitative Approaches in Social and Educational Research: The Life History Approach in Theory and Practice*, University of Hull, 1987.

Atkinson, D. and Williams, F. *Know Me As I Am*: *An Anthology of Prose, Poetry and Art by People with Learning Difficulties,* Hodder & Stoughton, 1990.

Blair, A. et al, *Facing Goliath: Adults' Experiences of Participation, Guidance and Progression in Education*, SCRE, 1993.

Blair, M. et al (eds). *Identity, Diversity and Gender and the Experience of Education*, Open University Press, 1995.

Boud, D. and Griffin, V. *Appreciating Adult Learning from the Learner's Perspective*, Kogan Page, 1987.

Courtney, S. *Why Adults Learn: Towards a Theory of Participation in Adult Education*, Routledge, 1992.

Burnett, J. *Destiny Obscure: Autobiographies of Childhood, Education and Family from the 1820s to the 1920s*, Penguin, 1982 and 1994.

Edwards, R. *Mature Women Students: Separating or Connecting Family and Education*, Falmer Press, 1993.

Federation of Worker Writers and Community Publishers. *Once I Was a Washing Machine: The Working Class Experience in Poetry and Prose*, FWWCP, 1989.

Fieldhouse, R. '"Mythmaking and Mortmain": A Response', *Studies in the Education of Adults* 28, 1, April 1996.

Hoar, M. et al (eds) *Life Histories and Learning: Language, the Self and Education*, Centre for Continuing Education, University of Sussex, 1994.

McGivney, V. *Education's For Other People: Access to Education for Non-Participating Adults*, NIACE, 1990.

McLaren, A.T. *Ambitions and Realisations: Women in Adult Education*, Peter Owen, 1985.

Pascall, G. and Cox, R., *Women Returning to Higher Education*, Society for Research Into Higher Education, and Open University Press, 1993.

Plummer, K. *Documents of Life*, Allen & Unwin, 1983.

Pye, J. *Second Chances: Adults Returning to Education*, Oxford University Press, 1991.

Russell, W. *Educating Rita, Stags and Hens and Blood Brothers*, Methuan, 1988.

Thomson, A, 'Writing About Learning: Using Mass-Observation Educational Life Histories to Explore Learning Through Life', in J. Swindells (ed.), *The Uses of Autobiography*, Taylor and Francis, 1995.

Vincent, D. *Bread, Knowledge and Freedom: a Study of Nineteenth Century Working Class Autobiography*, Methuan, 1982.

West, L. *Beyond Fragments: Adults, Motivation and Higher Education*, Taylor and Francis, 1996.

# Abbreviations

| | |
|---|---|
| ABE | Adult Basic Education |
| AGM | Annual General Meeting |
| 'A' level | Advanced level GCE |
| ARICS | Associate of the Royal Institute of Chartered Surveyors |
| ATC | Army Training Corps |
| BA | Bachelor of Arts |
| BSc | Bachelor of Science |
| BSE | Block School Experience |
| BTEC | Business and Technical Education Council |
| CETS | Continuing Education and Training Service |
| CLAIT | Computer Literacy and Information Technology |
| CMA | Computer marked assessment (OU) |
| CMS | Certificate for Mature Students |
| CSE | Certificate of Secondary Education |
| CV | Curriculum Vitae |
| DCI | Detective Chief Inspector (Police) |
| DTP | Desk top publishing |
| EFW | English for Work |
| ESOL | English for Speakers of Other Languages |
| GCE | General Certificate in Education |
| GCSE | General Certificate in Secondary Education |
| GMTV | Good Morning Television |
| GNVQ | General National Vocational Qualifications |
| HMI | Her Majesty's Inspector |
| HNC | Higher National Certificate |
| IT | Information technology |
| JIG-CALS | Job Ideas and Information Generator – Computer Assisted Learning |
| LEA | Local Education Authority |
| LOCF | London Open College Federation |
| LT Project | Learning Together (literacy) project |
| MD | Medical Doctor |
| MFI | Furniture retailer |
| MoD | Ministry of Defence |
| MSc | Master of Science |

| | |
|---|---|
| NACRO | National Association for the Care and Rehabilitation of Offenders |
| NATO | Northern Atlantic Treaty Organisation |
| NEC | National Extension College |
| NHS | National Health Service |
| NIACE | National Institute of Adult Continuing Education (The National Organisation for Adult Learning) |
| NVQ | National Vocational Qualification |
| OBE | Order of the British Empire |
| OCN | Open College Network |
| 'O' level | Ordinary level GCE |
| ONC | Ordinary National Certificate |
| OU | Open University |
| OUGS | Open University Geological Society |
| PCO | Peripatetic Care Officer |
| PPA | Pre-school Playgroups Association |
| RAE | Royal Aircraft Establishment (now Defence Research Agency) |
| RNIB | Royal National Institute for the Blind |
| RNLI | Royal National Lifeboat Institute |
| RSA | Royal Society of Arts |
| RSPB | Royal Society for the Protection of Birds |
| RSPCA | Royal Society for the Prevention of Cruelty to Animals |
| SYOCF | South Yorkshire Open College Federation |
| TEFL | Teaching English as a Foreign Language |
| TMA | Tutor marked assessment (OU) |
| TUC/JSA | Trade Union Congress/Job Seeker's Allowance |
| U3A | University of the Third Age |
| UWE | University of the West of England |
| WEA | Workers' Educational Association |
| WI | Women's Institute |
| WP | Word processing |
| WSCC | West Sussex County Council |
| YOC | Young Ornithologists' Club |

# Index

This index is arranged in two sections. The first section is an alphabetical list of the diarists who are quoted in the extracts in Part Two of the book and in the Afterward. The second section of the index is a list of institutions, organisations and places where the learning of the diarists takes place. We have not attempted to index the book thematically or conceptually: the diaries show the complexity of people's experience of learning, how it runs like threads interwoven throughout the fabric of their lives. We hope, therefore, that you will read the complete diaries in all their richness to gain an insight into that complexity.

## Extract Authors

Jackie Aggett, *162*
Shamima Aktar, *184*
Angela Mary Atkin, *177*

Genevieve Ball, *192*
Maxine Bancalari, *150*
Lesley Barber, *166, 195*
Linda Birch, *146*
Harriet Birungi, *183*
Nina Brittain, *193*
Claire Britton, *183*
Eliane Boyet, *165*
Debbie Brooke, *164*
Ian Brown, *172*
Doreen Bullock, *178*

Joan Chadwick, *147, 184*
Ann Clowes, *179*
Alistair Cumming, *185*

Fiona Dale, *176, 190*
Rosalie Darlington, *152*
Jean Day, *170*
Mary Diggle, *173*
Christine Durrant, *156*

Barbara Evans, *172*

Jennie Farley, *177*
Kathleen Ferrelly, *142, 180-182*
Grace Fielder, *150*
Marjorie Foy, *145*
Maureen Fradgley, *156*

Frances Gilbert, *147, 194*
Dorothy Gravell, *186*
Brian Gray, *143*
Kevin Gregory, *148*
Sarah Guilbert, *165*

Stewart Hardie, *192*
James Harkins, *193*
David Harvey, *197*
Lorraine Hayward, *163*
Marilyn Hayward, *166*
Pauline Henderson, *164, 178*
Pat Hewitt, *195*
John Heywood, *183*
Rebecca Hilton, *165, 170*

Dawn Inns, *193*

Hanadi Jardali, *160*
Jenny Jerome, *193*

Bilques Khan, *196*
Anne Kissane, *142, 197*
Rae Kozary, *163*

Jacqualine Lamb, *174*
Kevin Lange, *187*
Heather Lankshear, *186*

Sheila McKinnon, *151*
Mary McLean, *168, 182*
Cynthia Mbah, *196*
Jane Meah, *148*
Geoff Meeks, *151, 179*

Sylvia Mendham, *157-159, 204*
Vera Moon, *162*
Sandra Moore, *146*

Annetta Owen, *176, 190*

John Pearson, *198*
Sue Perrin, *182*
Pauline Peters, *196*
Emma Pickles, *175*
Karen Piesley, *193*
Angela Pinnell, *150*
Frank Pololi, *153*
Douglas Preston, *149*
Margaret Prett, *190*

Eric Ratherwood, *184*
Tina Robinson, *159, 166*

Lyn Smith, *135 (and cover)*
Trish Spence, *138*
Doreen Stowe, *164*

Joy Tomkins, *143, 204*

Doreen Whitehouse, *163*
Margaret Whiting, *144*
Theresa Williams, *159*
Frances Withall, *191*
John Woodward, *175*
Audrey Wythe, *152*

Rosemary Yonathan, *161*

Emma (Croydon), *191*

**Institutions, Organisations and Places**

Page numbers in **bold** refer to full diaries

Ambassador House, Thornton
  Heath, *51, 54*
Ancholme House, Scunthorpe, *12, 13, 16*
Ashburton Centre, *162*
Ashton-under-Lyne, Cheshire, *161, 166*
Attleborough High School,
  Norfolk, *165, 171*
Aylesbury, *170*
Birkbeck College, London, *185*
Birmingham **24-26**, *151, 164, 180*
Bournemouth **57-58**, *192*
Bournemouth & Poole College, Poole, *192*
Bournville College, *164*
Bradford, **107-111**, *148*
Bramhall, Cheshire, *47*
Brighton, *150, 173, 186*
Brigstock, *151*
Bristol, **20-23**
Buckingham, *171*
Burnholme Community College, *34*
Cardiff, *148*
Carers' Support Group, *173*
Carlisle College, *144, 147, 157, 159, 178, 195*
Chelmsford, Essex, *149*
Cheltenham, *164, 177, 178*
Chesterfield, *177*
Chobham, *62*
City Adult Education College,
  Leicester, *102, 104*
Coombe Cliff, Croydon, *191*
Cottingham Adult Education Centre,
  Yorks. **27-30**
Coulsdon, Surrey, *162*
Crawley, West Sussex, **6-7, 75-78**, *142,
  172, 183, 196, 197*
Cromer, *74*
Croydon Continuing Education &
  Training Services (CETS), **50-56**, *152,
  153, 162, 165, 183, 191, 192, 199*
Cyfle Arall, Gwynedd, *186*
Cyprus, *174*
Denman College, *171*

Decorative and Fine Arts Society, *173*
Dudley, Lancashire, *163*
Eastleigh, Hampshire, *182*
East Durham Community College,
  Peterlee, *144, 156, 164, 196*
East Midlands, **99-106**
Exeter, *146*
Forest of Dean, *162*
Glasgow, **81-84**, *197, 198*
Guernsey, Channel Islands, *165*
Hassocks, West Sussex, **128-130**
Highgate Centre, *4*
Hull, *35, 95*
Huntingdon Regional College,
  Cambs. *143*
Huntingdon Technical College,
  Cambs. *178*
Jersey, Channel Islands, *165*
Knuston Hall, Northamptonshire, *100*
Lancaster, *73*
Leeds, **36-40, 88-98**, *147, 184, 195, 204*
Leicester, *99, 102, 142, 180-182*
Macclesfield, *49,* **79-80**, *179*
Mansfield, *157, 204*
Merthyr College, Merthyr Tydfil,
  S.Wales, *146*
Middleton Skills Centre, Leeds,
  **88-98**, *195*
Mid-Kent College, *150*
National Extension College (NEC), *47,
  166, 174, 175, 182, 195*
Newark and Sherwood College, *158*
Newcastle-under-Lyme College,
  **121-124**
New Malden, Surrey, *163*
Nine Acres County Primary School,
  Newport, IoW, *159*
Northbrook College, Worthing, **68-71**
Northern College, *3, 4*
Norwich, **72-74**, *150, 156, 165, 168,
  182, 187*
Nottingham, *112*

Open College Network, *37, 102*
Open University (OU), *47,* **72-74**, *80, 100,* **112-120**, *156, 163, 165, 171, 173, 195*
Open University: Summer School, *112-116*
Open University: Study Tour, *117-120*
Oshwal Centre, *51*
Park Lane College, Leeds, **36-40, 88-98**, *147, 184, 195*
Peterlee, Co. Durham, *144, 156, 164, 196*
Peterborough, *176, 190*
Poole, *192*
Portslade Community School, E. Sussex, *161*
Poynton, Cheshire, **8-10**, *49, 79,* **125-127**, *179*
Pre-School Playgroups Association, *174*
Prince William School, Peterborough, *176,190*
Punshon College of Further Education, Bournemouth, **57-58**
Rathbones Employment College, *86*
Royal Forest of Dean College of Further Education, *162*
Royal School for the Deaf, Exeter, *146*
St. Albans, *143, 204*
Scunthorpe, **11-19**
Sheffield College, *193*
Sileby, Leicestershire, **85-87**
Sir Jonathon North School, Leicester, *142*
Sittingbourne, Kent, *193*
South Norwood, *54, 191, 199*
Stockport, **8-10**, **59-61**, *170*
Stroud, *136-137*
Surrey Heath Adult Education Institute, **62-67**
Sutton, Surrey, *190*
Swansea, *196*
Swanshurst School, Billesley, Birmingham, *25*
Tameside College, Cheshire, *159, 166*
Thomas Bennett Community College, Crawley, **6-7**, **75-78**, *142, 172, 183, 196, 197*
Thornton Heath CETS Centre, *51*

Tower Hamlets, London, *160, 166, 184*
Trittford Centre, Billesley, Birmingham, *25*
Trowbridge College, Wiltshire, *20,* **41-46**
TUC/JSA, *3*
University of Strathclyde, **81-84**, *197*
University of the Third Age (U3A), *168, 182*
University of the West of England in Bristol, **20-23**
Varndean College, Brighton, *150, 173, 186*
Wakefield, *3, 88*
Wakefield Centre for the Unemployed, *3*
Warrington, Cheshire, *152*
Wells, Somerset, *166, 195*
Wellingborough, *184*
Wensum Lodge College of Further Education, Norwich, *165, 187*
Wheelers Lane School, Kings Heath, Birmingham, *25*
Widnes, Lancashire, *163*
Wilmslow, Cheshire, *145*
Women's Institute, *165, 171*
Wolverhampton College of Adult Education, *176, 190*
Worker's Educational Association (WEA), *15, 31, 33, 168, 171*
Worthing, West Sussex, **68-71**
York, **31-35**

# Time to Learn
## A directory of learning holidays

*Time to Learn* lists thousands of residential courses running in Britain. Published twice a year to cover winter or summer courses, *Time to Learn* will enable readers to choose courses and locations to suit all tastes throughout the year.

There are courses to suit everyone: from arts and crafts to writing; from music to politics; and from literature to Tai Chi. And there are even courses entitled *Pudding Lane to Pie Corner* and *The whiskies of Scotland*! Favourites such as languages, photography and bird-watching always feature, and foreign study tours continue in winter: *Journeying through Chile to Tierra del Fuego* or *Spring in Andalucia*, for example.

Discover all the opportunities with *Time to Learn*.

ISSN 0955-5374

Winter and summer volumes are available @ £4.25 each inc. p&p. Orders must be accompanied by payment. Cheques to be made payable to NIACE. Send to Publication Sales, NIACE, Department AL, 21 De Montfort Street, Leicester LE1 7GE.

---

# Adults learning

*Adults learning* carries the latest news and views on matters concerning adult learning. Published ten times a year (September-June) by NIACE, it features in-depth analysis and thought-provoking articles. Looking at issues of policy and practice in the field, *Adults learning* is indispensible for debate, networking and sharing experience.

No provider of adult education, whether in the public, private or voluntary sector, should be without *Adults learning*. Practitioners, policymakers and everyone who wants to keep abreast of events and developments in the adult learning world will want to subscribe to the leading magazine in the field.

Subscription rates: individuals £17.50; concessionary rate for part-time tutors and adult learners £15.00; libraries and institutions £30.00.

All subscription enquires should be made to:
Subscriptions Department, NIACE, 21 De Montfort Street, Leicester LE7 1GE.

ISSN 0955 2308

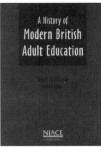